INTO THE ASSAULT

AINTO THE SSAULT

Famous Dive-Bomber Aces
of the Second World War

PETER C. SMITH

University of Washington Press
Seattle

Printed and bound in Great Britain

University of Washington Press edition first published 1985

Library of Congress Catalog Card Number 85-51519

0-295-96317-4

Contents

Illustrations

ILLUSTRATION SOURCES

1, 2: Mrs Kiyoko Egusa; 3: Commander Sadao Seno; 4, 6, 25: US National Archives; 5: Tadashi Nozowa; 7, 8, 9, 10, 11: Mesny Collection; 12, 13, 14, 16: Cesare Gori; 15: Nicola Malizia; 18, 19: Fleet Air Arm Museum/Major R. T. Partridge; 17, 20, 28, 29, 30: Imperial War Museum; 21, 24, 26: Colonel E. Glidden; 22, 23: US Marine Corps Official; 27: Frau Barbel Wilke; 31: Bundesarchiv; 32: Official Soviet; 33: Passingham Collection; 34, 35; Novosti, Moscow; 36: Tass, Moscow.

Diagrams

Acknowledgements

The author would like to express his thanks and appreciation to all those who so selflessly gave their time to answer the many questions concerning the lives of the seven men of this book. My thanks therefore to the following friends, enthusiasts and organisations for their many kindnesses and much patience. In alphabetical order:

Herr Baldes, Bundesarchiv, Zentralnachweisstelle, Aachen; Dale Birdsell, Chief Historian, Department of the Army, Alexandria, VA; William B. Black; Mrs. E. Boyd, Air Historical Branch, MoD, London; Herr Busekow, Deutsche Dienststelle, Berlin; Jean-Paul Busson, Conservateur en chef, Chef du Service Historique de la Marine, Vincennes; B.F. Cavalcante, Assistant Head, Operational Archives Branch, Department of the Navy, Washington DC; Danny J. Crawford, Head of Reference Section, History and Museums Division, Department of the Navy, Washington DC; Mrs Kiyoko Egusa; Major Elmer G. Glidden, jr, USMC (Rtd); Cesare Gori, Pesaro; Herr Havers, Bundesarchiv Zentralnachweisstelle, Aachen; Bob Henderson, Department of Printed Books, British Library, London; Pierre Herveaux; Captain Claude Huan; Amiral Francis Lane; Capitaine de Frégate Michel Lorenzi; Madame Hélène Mesny, Paris; Lucy Pakhoniva, Tass, London; Major R.T. Partridge RM (Rtd); Professor Amedeo Montemaggi, Rimini; Herr Kurt Scheffel, Schleiden; Commander Sadao Seno, IJSDF, (Rtd); Lieutenant-Colonel E. Smirnov, Assistant Air Attaché of the USSR, London; Neil Somerville, Senior Assistant, BBC Written Archives Centre, Reading; Madame Evelyn Stipanovitch; Richard A. von Doenhoff, Navy and Old Army Branch, Military Archives Division, National Archives and Records Services, Washington DC; Edwin R. Walker; Commander D.C.B. White, OBE, MRAeS, RN (Rtd), Director, Fleet Air Arm Museum, Yeovilton; Frau Barbel Wilke, Trisdorf-Eschmar.

Introduction

Dive-bombing is, by its very nature, an aggressive method of warfare. Even within the confines of aerial warfare to throw one's aircraft straight towards the waiting guns of the enemy requires considerable skill, dedication and a special type of courage. It is perhaps surprising, therefore, to find, on examination, that the greatest of its exponents, from all the combatant nations of the Second World War, were not in themselves aggressive men. Rather, the mould is of thoughtful, serious and even painstaking experts, highly trained in their special skills and meticulous in their application of them; not at all the mental picture conjured up by wartime or post-war media-influenced propaganda.

Perhaps this misleading picture is still coloured in the former Allied nations by the fact that it was the opposing nations, in particular Germany and Japan, which initially used the dive-bomber technique most widely and to the best effect. Certainly the heads of land-based air forces in Britain, France and the United States were not enamoured of the dive-bomber, wishing always to fight their own separate war with the heavy bomber. The fact that the dive-bomber scored victory after victory, while the heavy bomber almost invariably failed to hit what it aimed at during the first three years of the conflict, was not a palatable lesson to have to assimilate or accept, much less admit to. Their only riposte was to ridicule what they could not match through press and film and so well did they do so that the false impression they left then is still as fierce today among historians who should now know better.

Dive-bombers are often depicted as sitting ducks, easy targets, fighter bait. Despite the fact that scores of the much more expensive heavy bombers, along with their more numerous crew members, were destroyed month after month, attention tends to be concentrated on the comparatively few times that dive-bombers were so afflicted, although this amounted to but a tiny fraction of the heavy bomber massacres. In achievement, great acclaim is heaped on the rare occasions a heavy bomber unit, such as the famous 'Dam Busters', destroyed a precision target; while the fact that such bombers were not even hitting targets the size of cities in 1941 is often glossed over. Nor are the successes achieved by dive-bombers accorded their true merit yet. Given the chance, and the fleeting opportunities, even the minute dive-bomber forces of Britain, France and the United States did manage briefly to show how effective a weapon they could be if utilised correctly. In the same way the Italian and Soviet specialists made dramatic contributions to their respective theatres of war and it was dive-bombing which made the lasting impression on the battlefield itself, particularly against shipping targets, both mercantile and naval, in all the war zones.

Too often in the past heroism or skill has been presented as being the sole prerogative of the British (or whatever nationality the subject of the book belongs to). It is the author's hope that by presenting the lives of seven of the most renowned dive-bomber pilots from seven different nations, a truer perspective of what constitutes heroism and bravery will be shown and that such attributes recognise no frontiers.

Peter C. Smith
Riseley, Bedford
February 1985

1 Captain Takashige Egusa

Imperial Japanese Navy   1910–44

One of the most skilful and influential leaders in the field of
dive-bombing was Takashige Egusa of the Imperial Japanese
Navy. His fame became legendary, his units' achievements
outstanding, their influence compared to their numbers, enormous. As the fine tip of the red-hot spear that was the Japanese
navy's Nagumo Task Force, it was Egusa and his dive-bomber
crews who created the maximum havoc among the Western
Allies in the first year of the Pacific War and gave the Japanese
Emperor a unique succession of victories. Egusa – as much as
any of the men whose stories are told in this book – represents
the great effect that one well-trained unit could have on decid-
ing the outcome of great campaigns.

Takashige Egusa's wartime exploits, and also his death,
summarise the whole story of Japan in the Second World War.
At first the Japanese navy dive-bombers thrust through every
defence. But Japan, like Germany and Italy, relied on a
professional élite in order to prevail. Once those veterans began
to fall then it was to become a war of logistics in which resources
and numbers would ultimately tip the scales against any
amount of individual skill. As the tide of war changed, the
dive-bomber pilots found more and more that their own brand
of perfection counted less and less in the face of the big
battalions. This was particularly so in the case of Japan and
Italy which did not then possess the wide industrial base to
compete in a long war against the enormous resources of the
Soviet Union, the United States and, to a more limited extent,
Great Britain.

Although he was to become a noble warrior in the mould of
the samurai, Takashige himself was born the second son of a

poor farmer, one Kuemon Egusa. His father's chief claim to fame was that he was renowned as a 'heavy drinker'; he liked and could hold his sake, but he could also claim descent from a lord of a castle in the Izumo area (in the present Shimane prefecture) during the fabulous 'Era of Wars' 400 years previously. The Egusas had traditionally been a powerful family in the Fukuyama area. In this modest parentage Egusa was in good company: the great Isoroku Yamamoto, the Japanese commander-in-chief, was himself the son of a schoolmaster. Takashige was born on 29 October 1910, in the city of Fukuyama, in the prefecture of Hiroshima. Life was hard for the youngster and this was reflected in the youth himself. He grew up as a taciturn, self-possessed and stout-hearted adolescent, but it is recalled also that he was gentle and thoughtful in both manner and deed.

Japan had grown in the late nineteenth century into a major power, not least a major sea-power, and her navy was by far the most powerful in the Far East. Throwing many centuries of isolationism and adopting the best in the fields of the leading nations of the day, she had grown mighty and self-confident. This had been reinforced by a succession of victories, first over the Chinese and then, more dramatic in its effects and lasting impression, over the old Russian Empire of the Czar when the Japanese admiral, Togo, won the overwhelming naval victory of the Tsushima Straits in 1904. Coupled with the mystic faith that the Japanese were a chosen race protected by divine intervention, and destined to lead Asia into a new golden age, these achievements were a heady influence on the Japanese youth of the time. By the end of the First World War in 1918 and the succeeding Washington Conferences of 1922, Japan found herself elevated, with little effort on her part, to the position of the third naval power of the world, behind the British Empire and the rising power of the United States. Many young officers considered this ranking to be an insult to be avenged. Certainly the holding of Japan's battleship strength at two-thirds of that of her two main rivals gave the Japanese a spur to develop carrier aviation as an alternative to help redress that balance. In this she was helped by the fact that she was nominally still an ally of Great Britain, which at that time led the world in naval aviation. A British aviation mission, led by Lord Sempill, had been dispatched at Japan's request in 1921; twenty years later the results of this seeding flowered dramatically in the South China Sea. In that same year of 1921 Japan launched the first purpose-built aircraft-carrier, the little *Hosho* and the Mitsubishi Company employed another Englishman, Squadron-Leader F.J. Rutland, who had flown from a seaplane-carrier at the Battle of Jutland, to help design special naval aircraft for her.

Takashige Egusa meanwhile had set his heart on a naval career. In late 1926, when he was sixteen, he passed the entrance examination for the famed (and feared) Naval Academy at Etajima. Built on the tough traditions of the warrior-caste and on similar adopted principles to the Royal Navy's Whale Island Gunnery School, where discipline was paramount and harshness inbuilt, Etajima either made you or broke you. Egusa needed every ounce of his dour spirit and resilience during the four-year course but he emerged from it triumphant. On 18 November 1930 he graduated and was commissioned as a midshipman.

He had already set his sights on aviation, but first he had to undergo the normal naval training at sea. Before sailing for his initial sea experience aboard the new heavy cruiser *Haguro* the young cadet underwent a further preliminary course to lay the groundwork for a future air officer appointment at the first opportunity. Egusa settled down to work still harder toward his chosen goal and, after eighteen months, he was rewarded by promotion to Ensign. This was on 1 April 1932. Five months later, on 1 September, he was, to his great delight, assigned to the Air Student Training Group.

The air training centre was based at Kasumigaura and was a copy of RAF Cranwell. Flying skills were imparted but so also were the manners of a gentleman officer. Despite this Egusa's sturdy farmboy independence was in no way knocked out of him and he still retained many of his old virtues of hard work and honest endeavour.

It was in this same year that the Imperial navy began its great strides forward in naval aviation that were to culminate in the crushing victories of a decade later. The Naval Aircraft Establishment was founded at this time and the *7-Shi* programme was put in hand. This latter was to create a whole new air fleet, comprising new fighters, carrier-based dive- and torpedo-bombers and land-based attack planes. Japanese observers had been much impressed by the accuracy and hitting power of the American Helldivers and were determined to utilise this method to achieve a high percentage of hits with a minimum of outlay. Like the massive shipbuilding programme of the same period, most of the new equipment was kept 'under wraps' from the West and great secrecy was maintained. From this and the earlier programmes the Nakajima Company produced two experimental carrier dive-bomber types which went out to the fleet for evaluation. The Nakajima N–35 Tokubaku was powered by a 650-hp Lorraine engine. The Yokosuka Company was also early in the field with a dive-bomber design.

Egusa quickly showed great promise as an aviator. Saying little but pondering much, he diligently and studiously absorbed the lessons imparted to him and applied his own logic. Despite his outwardly staid mannerisms he was a popular young pilot and was always to remain a caring and thoughtful officer. One description of him by a contemporary recalls how, 'He always considered his subordinates very much and became a great leader among his colleagues'. His own skill was obvious to all, his concern for those later entrusted to his leadership equally became a byword. The results were to be made manifest. But at this time he had to learn his dangerous new trade. Not only was flying from ships itself a relatively new skill but dive-bombing, in particular, was a novel and fresh concept in the Imperial navy. Originally used by British pilots of the old Royal Flying Corps in France in 1917–18, the art had fallen into neglect until, nurtured by the US Marine Corps and adopted by the US navy, it had re-emerged in the early 1930s as a potent force. Not only in the United States but also in Germany the dive-bomber concept was re-born, and, in her old tradition, Japan eagerly embraced this latest thinking.

The precision aspect of dive-bombing had a strong appeal to Egusa. He appreciated the economy of force and the maximising of effort contained in this method of bombing and saw it as the perfect solution for a nation which would always be outnumbered in combat but which might mitigate this drawback with skill and expertise. Egusa specialised early in divebombing. On 15 November 1933 he passed his flying tests with honours and was promoted to Sub-Lieutenant and a fortnight later he was assigned to his first regular unit, the Tateyama Air Squadron in the Chioa prefecture. Within a short time, on 20 April 1934, Takashige joined the aircraft-carrier *Hosho* operating in the China Sea. During two years of flight-deck operations, utilising the new dive-bombers, Egusa's skill became readily acknowledged. Unfortunately the aircraft themselves were not a success. Nonetheless a large amount of trial and experimental work was conducted which led to the establishment of tactics and procedures which were to endure with little modification.

It quickly grew clear that a more reliable design was needed to allow the dive-bomber to reach its true potential. A number of aircraft-carriers were now in commission and, more and more, the aviation side of the navy regarded itself as the true fighting power of the fleet. This view was not shared by the majority of the admirals but a few were far-sighted enough to back this thinking, among them Yamamoto himself. Again Japan turned to foreign designers to help her find the answers to her needs and the Aichi company imported a Heinkel He66 single-seater dive-bomber from Germany for evaluation. Under the terms of the new *8-Shi* programme Aichi's design team under Tokuhishiro Goake modified this aircraft, making it into a two-seater with a stronger undercarriage and a Nakajima radial engine. As the Aichi Special Bomber this aircraft was tested in comparison with home-built products and found to be superior. The navy therefore placed production orders in 1934 and, as the Aichi D1A1 or Type 94 Carrier Bomber, this sturdy aircraft gave the Japanese navy a powerful base on which to advance the art further. Together with the subsequent D1A2 a total of 590 aircraft were built, numbers far in excess of any equivalent dive-bomber anywhere else at this time, showing just how highly the Imperial navy rated this method of attack. Egusa was to be in the forefront of its testing and application at sea.

Further advancement was swift as the navy expanded. On 16 November 1936, Egusa was given his first command, a company in the Saheki Air Squadron, and a month later (on 1 December) he was promoted to Lieutenant. Intensive testing in peacetime exercises involved the bombing of fast-moving targets and this quickly proved the effectiveness of dive-bombing over altitude attacks. The obsolete battleship *Settsu* was converted to such a target, being radio-controlled much like the Royal Navy's *Centurion* and similar results were obtained. But soon Egusa was to become involved in a real shooting war in which the theories were put into practice.

The so-called 'China Incident' first erupted on 7 July 1937. Following the initial flare-up, preparations were made for a quick campaign and the army prepared itself to advance on Peking. In support, because they were the most readily available air units, was the navy's Second Combined Air Flotilla, commanded by Rear-Admiral Teizo Mitsunami, based initially at Ohmura and later at Shanghai. This force included the 12th Air Corps under Captain Osamu Imamura, with twelve of the Nakajima Type 94 dive-bombers on its strength. By December the fleet had moved 1 and 2 Carrier Divisions to the China coast to support the army further as the situation developed into a full-scale war. Aboard the carrier *Ryujo* were fifteen Nakajima Type 95 dive-bombers, while aboard *Kaga* of 2 Division were twelve more Nakajima Type 94s. *Hosho* initially had no dive-bombers aboard, but on 11 July 1937 Egusa was appointed as Commander of 12 Air Squadron and posted once more to that ship.

In central and southern China fighting was intense and the dive-bombers were in the thick of it. Japan seized Peking on 8 August, reached Shanghai on 9 November and Nanking, the capital, by 13 December. All these thrusts were supported by navy dive-bombing. Initially all did not go well and some severe losses were suffered but gradually the upper hand was obtained and the missions achieved some notable successes. Egusa and his compatriots had not been trained in the role of supporting land warfare – hitherto all their efforts had been concentrated on attacking shipping – but the inherent accuracy of the dive-bomber proved itself invaluable in this new role. Improvisation saved the day and the young airmen and their supporting ground-crews proved adaptable to a degree matched only by the Luftwaffe in the early stages of the Second World War. Under Egusa 12 Air Unit was equipped with a dozen Type 94 carrier bombers on 15 July, while 13 Group had eighteen Type 96s. The latter unit began preparing for the shift to mainland China on 7 August and had arrived at Chou Shui Tzu via Korea by 11 August to operate in the Shanghai area.

The pressure on Egusa and his pilots was intense and operations were conducted at full stretch. During the advance on Shanghai in August, 1 Carrier Air Division had been ordered to mount all-out assaults on Chinese positions on 15 August, but typhoon-like conditions kept them grounded. Next day, taking advantage of the Japanese aircraft's absence, the Chinese army launched a counter-offensive and, for a time, the situation was critical. Both *Hosho* and *Ryujo* were operating from the vicinity of Ma-an island and began launching their aircraft early that morning despite heavy seas. Despite difficulties in taking off fully laden from the pitching flight-decks, all the carrier aircraft got airborne and bombed Chinese airfields at Chia-Hsing, Hung-Chiao, Chiang-Wan and Ta-Chang-Chen. Their accuracy was first-rate and great success was achieved, ten enemy aircraft and a large hangar were destroyed at the latter base, for example, and the nearby railway was also wrecked. Two opposing Chinese fighters were also destroyed in aerial combat. This set the pattern for future navy dive-bombing support from both carrier and land bases.

Bomb-loads at this stage were primitive. When 1 Attack Unit flew into battle on 22 September, each of the twelve Type 92 carrier-based bombers were armed with six standard 60-kg bombs only. Nonetheless they were able to place these where they were required, on the target. Throughout that month the dive-bombers of Egusa and his unit had been constantly in demand. On 10 September three carrier-based dive-bombers attacked Chinese field-artillery positions on the Pootung side of the river. Next day fifteen bombed large enemy concentrations on the Hangchow road. Four dive-bombers carried out an armed reconnaissance of Haimen, Tung-Chou, Soochow, Kahsing and Chiang Chiao on 12 September and the same day saw another twelve hit large enemy units at Ta-Chang-Chen and Liuchiahsing. On 13 September Egusa led his bombers in support of the army during the intense fighting between Ta-Chang-Chen and Nansiang and strafed the retreating Chinese troops during the ensuing rout. On 14 September they were flying missions in support of Japanese marines hard-pressed at Te-Chih. And so it continued. By 1 December Egusa had been assigned to command the Air Company of the aircraft-carrier *Ryujo* and the missions continued.

The carriers eventually returned home to refurbish their air groups. Life was not all fighting and war for Egusa at this period, however, as this lull would show. In the brief periods of leave back home in Japan he courted and won the heart of Kiyoko Okamura. Although the nation was advanced in technology much about Japan remained traditional and their courtship was in the highly formal and stylised manner which, in the West, would have been considered 'Victorian' in the extreme. It was the practice then for influential parties to bring together suitable young couples with a view to marriage but it was the sister of another navy pilot that had caught Egusa's eye. Motoharu Okamura was to become as famous a pilot to fighters as Takashige Egusa was to dive-bombers, and in the last years of the Second World War, he was appointed commander of the 'Divine Thunder' Corps of kamikaze pilots. But that lay far ahead and undreamt of. Attracted though the couple were to each other the correct formalities had to be undergone and it was through the good offices of Rear-Admiral and Mrs Takijiro Onishi (later also to be known as the father of the 'Special Attack Forces') that their marriage was finally arranged. This took place on 20 December 1939 and Egusa shaved off his moustache, of which he was particularly proud, especially for the occasion at his wife's request. Their son, Hiroyuki, was born in July 1940.

The newly-weds were not to know many years of undisturbed happiness but their marriage was given an excellent start for ten days later Egusa was assigned as Company Commander and Instructor of the Yokoshuka Air Squadron. This was at the main dockyard of the Imperial navy, situated some twenty miles from Yokohama City itself. Although operational units were periodically based at the Naval Air Station, its main function then was for the training and evaluation of men and machines. As the months slipped by this training went into high gear. It was not hard to see the reasons for this. Already in Europe Poland had fallen to Nazi Germany, largely through the effectiveness on the battlefield of the dive-bomber. The omens for Egusa, Japan's leading exponent of this form of warfare, were obvious. Relations with the United States were strained almost to breaking point by the war in China and the later imposition by the West of an oil embargo only set the seal on the inevitable. Meanwhile Japan was given two years' breathing space to prepare for the final battle and Egusa was to use that time imparting his extensive knowledge to the navy's new dive-bombing recruits.

The old biplanes of the China War were now steadily being replaced by a new dive-bomber, a sleek monoplane, but with a fixed, spatted undercarriage similar in style in many ways to the famous German Stuka that was even then devastating Western Europe. This new Japanese dive-bomber was the Aichi D3A and had been developed as a result of war experience and from another Heinkel design, the He 70, which had also been imported and studied in depth. Powered by a Nakajima Hikari 1 radial engine this sturdy little aircraft made its maiden flight in December 1937 and had been steadily developed and improved ever since. It featured the slatted dive brakes and the engine was changed for the larger 840–hp Mitsubishi Kinsei 3. During competitions held in 1939 the Aichi bomber came out top over the Nakajima D3N1 and was placed in full-scale production as the Type 99 carrier-based bomber. Further increases in engine size and other modifications resulted in a first-rate dive-bomber and all front-line squadrons had been re-equipped with it by the eve of the Pacific War. Deck trials were conducted during 1940 aboard the carriers *Akagi* and *Kaga* and evaluation tests were conducted by Egusa at Yokosuka. It was to become his regular mount and in his hands and in the hands of his élite band of young experts, this aircraft, dismissed by the Allies as obsolete in 1941, was to create a fearful trail of havoc when war finally arrived.

By the autumn of 1941 the die was cast. The Japanese navy had staked all on surprise and the skill of its warriors. The best pilots were taken from the schools and training squadrons and given command of front-line units. Detailed plans were drawn up for attack on the United States Fleet at Pearl Harbor and that September saw intensive practice being undertaken against mock-up targets in the secret harbour of Kagoshima Bay in a remote part of Japan. Egusa was naturally the first to be so selected when the time was ripe and on 25 August 1941 he was assigned as Flight Leader aboard the new carrier *Soryu*. He was entrusted with the most important mission of all – the destruction of the United States aircraft-carriers – and was given the cream of the Imperial navy's dive-bomber crews. Eighty Aichi D3As were to be placed under his direct command from the six big carriers of the Nagumo Task Force. It was an awesome responsibility but characteristically Egusa met it head-on. Practice dive after practice dive was undertaken until his young crews were honed to perfect attunement and were eager and ready to show off their skills.

Proud as he was to be so chosen to strike the initial blow for Japan, Egusa had a secret burden when the fleet sailed from Tankan Bay in the fogbound Kuriles on 26 November 1941. Unbeknownst to his comrades their commander was concealing worries over and above those concerning the attack. His beloved Kiyoko was expecting their second child and it was proving a difficult pregnancy. But in addition their son, Hiroyuki, was fighting for his very life with a serious illness. Egusa could not be at their side at this grave juncture, and rarely can any commander have gone to war with so many burdens on his shoulders.

Egusa was now a Lieutenant-Commander, his promotion having been confirmed on 15 October on his appointment to the Task Force. Following the then current Japanese practice, the trail of his Aichi dive-bomber (or 'Val' as the Allies were soon to code-name it) was painted a brilliant red overall so that his various sub-sections could keep him in sight and close up formation prior to and, more important, immediately after an attack. The dive-bombers were very slow and their defensive armament was limited. Thus they relied to a great extent on the protection of their covering fighters, but in combat, once the bombers were committed to the attack dive, they were very much on their own. The danger point was after bomb-release. For a split-second at the bottom of the dive the pilots tended to 'black-out' and each aircraft broke away at low level and high speed as best it could from the wall of flak that met them. Enemy fighters usually chose this moment to attack and so it was essential that the dive-bombers rendezvous quickly and form up in tight sections for mutual self-defence. Painting the leader's tail a distinctive colour made recognition and formation easier to attain for the rest, and this followed the current practice among German dive-bomber units who painted their Wing Leader's tail yellow. However it also marked out to the enemy the leaders of the dive-bomber formations, a pride of place target which they accepted as an honour.

To understand something of the attitude of Egusa and his compatriots as the *Kido Butai* (Nagumo Task Force) sailed on its mission, one must recall that, although they were highly skilled technicians and twentieth-century warriors, their thoughts and way of life were viewed through the Shinto religion. Shinto means 'The way of the gods' and its message and practice permeated further than most Western religions into everyday life and custom. In its original form it evolved from primitive nature-worship and from that became associ-ated with the gods and spirits and the symbols of these in nature. Thus mountains and rivers were holy, the Emperor himself claimed direct divine ancestry, and everything had a mystic purpose. Self-sacrifice in the service of the Emperor, even to the supreme sacrifice of one's own life, was therefore the norm and although for a period this religion had been absorbed and superseded by Buddhism, when it was re-established in the mid-nineteenth century, State Shinto incorporated these values. Legends from the 'Time of Wars' laid down that Japan could never be defeated with such divine blessing and that to die in battle ensured the greatest worship open to any warrior. This almost lyrical way of life was reflected in the naming of Japanese warships and aircraft. For example, the carrier *Soryu*, in which the Egusa Air Group was embarked, translates as 'Blue Dragon', her sister ship *Hiryu* as 'Flying Dragon'. The great battleship *Yamato* with her nine 18-in. guns was named after the sacred mountain, and the lithe destroyers frisking about the great ship's flanks had the evocative names of winds, clouds and similar poetic ideas, such as 'Shore Breeze' and 'Summer Mist'.

It had never been the intention of Japan to mount what the Americans later claimed as a 'sneak attack'. Negotiations still proceeded, but the Japanese were realists and the oil embargo gave them little room to move or choose. It was either surrender or fight and nobody who knew the Japanese, as the American President Roosevelt did, would expect them to do the former without a struggle. Bad weather fortunately hid the ships during the early stages of their long roundabout journey towards Hawaii. Last-minute preparations were made and oiling took place at a pre-arranged rendezvous. On 1 December 1941, the die was cast and Admiral Nagumo received the signal '*Niitaka yama nobore*' ('Climb Mount Niitaka'), the final 'go' signal for the operation.

Egusa's main preoccupation was whether or not the American carriers would be present. These were the opponents most naval pilots wished to eliminate first. By contrast their senior officers were concentrating almost totally on the eight battleships which formed the core of the United States Pacific Fleet. The dive-bombers could not sink these monsters by themselves, but they could pulverise their upper decks and anti-aircraft (AA) positions to enable the torpedo-bombers to approach unmolested and finish the job. For attacks on battleships, however heavy, armour-piercing bombs were required. Such weapons were more suited to high-level attack and therefore these targets were originally to be bypassed by Egusa's first wave. They, with their smaller bombs and their precision, were to take the US carriers, but, should they not be present, they were allocated the airfields around the harbor and their rows of gleaming silver fighter planes as alternative targets. All depended on the final reconnaissance verdicts. They had initially hoped to catch six American flat-tops but, alas, by the eve of the attack, they knew (via an Intelligence report timed at 00.50) that none of them was left at Pearl Harbor. In fact three were in the Atlantic, one was on the US west coast and the other two were at sea, one ferrying Marine dive-bombers to Midway Island.

That same evening the crews of the warships were called up on deck and given the dramatic news. In a grand gesture the battle flag of Admiral Togo was flown at the flagship's masthead and a stirring signal by the same Admiral at that battle was received from Admiral Yamamoto aboard *Yamato* back in Japan which read like Nelson's signal before Trafalgar: 'The destiny of the Empire depends on this battle. Every man must do his duty.' Nobody knew better than Egusa that this was the case. The lifts began to bring the planes up on to the pitching decks to be made ready for the scheduled take-off at 06.00 on 7 December. The launching point was some 275 miles due north of Pearl Harbor. By 06.15 all 183 planes of the first wave of two planned waves were in the air.

There were 40 torpedo-bombers, 49 high-level bombers and 43 fighters in this wave, as well as 51 Aichi 'Val' dive-bombers, each one armed with a single 500-lb bomb. These were drawn from the total of 126 dive-bombers embarked in the Task Force which, in all, comprised 'Vals' of the Air Groups of the carriers *Akagi* (18), *Hiryu* (18), *Kaga* (18), *Shokaku* (27), *Soryu* (18) and *Zuikaku* (27), each crewed by the cream of the corps.

Much as Egusa wished to lead the first aircraft against the enemy, he knew that the men of the second wave would have the hardest time of it. They would not have the element of surprise on their side but would be attacking a fully alerted and vengeful opponent. Egusa knew his duty. The first wave was led by Lieutenant-Commander Takahashi, and Egusa himself chose to lead the second wave. He allocated to Takahashi, in the absence of the American carriers, the task of eliminating the air bases of Hickham Field and Ford Island. The former was believed to hold the long-range Flying Fortress bombers which might reach out against the Nagumo Task Force; the latter was thought to be a fighter strip (in fact it was only a seaplane base). The second wave consisted of 167 aircraft, 54 level bombers, 36 fighters and, the main force, Egusa leading his 80 dive-bombers on 'Targets of Opportunity', which, in the main, meant what remained of the battleship line, most of the American fighters having already been destroyed on the ground by the first wave. What few interceptors did get airborne were mainly handled by the deadly Zero fighters of his escort.

Egusa was in the air from *Soryu* at 07.15 and the mass formation quickly headed south. The flight towards the target was a long one, two hours pounding steadily onward, each man alone with his thoughts. Long before Pearl Harbor hove into view the columns of fire and smoke from the burning ships and installations gave them a perfect landfall and the knowledge that the attack had been pushed home hard. In fact, so intense was the smoke over the target that it caused a serious hazard in picking out suitable targets. Egusa took his dive-bombers in a wide swing around the mountains to the east of the harbor to attack from the direction least expected – this gave Lieutenant Saburo Shindo's fighters time to make strafing sweeps to pave the way. Then he led in, deliberately selecting, as best he could, those warships which seemed to have suffered the least heavy damage. Anti-aircraft fire was intense, and, in contrast to earlier, more accurate. Even so the red-tailed D3A1 bore a charmed life as Egusa deposited his bomb firmly into the still undamaged battleship *Nevada* which had tried to make a run for it. More 'Vals' went for the battleship *Pennsylvania* in dry-dock along with the destroyers *Cassin* and *Downes*. These targets were heavily hit and damaged, as was the destroyer *Shaw* in floating dock whose bows were blown off; *Nevada* ran aground; the other two destroyers were wrecked (although subsequently rebuilt) but damage to *Pennsylvania*, although extensive, was not fatal. The bombs could demolish upperworks but not penetrate the big ship's vitals.

The first wave had lost only one solitary 'Val' but Egusa's men, as expected, took the brunt of the alerted firepower and no less than fifteen Aichis failed to return to their carriers. After the intense concentration of this assault Egusa gathered his surviving aircraft about him and set course for the long trip back to the waiting Task Force. He could confirm that the American battle fleet had been dealt a heavy blow, but the shore installations, workshops and oil storage tanks on which subsequent American fleets would rely, were still largely intact. A third attack was clearly called for. However this was not to be. Despite his desperate tiredness Egusa tried to put over his viewpoint via *Soryu*'s commander but the commander-in-chief, Vice-Admiral Chuichi Nagumo, turned it down. Despite the acclaim he received as leader of the great Task Force he was not a carrier man at heart and was much concerned with the vulnerability of his ships, a concern which was later proven to be well founded. He weighed up the pros and cons and, much to the fury of the young airmen, decided he had done enough. The great carriers turned their bows about and headed towards home. Behind them, it is true, they left the shattered remains of the American fleet, but they also left a legacy of hate and revenge, and, more important, the US carriers remained intact. Around them an even greater fleet was ultimately to be built.

The Hawaiian operation, as the Japanese called the Pearl Harbor attack, was but one of the many assaults throughout the Pacific Theatre. Others were taking place against the

Philippines, Malaya, Hong Kong and Wake Island. Most were devastatingly successful, but the last-named was not and the Japanese invasion force sent to crack this small nut was repulsed. In order to soften up the island for a second attempt, Nagumo was ordered to detach *Hiryu* and *Soryu* with some escorts. They arrived within striking distance of Wake Island on 18 December and Egusa led a force of eighteen D3A1s against the island's airstrip. But in this and subsequent missions low cloud hindered the skill of the dive-bombers and made target selection difficult. Further attacks followed the next day and on 21 December so that, by the time the second invasion attempt was made, most of the Marines' heavy weapons had been destroyed and the island fell.

Rear-Admiral Yamaguchi's 2 Carrier Division then returned to Japan to refit in preparation for further assaults. Already the Japanese were swarming over south-east Asia, crushing such feeble resistance as they found and moving with speed and skill into Borneo, Celebes, Malaya, Singapore, Sumatra, Java, Timor and New Guinea, each step forward being a consolidation for the next.

Egusa had little time with his family, now safely through their own ordeals, before *Soryu* and her companion vessels were on the move once more, standing southward. Their initial objective was to provide air support for the invasion of the island of Ambon in the Northern Banda Sea to the east of the Celebes. An Allied garrison consisting of 2000 troops, hastily reinforced, attempted to stem the onward surge of the Japanese towards Australia. By 21 January 1942, a first-class fleet anchorage had been obtained by the Japanese at Staring Bay, south of Kendari in the Celebes, and from here the two carriers sailed to carry out their softening-up attacks. Two strikes were made on Ambon by the dive-bombers on 24 and 25 January, opposition was slight and much damage was done. When the Japanese troops stormed ashore a few days later this strategically important island joined the long list of Allied defeats.

Nagumo now re-grouped his forces at Davao on Mindanao in the Philippines and, with the same carriers that had hit Pearl Harbor (less *Shokaku* and *Zuikaku*), refuelled at Staring Bay and entered the Timor Sea. Their target for this strike was the northern Australian port of Darwin, the only sizeable harbour in reach of the threatened area and the main staging post for troops and supplies being rushed up towards the battle zone by the Allies.

On 19 February 188 aircraft were launched: 71 dive-bombers, including 18 'Vals' under Egusa from *Soryu*, 81 attack bombers and 36 fighters. These were joined by a further 54 land-based aircraft, and again they caught the Allies completely by surprise. The dive-bombers concentrated on the massed shipping in the crowded harbour while the fighters and altitude bombers eliminated the opposition defences and hit shore targets. Egusa's men, as always, scored devastating hits when they arrived over the base at 10.10 that morning. When the Aichis had finished they had lost only two of their number but the destroyer *Peary*, seven large transports and tankers totalling 43,429 tons, had been sunk, as well as many small craft, while the Australian sloop *Swan*, the US seaplane tender *William B. Preston*, nine large and many small ships had been badly damaged. In addition eighteen Allied aircraft were destroyed. This effectively finished Darwin as a threat for the rest of the invasion period.

By 21 February the Nagumo Task Force had slipped silently away and was back at Staring Bay. Here they rested and replenished while Java was invaded. At the beginning of March they again sailed for the waters south of that island along with the battleships of Admiral Kondo's Main Body, Southern Force, for the mopping-up of any survivors trying to escape by sea. Among these were the US destroyer *Edsall* (Lieutenant Joshua J. Nix). She had earlier been damaged by the explosion of one of her own depth-charges but, on 26 February, had sailed from Tjilatjap to rendezvous with the American aircraft transport *Langley* along with the destroyer *Whipple*. The transport was sunk by land-based bombers and *Edsall* had rescued 177 survivors. The destroyer then met the fleet oiler *Pecos* off Flying Fish Cove, Christmas Island, on 28 February to transfer survivors to that ship which she did while under air attack, completing that task by 1 March. She was then sent back to Tjilatjap, but never got there. On the way she ran into Admiral Kondo's heavy ships. There followed an epic struggle. Alone and unaided *Edsall* fought her last battle with grim tenacity, twisting and turning at the best speed her little hull and straining old engines could manage. They both gave the best performance of her long career. For a while she bore a charmed life. She was taken under fire by the heavy cruisers *Tone* and *Chikuma* as well as the battleships *Hiei* and *Kirishima*. Hundreds of 14-in. and 8-in. shells were fired at her but somehow she evaded them all and kept moving. For a time it almost looked as if she might get clean away. In frustration Kondo called up the *Kido Butai* to pin her down. Together with one wingman, Egusa took off from *Soryu* and quicky located the four-piper making smoke amid the shell splashes. Boring in from out of the sun he planted his bomb to score the first direct hit on the little ship. The crippled destroyer immediately slowed down to become a sitting duck.

No word ever came from her or her 150-man crew and it was not until the spring of 1952 that the Americans found out her fate. Damaged and unable to steam she was quickly overhauled by the whole Japanese force who used her for target practice. Under the fire of four heavy cruisers and two battleships she was mercilessly blown asunder. Film was taken from the cruiser *Ashigara* as the Japanese fleet pumped shells into her from point-blank range. Later five survivors got ashore only to die in POW camps. Nor did other ships long survive her; *Pecos* herself was destroyed by Egusa on the same afternoon. On 5 March he led a 180-plane strike force against Tjilatjap itself repeating the Darwin exploit. Two merchant ships were sunk and fifteen others so damaged they were scuttled before the port fell.

By now Egusa's victories were becoming legendary and his accuracy a byword in the fleet. To his crews he was inspirational. As one Japanese officer told me, 'He was called the "God of Dive-Bombing".' His group always achieved incredible percentages of bomb hits. Yet despite the tempo of operations thus far, Egusa's best work was still to come.

On completion of the Java mopping-up operations Nagumo took his carriers back to Kendari and here *Kaga* was replaced by *Shokaku* and *Zuikaku* once more. On 26 March the force put to sea again, steering south to pass north of Timor and then west, south of the Java and Sumatra barrier, to enter the Indian Ocean on 2 April. Their objective was to engage and destroy a scratch fleet hastily assembled by the Royal Navy under

Admiral Sir James Somerville to defend the Indian subcontinent. On paper it was a formidable force with five battleships, three carriers and numerous cruisers and destroyers. In practice the ships were a hodgepodge, many dating from the First World War, while the aircraft they carried were hopelessly outdated and outmatched by the Japanese (surprisingly, there were no dive-bombers serving in front-line units in the Royal Navy at this period although both Skuas and Chesapeakes were available). The Admiral contributed decisions during the battle which split his forces.

The first Japanese strike was launched on 5 April against Colombo in Ceylon and included 36 'Vals'. Although the Royal Air Force was alerted and waiting for them, and although huge claims were made at the time by Churchill (and since by those who should know better), Japanese losses were just seven planes, whereas the British lost 27, including 15 Hurricanes and four Fulmars. Egusa and his men hit and sank the destroyer *Tenedos* and the armed merchant cruiser *Hector* while damaging others and destroying submarine workshops. After casting blindly around in the hope of making a dusk torpedo-bomber attack on his Japanese opponent Somerville detached parts of his force for other duties. When news came in of the Colombo strike he attempted to re-concentrate them but it was then too late. Two heavy cruisers, *Cornwall* and *Dorsetshire*, were recalled but soon after midday on 5 April they were sighted by a scout plane from the Nagumo fleet, which reported them at first as destroyers. At once Egusa was dispatched with a full force of 80 'Vals' from *Akagi*, *Hiryu* and *Soryu* to hunt them down. A corrected sighting was received confirming the targets as cruisers. The British ships intercepted these reports and knew they were in trouble. They increased speed to 27 knots, their maximum, and went on to full alert. At 13.38 Egusa spotted their long wakes in the clear visibility. The two ships began a desperate zigzag but this served only to put their guns' crews off their aim. Approaching from out of the sun and astern, thus masking most of the defenders' guns, Egusa led in against *Dorsetshire* and scored a direct hit with his first bomb. Egusa's terse radio orders were intercepted on the Japanese flagship's bridge and the nineteen-minute assault was recorded for posterity in his own words:

'Sighted enemy vessels. "Get ready to go in." Air Group, 1 CarDiv, take the first ship; Air Group, 2 CarDiv, take the second ship.' [There was a brief pause, then:] 'Ship Number One has stopped, dead in water. Listing heavily. Ship Number Two is aflame. Ship Number One has sunk. Ship Number Two has sunk.'

Dorsetshire was hit quickly in succession on her aircraft cata-pault, the W/T office on the bridge, and in the engine and boiler rooms. Her rudder was jammed to starboard and she careered around taking further hits, including one which penetrated a magazine, and in eight minutes she had gone. *Cornwall* took something like fifteen bombs in seven minutes. She heeled over and sank bows first. One survivor wrote: 'The Japs by this time had formed up in squadrons and flew past in perfect formation, thirty or forty of them, and much to our relief flew away. We were quite expecting to be machine-gunned in the water.'

But Egusa did not fight in this way, nor did he allow his men to do so. After the attack the analysis was that this was an all-time record in bombing accuracy for the Japanese (or anyone else for that matter). They estimated that just about every bomb dropped had been a direct hit or a very near miss: 'So thick were the explosions from the rain of bombs that many plane crews could not determine whether they had actually released their missiles. Only after all our planes had assembled in formation and the pilots could visually check the racks of other planes could we tell whether or not several planes were still armed.'

After refuelling Nagumo took his carriers back to Ceylon on 9 April and launched another strike at Trincomalee. Events were almost an exact repeat of the first raid. Again the British fighters got a mauling, ships were sunk in the harbour and others damaged. Royal Air Force bombers mounted an attack in return, the first time Allied eyes had even seen the Nagumo ships, but most were shot down and they achieved nothing. Huge claims of victory were made over this failure back in Britain.

Another blunder was committed in sending all available ships to sea without any fighter cover. This gave Egusa his longed-for chance to destroy an enemy aircraft-carrier. It was not the big US carriers he had been searching for, just the small

British carrier *Hermes*, but it was a carrier. She had an escort of one lone destroyer HMAS *Vampire*. Once more 90 Aichis roared off from the Japanese carriers' flight-decks and headed west. Scanning the shallow waters off Trincomalee Egusa sighted the flat-top at 10.35 and began his attack. Within ten minutes *Hermes* was on the bottom, literally blown apart by the deluge of direct hits. An eyewitness recalled: 'The Japanese came in so low that, after dropping their bombs, they were in serious danger of being blown to bits by blast of their own making. Those in the look-out position in the fighting top, some 120 ft above the flight-deck, remarked later that some planes swept in below their level.

Hermes capsized and went down and those bombers left turned their attention to *Vampire* which they just as quickly dispatched, and various lesser vessels in the area. Not one dive-bomber was hit, let alone lost. As for the accuracy of Egusa's latest assault, one source summed it up thus: 'Shortly after the Indian Ocean Operation in which Egusa figured so prominently, we were able to have a reunion in Japan. I was preparing for the Midway and Aleutian Operations; I asked my old friend how his planes had sunk the British warships. Egusa looked at me and shrugged.

'It was much simpler than bombing the *Settsu*. That's all.'

'The *Settsu*. Simpler than bombing Japan's old target battle-ship.'

As well as the reunion with his old comrade Egusa was able to use the opportunity of the fleet's return to home waters, where they arrived in May 1942, to rejoin his family at last. He was able to see his second son, Toshimasa, for the first time, after the child's difficult birth at Kamakura in December. He also received a hero's welcome, as was to be expected. For six months the dive-bomber pilots had struck from the Nagumo Task Force like phantoms leaving a trail of destruction behind them unequalled in naval warfare. Little wonder the Japanese considered the tide of destiny was with them.

This leave was the happiest Egusa was to know, never again were things to be so perfect in every sphere. But the time soon passed and it was back into training for the 'Big Operation', the final reckoning with the Americans, the MI Operation, Midway.

The Indian Ocean sortie had marked the high-point of Egusa's career. Such a fantastic hit-rate in wartime would be almost impossible to equal, let alone surpass, no matter what the odds. But Egusa knew that destroying the British warships, with their antiquated concept of modern sea warfare, was a very different proposition to taking on the United States navy's aircraft-carriers. These, all still intact six months after Pearl Harbor, were the elusive prizes that he sought most eagerly. But would he hunt them down, or would they do the hunting?

How to lure these carriers into a set-piece battle and destroy them, leaving Japan master of the Pacific, was the principal problem to which her navy leaders now applied themselves. Their deliberations resulted in the Midway and Aleutians operations. By occupying both these strategic places simultaneously, Yamamoto reasoned, the enemy would be forced to come out and fight on ground chosen by the Japanese and so with the odds heavily in their favour. In theory this was an admirable idea, and indeed initially it worked perfectly. However it was the assumption that the Americans would always play by the Japanese rules that made the final outcome very different, also the fact that the very ease of Japan's conquests to that date had led her to disperse her forces over a vast area and thus over-reach herself. The army wished to push down the chain of the Solomon Islands to isolate Australia, and the navy, forced to dispatch three aircraft-carriers to support this objective, lost one in the Battle of the Coral Sea. The other two were damaged, thus all three were not available for the main battle. The Japanese still had a superiority in carriers but again they dissipated what they had, some being sent to cover the Aleutians operation far to the north, others split between the various Midway Task Forces. So, in the final analysis, it was only four aircraft carriers, *Akagi*, *Kaga*, *Hiryu* and *Soryu*, which were matched against three United States carriers. Over-confidence had reduced the odds quite needlessly from a ratio of 10 : 3 to a mere 4 : 3. The conflicting needs of having to attack both the island and the American carriers split still further the Japanese air strike forces as different types of bomb-loads were required for each target. The result was that, this time, it was the Japanese who were caught between two stools. The American marine and navy dive-bomber pilots did not miss the opportunity, and it was the turn of the Japanese to feel the weight of dive-bombing on exposed carrier decks. The result was equally devastating.

'Victory Fever' there may have been at home and in some elements at headquarters or in the army, but Egusa himself was under no illusion as *Soryu* put to sea once more from Hashira-jima, at 04.00 on the morning of 27 May 1942, with the Nagumo Task Force. She was just one of no less than 71 Japanese warships, including the whole battleship strength, converging on the tiny atoll for the final showdown.

Let us consider the composition of the Japanese air-striking forces as they were organised at this stage of the war. *Soryu* herself was a typical Japanese aircraft-carrier. Displacing some 15,900 tons, she could steam at 28 knots and carry a total of 71 aircraft – 63 operational and eight in reserve. She was completed in December 1937. She had a small 'island' bridge structure on her starboard side, and two smoke-vents discharged almost horizontally from the same side leaving her 711-ft planked wooden flight-deck clear for operations. Like contemporary American carriers, but unlike equivalent British carriers, she was unarmoured, being built to carry a large number of aircraft to strike hard, rather than to absorb punishment herself. She was, therefore, very vulnerable and relied heavily on her own fighter and gun defences to protect herself.

At this period of the war Japanese carriers had numerous fuelling points positioned around two large hangars so that aircraft could be fuelled below decks and then be brought up later ready to go. This made for speed but meant that under the flimsy wooden flight-deck they were wide open to bomb hits. Each hangar had two decks which were each almost completely sealed and isolated from the rest of the ship. Ventilation systems changed the air at ten-minute intervals, but any fumes from leaks could build up dangerously in that confined space. In the event of a major fire the hangar crews could not escape, nor get rid of flammable material, while the ship's own firefighters could not gain easy access inside, nor could other ships help very much. Still, up to that time, hardly any enemy aircraft and no ships at all had so much us sighted them, let alone made a serious attack, and little concern therefore was felt on this point.

As originally built *Soryu* lacked sheer in the bows, a fault which in her later sisters was rectified by the addition of further decks forward. This made her notoriously 'wet' and she would dip her prow into every sea and throw spray back over the flight-deck in sheets. No catapaults were carried, the heavily laden bombers taking off against the wind without assistance. A smoke-discharger forward gave wind direction and the carrier thus had to steer into it when launching. This again made them vulnerable as they then had to maintain a steady course during the landing operations. Once the aircraft had been fuelled and armed below decks in the large hangars they were brought up on the lifts and 'spotted' on the flight-deck in readiness for launch. The *Hikoochoo* (Air Operations Officer) controlled events from the bridge with the aid of two other officers, while the *Seibiin* (Flight-Deck Controller) was responsible for arranging the aircraft on the deck. Once the order was given to launch, the *Hikoochoo* raised a white flag from his position in the bridge wings and the aircraft flew off one by one at about 20-second intervals until all had become airborne, whereupon the flag was lowered. Destroyers were allocated to each carrier in the usual manner as 'plane-guard' to rescue any ditching aircrew.

Landing operations were almost as basic. Returning planes (priority being given to damaged aircraft) flew some 500 m from the carrier waiting for the *Seibiin* to signal by lamp that the flight-deck was clear. Abreast of the small bridge structure, the aircraft turned at a height of some 200 m and positioned itself astern. The pilot then used his own judgement to complete the landing. Eleven arrestor wires, normally lowered, would be raised across the rear portion of the deck and ensured that at least one engaged the tailhook of the aircraft and brought the plane to a halt. A large retractable crane and foam fire-fighting apparatus stood ready in the deck platforms for any cripples or mistakes by novices. No bomber was allowed to land with a bomb intact for obvious reasons, not that many of Egusa's skilled and proud pilots would contemplate bringing home his bomb-load while an enemy ship was available as a target. It was a point of honour among these veterans to make every bomb count.

The Second *Koku Sentai* under Rear-Admiral Tamon

Yamaguchi aboard *Hiryu* comprised that ship and *Soryu* commanded by Captain Ryusaku Yanagimoto. Both *Hiryu* and *Soryu* carried identical aircraft complements: twenty-one A6M5 (Zero) Sentoki (fighters), twenty-one B5N2 (Kate) Kogekiki (torpedo or attack bombers) and twenty-one D3A2 (Val) Kyukoka Bakugerkiki (dive-bombers). The latter were commanded by Lieutenant Masahiro Ikeda, while Egusa flew from the same aircraft-carrier in his distinctively marked 'Val' as overall Flight Leader and Attack Co-Ordinator for the whole strike force. The normal bomb-load for attacking ship targets with the 'Val' was a single 500-kg armour-piercing bomb, but SAP (semi-armour-piercing) and HE (high explosive) bombs were available if required, as were small fragmentation bombs designed to scythe down anti-aircraft gunners in their nests or infantry ashore. The defensive armament of the dive-bomber consisted of two 7.7-mm machine-guns in each wing and one flexible mounting of the same calibre operated by the wireless operator seated in tandem behind the pilot. The aircraft themselves were slow and relied on their own fighter protection for their immunity on the flight out to the target and back again. Once committed to their 60-degree plus dives only a direct hit by a large calibre shell (3-in. or 5-in.) could deflect them and this was not easy to achieve, even by experienced gunners willing to stand up to a screaming dive-bomber. Smaller calibre guns would score hits and eventually destroy a dive-bomber in the break-away at low altitude but by then the bomb was released and it was too late.

The aircrew complement aboard was about one-tenth of the entire ship's company, but they were the principals on whose achievements all the others depended and whom they served. As *Soryu* sailed to battle most of her Kyukoka Bakugerkiki aircrew were veterans, the crème de la crème, with only the slightest leavening of new recruits among them. Losses hitherto had been minimal. Each man thirsted for the sight of a 'Yankee' flat-top in his dive-bombing sights, and most were convinced that, when that opportunity arose, they would deal with it as positively as they had done with *Hermes*.

It was fated not to be. The American Dauntless dive-bombers found the Nagumo Task Force with all its bombers still sitting on the flight-decks awaiting take-off. Although the dive-bomber groups of *Akagi* and *Kaga* had been struck down to be re-armed for a second strike on Midway Island itself, the élite crews of Egusa's units, 18 'Vals' each aboard *Hiryu* and *Soryu*, remained ready for instant action, bombed-up and ready to go on a carrier-strike as they had been for a long period. Egusa and his men were eager to be off but, for some strange reason, Nagumo held them back too. They remained 'spotted' on the flight-deck fully armed and fuelled but chained impotently as the vital minutes ticked by. Attacks by land-based aircraft had been repeatedly beaten off by the fleet's fighters but, at 10.24 on 4 June, just a few minutes before the launch was finally to be accomplished, fate struck a cruel blow. Undetected in the general mêlée, powerful American dive-bomber forces arrived over the Japanese carriers and began their ear-splitting dives. Within a few minutes *Akagi*, *Kaga* and *Soryu* had been hit by a number of bombs which penetrated their frail decks, carved through the assembled aircraft which had their engines running, and exploded with devastating results inside the hangars among the reserve aircraft, fuel tanks and bomb and torpedo arsenals. It was a moment of utter devastation and, with this one attack, the whole élite team of the Japanese dive-bomber forces was annihilated. An eyewitness described the scene aboard *Soryu* at that fateful time as follows: 'When the attack broke, deck parties were busily preparing the carrier's planes for take-off, and their first awareness of the onslaught came when great flashes of fire were seen sprouting from *Kaga*, some distance off to port, followed by explosions and tremendous columns of black smoke. Eyes instinctively looked skyward just in time to see a spear of thirteen American planes plummeting down on *Soryu*. It was 10.25.'

The carrier took three direct hits immediately, one hitting the flight-deck forward of the main lift right on the great red 'meatball' of the nationality marking painted there, the other two on each side of the amidships lift. The fuel of the pulverised aircraft ignited and spread instantly through the hangar decks, bombs exploded and a chain reaction spread like wildfire through the great vessel's innards. Egusa himself, like many of his companions, hardly had time to realise the attack was taking place before explosions blew him violently overboard and into the sea. He was still alive but the searing agony of multiple burns was barely eased by contact with the warm salt of the sea. He survived the explosion, the catapaulting into the sea from the flight-deck, and the flames, and was finally pulled out, breathing but in a bad way, when the destroyers *Hamakaze* and *Isokaze* moved in among the wreckage and the survivors to retrieve whoever they could from the carnage. Egusa was hardly recognisable when taken aboard but prompt medical care soon restored him to a painful fitness during the long voyage back home to Japan.

It was a sad homecoming for the hitherto conquering hero. His burns were bad enough to ensure a short period of hospitalisation, but Egusa was indomitable. Not only did he recover quickly from his injuries but, once he was up and around again, he was campaigning to fly once more. Within a month he was given his wish, but not with a front-line unit. On 10 July 1942, he was assigned as an Instructor at the Yokosuka Kokutai. With the loss of so many of her fine and experienced aircrew, most of them without even the opportunity to strike back at the enemy, Japan's position was a very serious one. True the Aleutians were occupied but this had little revelance. The Americans were soon storming ashore at Guadalcanal in the Solomons as the first stage of the long fight back. The loss of the aircraft-carriers was grievous, the loss of so many front-line aircraft was sad, but these could be replaced. The aircrew slaughtered at Midway could never be replaced. From this moment on Japan was fighting a losing battle.

The urgent need was for the training of large numbers of replacements, and veterans such as Egusa became doubly valuable in this role, much as they may have wished otherwise. Somehow he had to impart his special skills and expertise to the new arrivals, knowing that when they faced the enemy the odds against them would have increased enormously. In fact the rest of the Pacific War saw the ever more frantic training of fresh aircrew, and their squandering in operation after operation without a decisive result. As their training period grew shorter and shorter so their ability to inflict damage on the Americans lessened. With the enormous industrial base behind them the first fleet of the United States doubled and quadrupled in a short period of time and never again did the Japanese have the advantage of numbers over their opponents as at Midway.

New aircraft were now on the drawing boards to replace the standard models. A powerful new dive-bomber for carrier work, the Yokosuku D4Y ('Judy'), showed great promise of speed and range, but suffered numerous teething problems which delayed its entry into service. New carriers were laid down or converted from oilers and the like, but for every one Japan commissioned the United States commissioned three. With her ring of island bases forming a series of bulwarks across the Pacific the Japanese husbanded their naval strength while seeking to rebuild their air arm. This gave the United States the breathing space she needed to outbuild the Japanese and then begin her assaults with overwhelming forces.

As Japanese carriers were at a premium the Imperial navy designed a powerful new twin-engined attack bomber for use from island airstrips. It was thus hoped that these, working from their 'unsinkable aircraft-carriers', would inflict enough damage on the attacking American Task Groups so to weaken them that the Japanese fleet would be able to tackle them on something like level terms. This new bomber was the Yokosuka P1Y Ginga ('Milky Way'), which the Allies later code-named 'Frances'. Taking the versatile Junkers Ju 88 as an ideal the navy *15-Shi* specification in 1940 called for the aircraft to operate as a fast strike bomber, torpedo- and dive-bomber. Powered by two Nakahima Homare 11 engines each of 1820 hp, the first Ginga made its operational flight in August 1943 and achieved speeds of almost 300 mph. It could carry an internal bomb-load of two 500-kg bombs or a single 1764-lb torpedo. It had a crew of three.

Egusa was one of the first of the navy's more experienced veterans to fly the Ginga as a test-pilot. On 30 November he had been assigned to the training carrier *Hosho* again to teach deck landings, take-offs and other techniques but, on 1 February 1943, he returned once more to Yokosuka. His job was now to test and evaluate the Ginga ready for combat use. The need was now urgent with the Americans everywhere on the advance and the latest batch of naval aircrew wasted in Yamamoto's abortive and costly *I-Go* operation. Numerous design changes were required as the test programme continued; in particular, although it was found to be an excellent aircraft in the air, the P1Y1 was a difficult and temperamental aircraft to keep operational. This was discovered during training, and it was realised that ground crews at the more primitive airstrips out in the atolls where they were to be based would experience even greater difficulties.

So confident were the builders in the machine's potential, however, that large numbers of Gingas were ordered off the drawing board. The engines were changed, the defensive armament increased and a host of other modifications all complicated production but, contrary to what has been written on this aircraft, the Ginga soon saw combat. The Americans were at any time expected to make their next major move and it had been decided to meet this thrust with every available ship and aircraft. In anticipation of this, experienced instructors such as Egusa were withdrawn from basic training and thrown into the fight. Thus, on 15 August 1943, Egusa was given command of the 521 Kokutai, the first complete unit of P1Y1s. With a select team he was ordered to develop suitable bombing and torpedo attack tactics in anticipation of imminent combat.

The 521 Kokutai formed part of the re-organised 1 Air Fleet of land-based aircraft under Vice-Admiral Kakuji Kakuta. This was built up over the next year to a strength of 1000 aircraft and was therefore, on paper, a formidable force. By May 1944 wind of the next American assault against the Marianas was received and Kakuta moved his units forward into the combat area in anticipation, setting up his headquarters on Tinian Island and distributing his forces on airfields in the Marianas, Carolines, Iwo Jima and Truk, from where they could island-hop to reinforce the threatened area once the American attack was committed. Unfortunately for the Japanese they allowed a large proportion of these aircraft to be withdrawn from this area and redeployed down to New Guinea for the Biak operation. Not only were large numbers thus destroyed there fruitlessly, but a number of aircrew were lost from malaria. This deployment proved a grave mistake, for when the pre-emptive American carrier strikes began to hit the island airstrips in the Marianas on 13 June, half the Japanese force which should have met it had already been thrown away. The main assault went in against Saipan at 08.40 on 15 June 1944, by which time Kakuta's remaining air strength had been decimated.

The original Japanese plan, Operation *A-Go*, had called for the land-based aircraft to co-ordinate their attacks with Vice-Admiral Jisaburo Ozawa's powerful main fleet, which had been rebuilt around no less than nine aircraft-carriers. This latter force was based at Lingga and in the homeland and was to rendezvous at Tawi Tawi, then move to the north-east of Palau and standby to meet the United States fleet in direct combat. By that time it was hoped that Kakuta's land-based aircraft, reinforced from Palau and elsewhere, would already have inflicted severe damage upon the enemy. Word about the approach of the American Task Force was received on 9 June and immediately what was left of the Biak diversion force was hastily ordered back. Other reinforcements were later sent in from the homeland and via Iwo Jima.

At the Yokosuka Naval Air Station there remained some 120–130 miscellaneous naval aircraft of all types, one-third only of the pilots being experienced, the rest novices. These too were to be thrown in. But by then it was too late. Heavy fighter sweeps were mounted from the twelve large carriers of Admiral Raymond A. Spruance's Task Forces and they so destroyed Kakuta's units both in the air and on the ground that the latter were unable to make any effective reply. Within two or three days almost all these aircraft were wiped out and, far from whittling down the odds for Ozawa, they had inflicted no damage whatsoever on the American fleet.

At the start of the attack, which the Americans code-named FORAGER and which was later to become known as the Battle of the Philippine Sea, Egusa's unit was based at No 2 Airfield on Guam Island and he had about sixty Gingas on his strength. These had undergone further training at Guam and Yap prior to their final deployment but it was all in vain. With the overwhelming numbers of the new Hellcat fighters at the Americans' disposal and the huge concentration of anti-aircraft firepower mounted by the massive array of warships in the American Task Forces, Egusa knew that he stood as little chance in a straightforward daytime attack as would Somerville's antiquated biplanes have had against the Nagumo Task Force back in 1942. Like Somerville then, Egusa knew that his only hope of even getting close to the American carriers – which over and over again were reiterated as the number one and only target for all Japanese flyers in the islands – was by a low-level dusk approach under their radar. To inflict the most damage by such methods dive-bombing was ineffective, shallow bombing was not decisive enough and so the adaptable Ginga was equipped for torpedo attack.

Even before they could mount their raid the unit suffered grievous losses as the American naval fighter aircraft swarmed over Guam throughout the daylight hours, bombing and machine-gunning everything and anything that moved on the tiny airstrips. Their tormentors were the flyers of Task Group 58.1 under Rear-Admiral J.J. Clark with the carriers *Hornet (II)*, *Yorktown (II)*, *Belleau Wood* and *Bataan*, with four cruisers and 12 destroyers. On 12 June this force mounted 468 sorties against the two Guam airfields and Rota, although the Japanese were not using the latter. The American flyers lost 15 aircraft and claimed to have destroyed a total of 40 Japanese aircraft. Next day 339 sorties were made, with the loss of four aircraft and claiming the destruction of seven more Japanese planes. On 14 June Task Group 58.2, under Rear-Admiral A.E. Montgomery, took over. He had the carriers *Bunker Hill*, *Wasp (II)*, *Monterey* and *Cabot* with a similar strength screen. They launched 80 sorties and claimed a further 13 Japanese aircraft for the loss of two of their own.

It was obviously useless for the men of 521 Kokutai to sit and endure any more of this slaughter. They were being annihilated piecemeal and, if they waited for Ozawa to come up as planned, there would be no aircraft left to co-operate with his carrier bomber force anyway. Egusa decided to launch his attack that evening while he still had some planes left intact. All in all it was a pathetic attack group he was able to muster on the afternoon of 15 June: a few Susei dive-bombers and 10 Gingas still airworthy. All along Egusa had known that his next battle might well be his last – a forlorn hope against the mighty strength of the United States. Gone were the halcyon days of 1942. In his last conversation with his wife, just before he left homeland Japan for Tinian in May, he told her: 'This is *Minato-gawa.*' *Minato-gawa* means that one has made up one's mind to go out fighting despite the certain knowledge that one is to be killed in a defeat. Two years on from his great victories, the Japanese air attacks were now as puny as spear against

armoured plate. Nonetheless enough of the old skill remained
to ensure that even this tiny force was to give the Americans the
only real fright they had in this one-sided battle. The aircraft
took off just before dusk, evading enemy patrols and flew
towards the hidden enemy Task Force.

Egusa had deployed his force in two groups. The first 10
'Judys', the second a mixed group of another 10 Gingas, three
'Judy dive-bombers and six Zero fighters – all that remained.
The Gingas were variously reported as 'Betty' navy bombers
and 'Sally' army bombers in a few subsequent reports and even
in many later books, although no aircraft of either of these types
were in the islands at this time. Even the very existence of 521
Kokutai is not acknowledged in the 'definitive' histories. Thus
Egusa's last mission has, hitherto, been totally misreported.
But there is no need for any of this inaccuracy, since the
contemporary reports of both the Japanese and the American
survivors give accurate and precise details.

The objective of Egusa's last mission was in fact Task Group
58.3 under Rear-Admiral J.W. Reeves with *Enterprise*, *Lexington
(II)*, *San Jacinto* and *Princeton* with four cruisers and nine
destroyers. Vice-Admiral W.A. Lee's 'Battle Line', Task
Group 58.7, comprising the battleships *Washington*, *North Carolina*, *Iowa*, *New Jersey*, *Indiana*, *South Dakota* and *Alabama*, four
heavy cruisers and 12 destroyers had formed an advance wall of
steel upon which Japanese air attacks were to dash themselves
in vain. They were in position, bearing 291 degrees, 19 miles
from Reeves' carrier group at 18.48 that evening, when Egusa's
Gingas slid in softly out of the twilight sky towards them.

The earlier raid had been plotted by radar and intercepted
by the Combat Air Patrol from *San Jacinto* which shot down six
of the Susei dive-bombers of a force of ten (and identified them
as 'Tonys'). They were thus drawn out and enabled the Gingas
to get in close enough to make a determined attack. *Lexington
(II)*'s report read as follows:

> The USS *North Carolina* began firing to port at 19.03, and firing was
> seen on the horizon dead ahead. At 19.07 lookouts reported ten
> low-flying multi-engine planes dead ahead at 10,000 yds. These
> planes were lost until at about 4000 yds where they were reported
> coming in from dead ahead and on the port bow. All the ships in

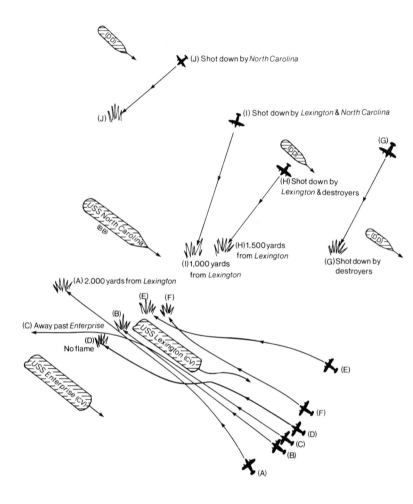

(J) Shot down by *North Carolina*

(I) Shot down by *Lexington* & *North Carolina*

(G)

(H) Shot down by
Lexington & destroyers

USS *North Carolina*
(BB)

(H) 1,500 yards
from *Lexington*

(I) 1,000 yards
from *Lexington*

(G) Shot down by
destroyers

(A) 2,000 yards from *Lexington*

(E)   (F)

(B)

(C) Away past *Enterprise*

(D)
No flame

USS *Lexington* (CV)

(E)

USS *Enterprise* (CV)

(F)

(D)
(C)
(B)

(A)

Fig 1 USS *Lexington (II)*'s track chart of attack by Egusa's squadron
on 14 June 1944: At 19.13 *Lexington* ordered Emergency turn
left 50° to 090. Used full rudder to about 080, right full rudder
to about 100, steaded on 090. 19.15 Emergency turn right 40°,
to 130 using standard rudder

the Task Group began firing. During the next four minutes a total of eight planes attacked this ship, and four were shot down in flames and one hit the water without burning. Five sure and two sure sure assists were claimed by the USS *Lexington (II)*. Four definite torpedo wakes and possibly a fifth were observed, two of which were within 10 yds of the hull running down each side. [The report goes on to state, correctly, that:] It is the opinion of this ship that the attacking planes were 'Milky Ways', new type enemy light bombers. This action with the enemy aircraft resulted in eighteen casualties, of which eleven were of a minor nature, and seven were considered serious enough for admission to the Sick List. One man suffered a serious shrapnel wound in the chest, three suffered multiple shrapnel wounds, one had both eardrums ruptured, and two received flash burns to the face.

The *San Jacinto*'s report makes similar reading:

In spite of the success of the CAP (Combat Air Patrol) eight enemy aircraft reached the disposition and attempted torpedo attacks. Formation 5V was effected and the group was manouvered in a series of evasive turns by OTC while all ships opened fire. All eight enemy aircraft were shot down by ships' anti-aircraft fire and no damage was inflicted on any unit of the TG by the enemy, although a bomb was dropped off the port quarter of *Enterprise*, doing no damage. *San Jacinto* shot down one 'Betty' [*sic*] making a turn by her port quarter with *Enterprise* as her apparent target. Enemy attacks all appeared to be concentrated on the two large carriers.

Surprise had been achieved but, despite their gallantry, Egusa's forlorn hope had been wiped out in vain. Thus passed almost unnoticed by friend and foe alike, Japan's and, arguably, the world's leading naval dive-bomber pilot. He died in combat as any good samurai should. His achievements remain unique and special in the annals of air/sea warfare. His passing typified the ultimate issue of the Pacific War: the age of the skilled warrior had been overtaken by the age of massed firepower.

Four days later at home in Japan Kiyoko lay sleeping and, as she later recounted, in her dream Takashige Egusa appeared to her to tell her of his fate. It was dawn on 19 June 1944. Several weeks were to pass before she received official confirmation that her husband had failed to return from his mission. He was given a most exceptional posthumous promotion, by two ranks, to Captain. Three months after his death Kiyoko gave birth at Kamakura to their third child, a daughter, whom she named Haruko.

Eleven years later Kiyoko, by then a practitioner at the Kochi Medical College, was returning from the United States after a one-year study course when her ship passed close to the spot where her husband had fought his final battle. She dressed up in her national costume and, at the nearest point to Saipan, threw a wreath of flowers into the sea. Takashige Egusa was not forgotten.

2 Rear-Admiral Gerald Mesny

French Navy   1908–76

War brings about many strange events, some of which are so paradoxical that, had they been suggested before the event, they would have seemed ludicrous. Thus the idea that a small force of French naval flyers, operating from land bases and using American dive-bombers to stem an attack by German troops in The Netherlands, would have seemed insane prior to May 1940. Yet within less than a month this was the situation in which the young Lieutenant de Vaisseau Gerald Mesny found himself. The fact too that this Anglophile would be found later in the war serving with the Vichy French-controlled forces in Casablanca was yet another contradiction of accepted history, yet that too was to be his destiny.

Gerald Joel René Mesny was born at Granville, in the district of Manche, on 24 July 1908. This pleasant coastal town overlooks the Bay du St Michel and the famous Mont-Saint-Michel is due south. Across the bay stand Dinard and the docks of St Malo while to the north-west lie the Channel Islands. Growing up on the coast it was perhaps natural that Mesny should set his heart on a naval career. Maybe the close proximity of England and the traditions of Normandy influenced his long-held affection for his British cousins – certainly the two feelings were to feature largely in his life. Be that as it may, it was at the age of nineteen that the young man took the first steps to achieve his ambition, entering the Ecole Navale, situated at the great naval base of Brest, on 30 September 1927, as a cadet Officier de Marine. One of his closest friends there was to become another of the French navy's dive-bomber aces, the Capitaine de Frégate Michel Lorenzi. He told me that he always remembered Mesny from this period with affection as an excellent comrade in every sense. A third young cadet destined for the same career was the Admiral Francis Laine. He too recollects with fondness that early comradeship: 'I can tell you that he was a good friend, rather reserved and not given to much talking. In appearance he was what I can only describe as "British looking" in both aspect and mannerisms.'

Mesny emerged from the two-year course with a School Leaving Certificate in Sciences to complement his excellent English-language ability and with the rank of Enseigne de Vaisseau Class 2. On 2 October 1929 he was posted to the old 13,847-ton armoured cruiser *Edgar Quinet* for his sea-going training. She was the same age as himself and when she was wrecked on 9 January 1930 Mesny survived and was transferred to the modern light cruiser *Lamotte-Picquet* to continue his lessons in more secure conditions. Later that year the cadet officer voyaged to the Far East and, along with the other young officers, Mesny was transferred to a smaller ship. This took place in November 1930, and his new vessel was the little Yangtse River gunboat *Francis Garnier*. Along with British, American and Japanese vessels of the same type this little man-o'-war spent her time patrolling up and down that enormous river maintaining a precarious peace amidst the chaos of warring factions, pirates and natural disasters such as riot and flood. In the two years Mesny served aboard her he managed to see brief periods of action and was rewarded, on 1 October 1931, with promotion to Enseigne Class 1. He returned home a year later for the regulation period of service ashore, being based at the bustling Mediterranean Fleet base of Toulon.

This frustrating period determined the young officer to branch out into fresh fields and, like so many young men in the world's armed services at that time, the lure of the air beckoned him. He applied to transfer to the Naval Air Arm, the Aeronavale, at the first possible opportunity, and joined the Air Training School (Ecole d'Aeronautique) at Versailles in January 1933. Mesny graduated a year later holding a Certificate de pilote d'aviation – as a fighter pilot –(Brevet d'Aeronautique) to find himself posted to the Base d'Aeronautique Maritime at Brest to continue advanced training.

Other things besides flying aroused Mesny's passionate interest at this time. The principal one was Helène, one of the Gouzien girls, daughters of the English wife of the British

Consul-General stationed at the Brest naval base. Gerald started going out with Hélène and they married at the tiny village of Landunvez, near Kersatin-Portsall, on 21 March 1939. His daughter Evelyn, now Madame Stipanovitch, remembers her father: 'As an individual my father was a very interesting man. He was extremely well read and cultured. He wrote well and was good at versifying. He had a dry sense of humour and much wit. Physically he looked very much like Alec Guinness and dressed elegantly. As a matter of fact his fellow officers used to nickname him "Sir Gerald" because of his looks and his sense of humour was strikingly English.'

At this time the Aeronavale was very run-down as a result of the general lack of funds for the navy and the French government's indifference to naval matters. As one of the great naval powers France had not taken kindly to being relegated to a position below Japan at the 1922 Washington Conference; but great reforming Ministers of Marine such as Georges Leygues and François Petrie, and leaders such as Admiral Darlan, gradually began to rebuild the fleet. In the matter of naval aviation an early lead in dive-bombing experience, with experiments conducted at the St Raphael school by Lieutenant Teste with AC1 Squadron, had since been neglected but a new start was made with a specially designed plane for naval dive-bombing, the parasol-winged Gourdou-Leveurre GL430–B1, first flown in 1931. It was not a very advanced design, however, and French naval aviation, like the British, lagged far behind developments in the United States and Japan. The French navy in fact possessed only one true aircraft-carrier, *Bearn*. She was typical of her time, forming part of the post-Treaty fleet and was converted from an incomplete battleship of the *Normandie* class in the same manner as British, American and Japanese aircraft-carriers of the same vintage. This meant that she was always too slow to be a really efficient ship but she served several generations of French navy airmen as the only sea-going platform from which they could operate. She was of some 22,146 tons displacement, had a 590-ft flight-deck, and was equipped with three electric lifts but only a single hangar. She was limited therefore to a small aircraft complement of about forty machines.

It was in August 1935 that Mesny was appointed to his first

operational unit Escadrille 4T1 and embarked aboard *Bearn* to undertake deck landings and the like in the Mediterranean. At this period the chief naval rival of France had been the new Italian fleet being built up by Mussolini, but the tension over his invasion of Abyssinia soon faded and warlike preparations were left mainly to the Royal Navy. The rise of Hitler over France's eastern borders was now beginning to pull attention back more to her traditional enemy.

After his first stint Mesny was promoted to Lieutenant de Vaisseau on 7 October 1935, and transferred to Escadrille 7S1, also aboard *Bearn*. A year later, still based at Toulon with *Bearn*, Mesny was appointed leader of Escadrille 7B1. This appointment was a special assignment and marked the beginning of the most important phase of his career. It was at the end of May that the transformation from the antique PL7s flying escort missions over Atlantic and Channel convoys, to the new experimental unit set up at Lanveoc-Poulmic airfield near Brest, took place. A new French dive-bomber was finally under development, the Loire-Nieuport LN40, and great hopes were held out that, at last, the French navy would catch up and embark a modern monoplane bomber. Alas, development work proceeded slowly. The little bomber was an excellent aircraft but its size restricted its bomb-load and its top speed was not high. Even so it would have been welcome enough, but design testing took far longer in France than was normal. With the sands of time clearly running out, as a third Fascist nation appeared on French borders with the ending of the Spanish Civil War, eyes were desperately cast around for a modern dive-bomber from a foreign source which could be supplied quickly to fill the gap. It was at this point that the American Vought V156F appeared on the scene.

In the United States there had been a great deal of development of dive-bombers for the US navy and Marine Corps, and among the first monoplanes to be accepted into service with these organisations was the Vought SB2U-1. It was a sturdy low-wing single-engined aircraft of composite construction which had first flown in January 1935. It featured folding wings and reversable propeller, although the latter was not a success. It also had very effective dive-brakes in the form of slats fitted to its trailing edges, but, because of their over-effectiveness, the

SB2U–1 was not a complete success as a full-blooded dive-bomber. (It was not until later versions that the name Vindicator began to be applied to this aircraft.) The American solution had been to lower the retractable landing-gear instead of the brakes during diving attacks.

It also suffered problems with its R1535–94 radial engine and did not enter American service until 1937. Although still in front-line service in 1938 its replacement, the Douglas SBD, was already on its way and, with American orders falling off, the company sought to sell its surplus models abroad. Accordingly a display team of test pilots was assembled and a European sales tour organised.

The initial display was undertaken in Paris in December 1938. Here an immaculate V156, as the SB2U had been re-designated, took pride of place as the Salon Aeronautique International and quickly attracted the attention of French navy officials desperately searching for a modern dive-bomber. Contact was quickly made with Vought and this contact expanded rapidly into a firm order for 40 aircraft. At once the further exhibition of the plane was cancelled, although foreign pilots were still allowed to view the French model (the V156F) and test-fly it from Vought's makeshift headquarters at Orly airport.

With his perfect speaking knowledge of English and his experience with 7B1 Gerald Mesny was the natural choice for Project Leader and Liaison Officer for this purchase which soon got under way. The Vought team familiarised him with the bomber which he found a joy to handle after the obsolete aircraft he had hitherto been saddled with. Even the new LN40s lacked the V156's power and speed. The only reservation was whether time would allow them to equip before war broke out. Preparations therefore went ahead at great speed and Mesny was instrumental in smoothing as much as possible the many obstacles in their way. During January and February 1939, the team was hard at work evaluating the aircraft and assessing particular French needs. In practice these resolved themselves into relatively few modifications over the original design. The instruments and panels were graduated in metric measurements, the wing dive-brakes were reinstated, and the French machines were fitted with a reverse operating throttle.

Perhaps the biggest setback was in the bomb-load carried. The French did not possess the 1000-lb weapons used by the US navy and the heavy swing-out crutch was omitted from their models. Instead, underwing racks to take the vastly inferior French 330-lb bombs were utilised. French Darne 7.5-mm machine-guns were fitted one to each wing, with a third free-swivelling mounting in the wireless operator's cockpit firing astern. These particular weapons were not noted for their efficiency and tended to jam up after a dozen rounds or so. A wireless of French manufacture was fitted and was also notoriously unreliable, having an operational life-expectancy of about twenty minutes. Pilot and maintenance handbooks had quickly to be translated into French and printed in sufficient numbers, ground crew had to familiarise themselves with this modern concept of flying, and its airborne potential had to be completely evaluated by Mesny and his team.

When the prototype was returned to the United States in February Mesny accompanied it and supervised the production, testing and crating-up ready for shipment of the first five production V156Fs at Vought's plant at Stratford, Connecticut. Five planes were ready after flight testing by July in which time the government had placed urgent orders for another 50 aircraft. These latter were destined never to reach France but they did see limited war service with the British Fleet Air Arm, although never used operationally.

The first five of the original batch left for France early in July and work began at once at Stratford on the next batch of three. By the time these too were ready for shipment at the end of July Mesny was taking passage back to France where he arrived on the last day of the month. The situation in Europe was increasingly tense and the work was pressed ahead with all possible speed. The crated aircraft first had to be re-assembled in the old airship hangars at Orly, then a grass field on the outskirts of the capital. This took two days to do and then flight testing had to take place by Vought's own pilots which included Earl 'Ike' Irwin, John T. Hamlett and Boone T. Guyton who had flown the SB2U with the US navy earlier. Although under Mesny's direction the work proceeded satisfactorily, the outbreak of war at the beginning of September almost saw the ruin of the project. The 7B1 was immediately re-designated

AB1 (Attack Bombardment 1) with Mesny as its Commanding Officer but simultaneously the United States' much-heralded 'neutrality laws' caused difficulties as, technically, the test pilots were forbidden to fly aircraft of either combatant.

The way around this impasse was found by declaring the V156Fs to be still the property of Vought's until officially accepted into service by the Aéronavale and the testing continued unabated. With the opening of the submarine campaign by Germany the crated parts, in common with the stream of other vital war goods flooding into France from the United States, were 'combat routed' – in other words, to save the loss of one ship meaning the loss of an entire consignment they were split between destinations. This meant that when the ships arrived at the various French ports their crates had to be re-diverted to Brest where they were finally unloaded. A great deal of organisation was necessary to bring together all the various crates at Orly. But it was done. By October 1939, 19 V156Fs had been assembled somehow, tested and accepted by the French navy. To speed the process as much as possible the whole organisation moved back to Brest and enough aircraft were available for Mesny officially to form them into AB1, France's premier dive-bomber Escadrille.

A second unit was planned at Cherbourg, to be commanded by Lieutenant de Vaisseau Pierret. Each was to consist of 12 Voughts plus reserve aircraft, and these two units, along with AB2 and AB4 equipped with the Loire LN401s, made up Flotille F1A under overall command of Capitaine de Corvette Corfmat. In the existing circumstances the training of the French naval pilots and of their groundcrews was brief and hardly adequate. By November 1939 Mesny's squadron was considered suitable to undertake warlike patrols and was transferred to Alprech airfield near the Channel port of Boulogne. Here they undertook limited anti-submarine and recce patrols over the English Channel and up as far as the territorial waters of neutral Belgium. These patrols were totally uneventful, which was probably just as well, but it enabled the aircrew to get to know their new mounts. The assembly of the remaining V156Fs was not finally completed until April 1940, whereupon the American team left, just in time as it transpired. In this period of the so-called 'phoney war', Gerald himself recorded how: 'We never saw a U-boat and had only some brief glimpse of German aircraft, which always turned back thinking probably that we were fighters. We had as much training as we could get in during the winter months, enough to ascertain that the two fixed .30 cal Darne machine-guns, which replaced the American .50s, would never fire more than a few rounds before jamming and that the voice radio was hopelessly useless. We learned not to rely on any of them and we could never use them in actual operations. But the rest of the plane, engine and equipment was splendid.'

After a short period of such operations it was decided to relieve Mesny's unit and their place at Alprech was taken by the now formed AB3 who continued their patrol, one of their aircraft carrying out an attack on a suspected U-boat on 14 April and causing it damage. It later transpired that the vessel concerned was the neutral Dutch submarine clearly marked with large orange triangles. Mesny later recalled the reasons behind this move: 'We went south [to the airfield of Hyères-Palyvestre] near Toulon to start carrier training on our one and only carrier. The old *Bearn* had left Brest soon after the declaration of war to take on a load of American-built planes for our Armée de l'Air and had not been available for training us. We were very anxious to know how the V156Fs would behave on deck landings because they were the first modern aircraft used on *Bearn* and our methods were very different from the Americans. It all went quite smoothly and all our pilots, some of them deck landing for the first time, were cleared in a month.'

It is interesting to note here that, when the British Fleet Air Arm took delivery later of the second batch of Voughts – delivered to Great Britain as the V156B1 and renamed the Chesapeake 1 – they were assembled near Liverpool in 1941 and assigned to No 811 Squadron based at Lee-on-Solent in July. They were similarly flight tested by British naval pilots whose verdict was the same as the French had been the year before. One later wrote: 'The question we had to answer was whether our glamorous "Cheesecakes" (as they had been instantly dubbed) were suitable for the rough-and-tumble of hunting U-boats from a small carrier in mid-Atlantic . . . Our exhaustive three-month trials had shown no defects, drawbacks, shortcomings.'

Needless to say the Admiralty rejected the Voughts and re-equipped the squadron with, of all things, Swordfish bi-planes.

'It seemed totally inexplicable, a perverse step backwards to what we'd thought *temps perdu*, as though My Lords were determined at all costs that navy pilots should never have a half-way modern kite to fly.'

French admirals, reading Mesny's reports, were far more enlightened. It was just as well. Half-way through their successful carrier flight-deck trials the 'phoney war' came to an abrupt halt as, led by hordes of dive-bombing Stukas, the German Panzers crashed through the Meuse at Sedan. Mesny's unit was now the West's only experienced dive-bomber group available as a counter. The reason for this is that, despite the nine-month wait, the initial air strikes by the Luftwaffe on 10 May caught the Allies by surprise all along the line. Typical of the destruction wrought was the fate of Mesny's companion Vought unit, AB3. They still followed the peacetime practice of storing their aircraft in their hangars at night instead of dispersing them around the airfield in separate fragment-proof bunkers. Consequently, when the German bombers arrived and scored direct hits on these easy targets, the collapse of the hangars destroyed all 13 Voughts in one blow. Although most of the crews survived the onslaught they had to go to Brest to re-equip with fresh mounts and were thus out of the battle for a crucial fortnight, not rejoining until 23 May by which time it was too late.

The alarm call went out to Mesny aboard *Bearn* and with the utmost haste the unit flew ashore and made a rapid transition up through France towards the war zone with bad news constantly assailing them as the Allied front burst asunder and collapsed. By 13 May Mesny and his men had reached Boulogne and there, for the next three frenetic weeks, they were committed totally to trying to stem the unstoppable tide – some four dozen dive-bombers in a forlorn attempt to match on the French side what ten times that number were doing so easily and conclusively for the Germans. Although AB1 was for a time the only Vought squadron available, the two Loire-Nieuport squadrons came through the initial German onslaught relatively intact and were also thrown into the battle, so that all the French navy dive-bombers acted together for most of this period.

AB1 arrived at Alprech with 13 operational Voughts, while AB2 under the command of Lieutenant de Vaisseau Lorenzi, based at Berck, had 12 LN 401s, and AB4, commanded by Lieutenant de Vaisseau Laine, had 12 more LNs formerly belonging to the Armée de l'Air, initially stationed at Alprech. Fortunately this unit was ordered to concentrate at Cherbourg Chantereyne airfield in early May ready to be relieved by AB1, so that they could fly down to Hyères for their own turn at deck landing trials. Both these squadrons were therefore not so badly knocked about as they might have been and were soon in action.

All these aircraft and their personnel should have been embarked in the carrier with F1A, the whole group being known officially as the *Flotille du Bearn* commanded by Capitaine de Corvette Corfmat. Their real role was to have been operating from the carrier with the other fleet units in the Mediterranean, but they were now to work exclusively as shore-based aircraft and in the theatre of war controlled by the French Amiral Commandant en Chef les Forces Maritimes du Nord. The two Loire squadrons took part in several attacks in support of Dutch and French troops attempting to hold *Festung Hollandia* in the islands of the Scheldt estuary, the principal bastions of which were Walcheren and South Beveland. Although the main cities and defences of The Netherlands had been quickly overrun by the Germans there was some hope that they could be held in the islands and, despite British demolition of the port of Flushing and the Dutch capitulation on 15 May, considerable reinforcements had already been sent there by the French on 11 May and they had to be supported by Allied naval units and aircraft.

Mesny joined in these missions with his Voughts on 16 May. The Hook of Holland at the northernmost exits of the Maas river had fallen to the Germans but the key to the control of the vital East and West Scheldt estuaries lay in the islands and here the rearguards now held out under increasing attack. Northeast of Antwerp itself the narrow peninsula that joined South Beveland to the mainland was cut by a straight north-south canal and here a bitter struggle had developed to hold this

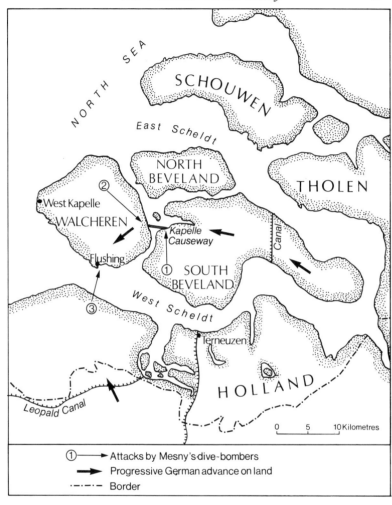

Fig 2 Mesny's attacks on the Kopelle Causeway, Walcheren Island by
French Navy Vought V156s in May 1940

slender waterline. Joined to the peninsula by an equally narrow
east-west causeway and railway Walcheren Island itself was
also invested from the south by the German penetration of
Belgium via Ghent and the crossing of the Leopold Canal line.
Walcheren Island was the final redoubt for the French forces
attempting to control this vital waterway, which for generations had been seen as 'a pistol pointed towards England's
heart'.

The overwhelming influence of the Luftwaffe was very apparent. Stuka attacks forced the Allied line back and patrols by
RAF Blenheims and Hurricanes were largely ineffective in
preventing them doing so. The same day, as the Dutch surrendered, the British destroyer *Valentine* was sunk and the destroyer *Winchester* was badly damaged by Stukas in the Scheldt
estuary. Following urgent telephone calls from Headquarters,
Admiral Abrial, the local French naval commander-in-chief,
immediately sent in reinforcements, four destroyers and all his
available dive-bombers, in a last-ditch attempt to save the
defenders.

Together with nine Loires from Lorenzi's command Mesny
took off with a similar number of Voughts early on 16 May.
Their targets were the Walcheren locks and the sluice-gates
along with the causeway linking the island to South Beveland.
The dive-bombers were provided with a strong fighter escort of
Potez 631s of 1 Flotilla based at Calais, and some Curtiss 75s of
G/C 1/4 to protect them. The War Diary of the fighter unit
records that they missed the planned rendezvous over Mardyck, which might have been fatal, but contact was effected
seven minutes late on the other side of the island and the attack
was continued without incident. The dive-bombers made their
attacks on the Kopelle bridge as planned and all returned
safely. Some Allied sources later stated that the mission had
been most successful in holding the German advance, but
Mesny contented himself later with the laconic remark, 'Résul-
tats inconnus.'

By the evening of the same day the German advance formations were pressing hard on the retreating Allies, having crossed over into Walcheren itself in considerable strength under
cover of nightfall and final evacuation was decided upon
without further delay. The Allied troops fell back on Flushing

in the south of the island, considerable confusion being caused by continual bombing and the demolition work still in progress there. Mesny mounted the next attack on 17 May with 10 Voughts and eight Loires from AB2, in order to cover the withdrawal of French Marines. Their targets were along the line of the causeway again. They picked up their Curtiss Hawk escorts over Dunkirk and approached the target flying at 2500 m, arriving over their objective safely at 05.05 and carrying out a quick reconnaissance. Mesny then led into the diving attack in vics of three aircraft between 05.10 and 05.20, despite the appearance on the scene of three Heinkel He 111s which the French fighters chased away.

Yet a third dive-bomber attack was mounted at 23.00 that same night, Mesny leading two Voughts and three Loires for a night mission to attack a battery of heavy guns which had been established by the Germans at Flushing and which threatened the evacuation ships. During these sorties two Voughts were lost. But they did hold the enemy for a brief, but vital, period and the last Allied troops pulled out the same night. The Germans were left victorious and had the great port of Antwerp working again within three weeks. Further sorties quickly followed one another after these baptisms of fire. Mesny was to write how they quickly learnt and adjusted to the new problems of such warfare with only inadequate training behind them and no experience at all of attacking land targets: 'Attacks like these, against fixed objectives like bridges or sluice-gates, did not present any particular difficulties, but, later attacks on mobile targets, coupled as they were with only the vaguest information on their exact locality and of our own forces' positions, was much more hazardous. In addition our aircraft were regularly taken as the prime targets for any Allied troops we flew over, Allied aircraft and our own unfamiliar silhouette combining with the rarity of friendly aircraft to make us fair game.'

In the disintegrating and desperate situation developing, there were also many confused commands and counter-commands received, especially as they were naval units operating in a fast-changing land battle. To the east the German Army Corps were now seen to be advancing in two armoured wedges crushing the Allies between them. Their main attacks had penetrated through Dinart towards Cambrai and Arras while the second great thrust appeared to be through Sedan and Montherme towards Montcornet and the river Oise. In the face of these threats the air operations of the Armées du Nord became relatively less important. The British seemed already more interested in strategic operations long-term rather than the immediate tactical necessities of the situation and declined most opportunities to engage their surviving aircraft against tanks and vehicles. Thus it was that, on 18 May, the French General in command of ZOAN (Zone d'Operations aerienne Nord) hit upon the only solution open to him to mount any sort of precision air attacks on the advancing German tank columns. He turned to the navy to demand the release of the dive-bomber Escadrilles, save for Mesny's unit, which was that day re-grouping. Next day the LNs of the AB2 and AB4 were flying under army orders against the Panzers. In an attack delivered by 20 Loires in the Forest of Mormal, east of Berlaimont, no less than half of these were shot down and the others damaged.

Mesny and his men joined in this desperate battle on 20 May having received urgent orders at 16.30 to join and reinforce the remnants of the other French navy squadrons. There was, in fact, little left to reinforce, for only one aircraft from one unit and two of the other were fit for operations this day. They were ordered to form into a special combined unit at Berck under command of Enseigne de Vaisseau de Rodellec du Portzic and told to try and co-ordinate their attack with Mesny. Meanwhile AB1 at Alprech was made ready for the vital sortie requested by the army. The crucial road bridge between d'Origny and St Benoite, built across the canals of the Oise and the Sambre, north-west of Laon on the Aisne, had somehow fallen intact on the advancing enemy columns. It lay directly on the route of the Panzer armies that were sweeping north of Paris towards Abbeville and the sea, and it was in constant use by them. Its destruction was considered essential if the onrush was to be stemmed at all.

The distance to the target from Alprech was 190 km, from Berck 164 km. The Loires were much slower than the Voughts but it was hoped that, having less distance to cover, both units might arrive over the target together. As the bulk of what was left of the Armée de l'Air was engaged further east fighter cover was promised by a Royal Air Force Hurricane squadron which was to meet them along the route. This expected fighter cover failed to materialise and the Frenchmen saw only German fighters that day, and more than enough of those. Mesny's command consisted of 11 Voughts for this attack, piloted by Lieutenant de Vaisseau Martin, Enseignes de Vaisseau Feltz and Leveille, Maître pilote Even and S/M pilotes Bunot-Launay, Lucas, Saulnier, Le Connet, Piquemal and Davonneau. They took off at 09.30 and followed a diversionary route via Amiens and St Quentin in a vain search for the RAF before continuing towards the target. The three Loires were left behind and made their approach separately but this proved a blessing in the event. Mesny was to recall that: 'The weather this day was good, with some cumulus, while the visibility was excellent. Our payload consisted of two 150 kg [330 lb] bombs one under each wing, and our planned attack method was en pique à la verticale. Our altitude during the approach was 2500 m and our formation was single-line, staggered down to the right. We orbited for several minutes at our rendezvous point waiting for our escort, but when they failed to appear, our fuel situation demanded that we press on without them towards our objective.'

They were still some twenty miles short of the vital bridge, flying in loose line ahead at 6500 ft by this time, under a cloud ceiling which they hoped would shield them from enemy fighters. It was a vain hope. Instead of the British fighters the squadron was 'jumped' by 12 Me 109s which dived down from above the cloud base. They had obviously been maintaining a defensive watch over the bridgehead and were ready and waiting for them. The slow Voughts stood no chance at all against the lithe fighters attacking with the twin advantages of height and surprise. Five dive-bombers were hit and destroyed in the first German pass. Maître pilote Even, shot down in the first sweep, survived the crash and, after three days and considerable hardships managed to rejoin his unit; Enseigne de Vaisseau Leveille, also survived, badly wounded, and was taken to a Paris hospital, while the other three victims, Martin, Feltz and Le Connet, were lost with their aircraft. Mesny had no choice in the circumstances but to order the surviving six Voughts to abort the mission and try and get back to base.

Fortunately, while the enemy fighters were fully engaged with the Voughts, the three inverted gull-winged Loires managed to slip through unnoticed (or else were mistaken for Stukas by the German fighters) and began their dives on the bridge. German flak gunners were late in recognising them also, but soon hit one aircraft, Hautin's, which was destroyed though he managed to achieve the crucial direct hit required before he crashed. The remaining two returned safely to their base by 18.45 that evening, both badly damaged. Meanwhile AB1 had another of their aircraft written off when it crashed on landing back at Alprech.

On 21 May the C-in-C of the Navy, Admiral of the Fleet Darlan, Commandant en Chef des Forces Maritimes Françaises, issued the following order No 1175:

> *Cité à l'Ordre de l'Armée de Mer:*
> *l'Escadrille AB1 avec le motif suivant: Commandée par le Lieutenant de Vaisseau MESNY (G.J.R.) s'est élancée, avec une magnifique hardiesse, sur le front des armées le 20 Mai 1940, y detruisant l'objectif assigné au prime de près de la moitié de son effectif.'*

It was a well-deserved tribute but Mesny knew he had failed to complete his mission personally and vowed to avenge his comrades.

Mesny's unit was now down to five or six flyable aircraft, but, worse yet, the Panzers were rapidly approaching their own base, the spearheads being spotted not far from Boulogne early on 21 May. Four of the Voughts were quickly evacuated north to Dunkirk, landing at Mardyck airfield, but a fifth crashed during this transition. This machine was quickly replaced but most of the squadron's groundcrew and supplies were captured intact by the advancing enemy columns soon afterwards and the surviving Voughts were very much orphans.

Dunkirk itself was invested by the next day and the remaining five V156Fs were led by Mesny to Cherbourg's Chantereyne airfield, making attacks with their small bombs on an enemy tank column at Neufchâtel and Somer near Abbeville during their passage. Meanwhile, at Boulogne, British troops had been sent to stiffen the defences but the vital Fort de la

Crèche overlooking the harbour had already fallen into German hands and several British destroyers were badly damaged by shells from this redoubt as they attempted to evacuate wounded and civilian refugees. In an attempt to neutralise these guns an attack was put in by Mesny's dive-bombers during the afternoon of 23 May in conjunction with a bombardment by French destroyers. Mesny sortied at 14.00 and took his aircraft in a sweep out to sea and circled around to approach the target from the northern side, thus avoiding heavy AA-fire from the Allied warships who were under almost continual Stuka attack all the time with no sight of defending fighters. Taking advantage of cloud cover as well the four Voughts made their dives and chose several large enemy tanks parked within the confines of the fortress as additional targets. Again, each Vought delivered two 330-lb bombs, scoring hits but failing to stop the batteries. Back at Cherbourg AB1's four dive-bombers were joined by three more Voughts from the reserve maintenance unit and all seven made a second attack on the same fortress later that day, losing one of their number in the process when it crash-landed on the return flight.

There was now little time for rest or recuperation as one chaotic day followed another. No sooner had the surviving aircraft landed than there was a rush to refuel and re-arm them immediately. The Germans were now swarming all along the French coast at will, with Walter Enneccerus's Stukas operating from airfields at St Quentin. They now had the ports well in range and were taking a heavy toll of Allied shipping going to the aid of the BEF.

Until the end of May Mesny remained at Cherbourg for operations, but on 1 June he led his aircraft across the Channel to RAF Tangmere, near Chichester in Sussex, in order to make an attack to the south without crossing the dangerous fighter and flak zone in between. At Tangmere they were safe from being overrun by tanks but even less secure from 'friendly' fighters and AA-fire. In this they shared the tribulations of their Fleet Air Arm opposite numbers who were flying the only other Allied dive-bombers to get into action in this campaign. These were the Blackburn Skuas of 801 Squadron who were operational from RAF Detling against German land targets in much the same way as the Voughts. They too had lost several of

their number due to 'mistaken identity'. Old Swordfish and
Hector biplanes, along with spotter aircraft like the Westland
Lysander, were all being thrown in as well as makeshift dive-
bombers, the Royal Air Force having always turned its back on
the type and coming rather late to the realisation of their true
value.

Taking off from Tangmere on 1 June Mesny led an attack
with six Voughts on German tank columns at Furnes,
to the south of Dunkirk and against similar targets located at
Bregues. Once more they carried out their mission perfectly,
claiming destruction of their targets, but, during the break-
away, the unit became dispersed under heavy ground-fire. Four
of the Voughts landed back at their old base near Cherbourg,
one arrived back at Tangmere as planned, refuelled and went
on to Cherbourg, while Mesny himself got down at RAF
Hawkinge by mistake, after trying to land at Lympne. He also
joined the others at Cherbourg. These visits by the French
aircraft led to reports in the British press later (which were
sustained by some post-war historians) that the Germans were
using captured Voughts against British airfields. At 18.30 that
same evening all six V156Fs were airborne once more dive-
bombing advancing enemy columns near the coast at
Gravelines.

The reconstructed AB3, along with what was left of AB2
and AB4, was evacuated from northern France at this time
because of the rumours that Mussolini was preparing to enter
the war. On 2 June they flew down to the Mediterranean area.
They were to rejoin the Mediterranean Fleet as it was expected,
correctly as it turned out, that Italy would seek to open up a
southern front to grab her share of the spoils. So it was left to
Mesny's dive-bombers to continue the fight at odds on their
own in the north. There was a brief and ominous lull as the
German army consolidated its enormous gains and prepared
itself for the finale. As it gathered its might along the line of the
River Seine, desperate attempts were made at pre-emptive
strikes by the French, but in truth there was now little left to
hold the line, let alone reverse it. Still under the command of
Armée de l'Air which, like its British counterpart, still had no
realistic conception of how correctly to use dive-bombers,
despite the object-lessons they had been given, Mesny's few

remaining aircraft were thrown in piecemeal to make forlorn gestures of defiance.

The first of these took place on 9 June when Mesny led six V156Fs from Deauville against a lurking tank column near Rouen. During the attack one Vought, piloted by Bunot-Launay, fell to the numerous light flak guns which the Germans deployed with such skill, and another was damaged on landing back at Cherbourg. Next day Mesny led four Voughts against a bridge across the Seine at Elbeuf as the Panzers swarmed south. Le Havre fell on 13 June and AB1, with just four aircraft remaining to it, was sent to operate further west, to Brest. By 17 June the German advance columns had reached Cotentin and were threatening to cut off the whole Cherbourg peninsula.

Mesny flew his surviving aircraft out in a dusk attack this day against a motorised column in the Coutances region. Next day two bombing attacks were mounted by them against similar targets at Cotentin itself. No losses were taken and, after the second sortie and with the enemy at the very gates of Brest, another rapid shift was made, this time all the way down from Querqueville on the Atlantic coast, to Bordeaux, where they flew into the airfield at Hourtin in the Gironde region, after a stop-over at Lanveoc. On 21 June they made a final sortie, this time against a bridge over the Loire. By this time the last of the armies of France were shattered and the German advance was taking on more and more the semblance of a motoring tour. Time was rapidly running out.

'I had two days in Hourtin,' Mesny was to relate later, 'and as the Armistice was signed I headed for the south coast, which was in the so-called "Free" Zone. The weather was bad and two planes turned back so that I finished that part of the war with only two. These were absorbed by AB3.'

With only his solitary wingman Mesny arrived at the airfield of Saint-Laurent de la Salanque on 24 June 1940. The planes were the only survivors of the original sixteen allocated to AB1 which had finally reached Hyères on the Cote d'Azur, just east of the Toulon naval base, by the beginning of July 1940. As well as the two pilots and two crewmen of these aircraft nine more AB1 personnel managed to make their way by diverse routes through enemy lines to rejoin their commander in exile. This marked the end of the initial French dive-bomber experience in the Second World War at least for the next four years. Later in the war two dive-bomber units were reinstated with the Navy and two more with the Army. They were all equipped with the Douglas SBD Dauntless, and in the fighting in France in 1944–5 they achieved numerous successes with very slight losses. But this was not part of Gerald Mesny's own story. As for his gallant Voughts which had survived so much, both were partially dismantled under the terms of the Armistice and neither flew again. Others managed to escape to Corsica and yet others reached North Africa but again, no Vought ever flew in combat again for the French.

After the disarmament of AB1 Mesny was assigned to the Demobilisation Centre (Centre d'Acceuil no. 1) at Chindrieux before being posted to the Camp de Pilotins at the former Navy Air Test Centre of St Raphael in southern France in March 1941. Here he flew fighters such as the Hawk, also an American import, many of which were transferred to bases in French North and West Africa following the various warlike incidents between the British and Vichy French forces. These clashes were serious. At Mers-el-Kebir, near Oran, a British fleet under Vice-Admiral Sir James Somerville, carried out a half-hearted attack which, nonetheless, caused heavy casualties. The Free French landings at Dakar followed, and although they were easily repulsed the fear of further attempts was to continue and the Axis authorities gave their blessing to the Vichy Government's desire to reinforce all their forces in those areas. Strong bomber attacks were made on Gibraltar by the Vichy French in reply, and for a time tension was very high indeed. Fortunately it never came to outright war between the two nations.

In October 1941, Gerald was transferred to Morocco. He was based at the Casablanca airfield with the Etât-Major Marine Maroc. Shortage of fuel kept all flying to a minimum during the next year and operations were very restricted, consisting mainly of patrols by Maryland bombers and defensive sorties by Hawk and Moraine fighters. But the command's resources were very limited. When Helène joined him there later, as she recalled to the author, she sailed in a convoy across the dangerous western Mediterranean to Oran. She was to remain at his side throughout the subsequent difficult years and their family was raised in this exile. Their daughter Evelyn was born on 24 May 1942, and their son, Axel, on 6 October 1943, both in Africa. Casablanca was one of the principal targets for the Allies during the landings in North and West Africa in November 1942. This area was assigned to American forces and a three-pronged assault was mounted on 8 November by their Western Task Force. This powerful concentration was commanded by Rear-Admiral H. Kent Hewitt, USN, and comprised an Assault convoy, UGF 1, of 38 transports with destroyer escort, and a covering force, Task Force 34, consisting of the battleships *Massachusetts* and *Texas*, five aircraft-carriers, seven cruisers and 38 destroyers as well as lesser vessels.

This awesome force was charged with the job of setting ashore the land forces under Major-General Patton which hit the beaches north and south of Casablanca at Melidia and Safi as well as at Fedala. The lack of aviation fuel had meant that this vast concentration of shipping was not spotted at all during the period of its approach and thus Vice-Admiral Fritz Michelier was awoken at midnight on 7/8 November and told that the Allies were everywhere ashore. At this period of the war there was a German Kontroll-Inspektion im Afrika (KTA) with a staff in Casablanca with representatives of the Navy, Army and Air Force. Their job, under agreements with the Vichy French, was to check all traffic with the United States especially to make sure the French did not try to evade or abuse the Armistice restrictions. The French liaison staff worked directly down from Michelier and his Chief-of-Staff, Missoffe, to the 4ème Groupe under Capitaine de Vaisseau Loisel, whose official title was Officier de liaison auprès de la Commission d'Armistice and Gerald Mesny was one of the two lieutenants assisting him in this office capacity. Mesny was thus not directly involved in the air fighting that followed the US landings. The American aircraft-carrier *Ranger* launched her first air strike of SBDs and Wildcat fighters at 07.30 and the Frenchmen managed to intercept them en route to their targets. However the French aircraft were hopelessly outclassed by their US counterparts. A furious dog-fight developed during which five American aircraft were shot down along with seven French fighters. Air attacks by the limited numbers of planes at the disposal of the Etât-Major against the transport, beach-head and landing craft were met by swarms of Wildcat fighters from the carriers and beaten off, with the loss of 15 pilots and crew. Renewed assaults by the US navy's dive-bombers were made on 10 November on the fortress of Kasba and fighter sweeps finished off most of the few remaining French aircraft. By the end of the day this brief but tragic little episode was over and hostilities were suspended.

With France mainly once more back in the Allied camp and fighting against her real enemies it was a time for rebuilding her shattered armed forces in order to play some role in the liberation of their homeland. Reconstruction was slow but, with Allied help, a start was made. Mesny was appointed commander of the reconstructed AF1 and then, in January 1943, he became also the Commandant of the Base Aeronautique Navale at Agadir. Here he worked closely with the British and, again, language and affinity stood him well in this situation. He served in this capacity for exactly a year and then assumed the same responsibility for the Thiersville Air Base for another three months. In April 1944, Mesny was promoted to Capitaine de Corvette and with this elevation in rank came another shore appointment to the command of the Port-Etienne base. This was a job he held for a further thirteen months before being moved back to Casablanca in May 1945, to the Forces Maritimes Ouest-Afrique, the general head-quarters for this area.

He had now been in West Africa for five years, a long enough period away from home. The war was over and won, the run-down of the maritime forces followed, as in all Western countries. In February 1946 Mesny was called back home and took on a fresh post in Paris itself, Etât-Major Générale de la Marine (Service Central de l'Aeronautique Navale).

The post-war years saw a similar series of appointments ashore in various French bases. Promoted to Capitaine de Frégate in December 1947, he became Commandant of the Port-Lyautey Air Base, a position he held until May 1949 when he moved to Toulon as Etât-Major Amiral Escadre. After such a long spell ashore it must have come as a great delight to be given a sea-going command, even if he was an aviator still at heart. His command was the ex-Royal Navy River class frigate *Moyola* which had been transferred to the FNFL in 1943–4 along with five sister ships. She had been renamed *Tonkinois* and was the flotilla leader of 5 Destroyer Escort Flotilla based at Toulon as the Groupe des Frégates du GASM, a training group for anti-submarine warfare. Mesny now became the commandant of this Group for fourteen months between May 1951 and July 1952, working in the Mediterranean area as part of NATO to which France still belonged.

However on the termination of this period Mesny returned to his first love, aviation, when he was appointed to the staff of the Etât-Major 2 Aero Region based at his old wartime base near Brest. Pistol-engined aircraft were at this time being replaced by jets in the French navy, although in the vicious wars in French Indo-China that were still raging the French navy was still utilising American dive-bombers – Curtiss Helldivers – which, flying from the ex-British carrier *Arromanches*, were in continuous combat against Vietminh forces. This dependence on a hodgepodge of ex-British, American and German ships and aircraft had continued for several years after the end of the war since France was in no position to rebuild her forces, but it was far from satisfactory for a major power. A new policy was adopted in the 1950s and a series of French-designed and French-built warships and aircraft began to be laid down for the new French navy. Included in these expansion plans were two brand new aircraft-carriers. The two ships planned in 1939, *Joffre* and *Painlevé*, were both cancelled as a result of the war but this enabled the new ships to benefit from the latest developments in Britain and the United States and incorporate them in their designs, plus the experience of wartime flyers like Mesny to plan their aircraft tactics.

In October 1954, the Mesnys returned once more to the United States, where Gerald was appointed to the NATO defence post of SACLANT based ashore at Norfolk, Virginia, and in December of that year he was promoted to Capitaine de Vaisseau. He served in this demanding post for three years, returning home in September 1957, to take up a new appointment as Commandant Aeronautique Navale at Hyères Air Base, the wheel having come almost full circle since his dive-bomber days. This enabled him to resume home life in full with his family. He was now fifty and able to enjoy the pleasures of a settled life within the confines of a service career.

His daughter recalls: 'He loved gardening and could do just about everything around a house. He was very much respected in his family and entourage. To my children he was the ideal grandfather, not the doting kind – he was quite reserved – but the kind which children like best because they treat them as equal fellow adults and not as inferiors. He taught them all kinds of things and awakened their minds to the real world about them.'

In November another office job took him back to Paris, but in July 1960 he received his crowning appointment, and one for which he was perfectly suited and of which he was very proud: the command of the new aircraft-carrier *La Fayette* and her fine new air group. He took her over at Toulon and his period with her was the culmination of his life's work. This period was all too brief for, after one and quarter years in command, he had to go ashore once more.

He became Liaison Officer with the French National Assembly in Paris, where his great experience was invaluable in mapping-out France's future defence needs in accordance with a fixed budget. It was stern and forbidding work trying to preserve the navy against the inroads and the infighting of the politicians. After three years of this he was appointed to Flag Rank, becoming Contre-Amiral (Rear-Admiral) in March 1964 and being appointed Commandant l'Arrondissement Maritime at La Pallice. This six-month period was his last service appointment. Gerald had decided it was time to make way for younger men. At his own request, under the terms and conditions of Article 6 of the Navy Law of 30 March 1928 (as decreed on 16 July) he was placed on the retirement list of l'Aeronautique in September 1964. His retirement followed the usual naval pattern. He was placed on the books of the Brest naval base as unavailable for further service that month and was also listed in 2 Section of the Cadre des Officiers Généraux de la Marine from that August, as a Reserve Officer.

At fifty-six Mesny was now free to enjoy himself as he wished while young enough still to make the most of his retirement. As well as his home and family he had other hobbies and joys to see that he did not stagnate. He was hardly the sort of man to take kindly to inactivity. The Mesnys settled in a beautiful home in Deauville, overlooking the Seine Estuary and towards southern England, and not too far from his birthplace. Here he became manager of the local Yacht Club and busied himself in the summer months with organising their regattas and cruises and was thoroughly content. Thus the years passed until, on Boxing Day 1976, Gerald Mesny died after a short illness at his beloved Tourgeville in Calvados. He left his wife, his architect son and his daughter as well as four grandchildren. They all still live in Paris and remember him with great affection and love: not as one of the gallant 'few' of France, hurtling into action against the German hordes, but as a kind and deeply respected husband, parent and grandfather.

'So many years later,' his daughter told me recently, 'we still feel the loss which his death inflicted upon us all, family and friends. As to his career there is really little I can add to what you have unearthed yourself, for, as I told you before, he was extremely reserved in this and never ever talked to us about it. Nor did he keep souvenirs and the like.'

It is in this tradition of reserve, in which he was so frequently compared by his friends and comrades to the British, that, Gerald Mesny, as one of France's most gallant airmen, is to be remembered.

3 Major Giuseppe Cenni

Royal Italian Air Force 1915–43

It is not surprising that many of the most famous of the world's dive-bomber aces came to the art by way of fighter aircraft. The skills required are, after all, similar in many respects: speed of reaction, alertness, physical fitness and, above all, the ability to make instant and precise judgements as a normal reflex. One of the most renowned of dive-bomber pilots, the German ace Hans-Ulrich Rudel, told me how his first desire on entering the Luftwaffe was to become a fighter ace, but that once he had discovered the special skills and quality of the Stuka he was more than happy to stay with dive-bombing.

The very first recorded war combat mission to be officially recorded as 'dive-bombing' took place on the Western Front in 1918. It was carried out by a fighter pilot flying a fighter aircraft, Lieutenant Harry Brown RFC. This pattern was repeated often in many air forces and one of the most renowned fighter pilots to convert to dive-bombing was the young Italian, Giuseppe Cenni.

Cenni was born during the First World War, his birthplace being Casola Valsenio (Ravenna) on the coastal plain bordering the north-west Adriatic not too far from Lake Comacchio in the valley of the Po. As with many young men of his generation, flying exerted a special fascination on him and the achievements of early Italian aviators in the development of flight in the 1920s, encouraged as it was by the government, acted as an irresistible bait to bright and intelligent young lads from the industrial northern towns.

As a youth Cenni showed special promise in the fields of mathematics and applied technology. He became a bright student at the Istituto Tecnico Superiore and, at the age of nineteen, achieved his first ambition when he qualified as a glider pilot. A year later and he achieved his passes in all the necessary examinations to enter the Regia Aeronautica which was then being built up by Mussolini as a powerful instrument of his ever more aggressive foreign policies.

This was in 1935, the year of the invasion of Abyssinia (Ethiopia), and of the futile sanctions and near-war with Great Britain in the Mediterranean. The hostility that Italy encountered from the Western Powers during this period was to lead her ever more into the arms of Hitler's Germany, although such heady politics had little part in Cenni's thinking. It was the chance to fly which inspired him and which he grasped with both hands when he was enrolled as a Pupil Pilot (Allievo Ufficiale Pilota di Complemento). Giuseppe fulfilled the old adage that good pilots are born not made. He proved a 'natural', and in August of the same year he graduated to become a full aircraft pilot flying a FIAT AS1 at the training school. This purely basic course he completed within three months, with honours, and, in November 1935, he was nominated as a Military Pilot and moved on to flying the current biplane fighter craft, the CR20.

During the stormy winter of 1935–6 the training course was pursued steadily and diligently and in the following February Cenni graduated from the military course and was assigned to a combat unit, 143 Squadron, with the VI Stormo Caccia based at Udine. It flew both the CR Asso and the CR 32 fighter, the famous little El Chirri, a very versatile and manoeuvrable biplane, typical of the period, with fixed spatted undercarriage and tailwheel. On 2 June 1936, Cenni was formally commissioned as Second Lieutenant and posted to 6 Fighter Wing.

By this time the Spanish Civil War had broken out and General Franco's Nationalist forces were receiving much aerial support from Italy and Germany. By far the more powerful support, in terms of numbers of men and machines, was provided by the former, on ground, at sea and in the air. Among the units dispatched was the squadron with which Cenni was serving, and so the fledgling young officer became one of the first Italians to join the Campagna as a fighter pilot.

Up to that year, 1936, Italy had not developed the dive-bomber as a specialist aircraft in the same manner as had the United States, Japan and Germany. The main line of Italian air/ground co-operation was running towards the conventional strafing form of attack, low-level Assalto forces, built upon the normal fighter units of the day, but specialised to carry light bombs. These 'grazing' attacks were conducted in the main by the Caccia Stormo, the fighter units. But following experiments conducted against real targets in combat conditions in Spain more specialised forces were created known as the Assalto units. Cenni's squadron was one such formation, but it was as a fighter pilot pure and simple that Cenni's first combat missions were flown.

The first sortie made in earnest by the young pilot took place on 16 September 1936, when Cenni was flying fighter cover for a raid on the Spanish stronghold of Andujar. In attacks on Republican air bases there, Cenni was credited with the recorded destruction of two enemy fighters on the ground. His first dogfight in the air took place soon after this blooding, on 25 September, but it was inconclusive. The following day Cenni was in the thick of the fighting again and this time he managed to out-fly his Republican opponent in a French Breguet fighter and scored his very first kill. Some men, as already mentioned, are born aerial combat flyers. Giuseppe Cenni was one of those who had developed such natural ability in the air that he became as one with his aircraft. He had to wait until 16 October, however, before he found his next victim and on this date he shot down another French aircraft (an Avionet) after a brief skirmish. This was followed by a third confirmed victory on 6 November when he destroyed a Curtiss fighter in the same region of the front.

A brief period without combat followed this initiation but Cenni was back at the front in 1937, having in the interim been transferred to 25 Squadriaglie Legionaria. On 29 January he was flying an escort mission with a bomber force when another CR collided with his machine. Cenni was forced to bale out by parachute as both aircraft plunged to the ground over enemy lines. His likely fate seemed grim, as the Republican forces were none too particular with Interventionist pilots who fell into their hands, because they had suffered much from their activities. Somehow Cenni landed safely without being hit by ground-fire or being injured. He managed to hide his parachute and himself from the enemy infantry patrols and for three days and nights he lived a fugitive's existence. Despite weariness and fatigue, and without proper food, he managed to evade capture during this time, but eventually he was so reduced by hunger and tiredness that he was surprised in one of his hiding places and made prisoner.

He was subsequently subjected to all manner of abuse and every form of deprivation at the hands of his captors. Threats and beatings were part of the routine 'Interrogation' methods used by Republican forces on their opponents and it is doubtful whether Cenni would have long survived such treatment but for a near-miracle. This took the form of a parley between the two sides and the exchange of specially important POWs through the International Red Cross. They passed him through the front lines to safety and he was finally invalided back home to Italy to enjoy a well-earned respite and spend some time with his fiancée and childhood friend, Tina Zoratti.

As with so many of the men described in this book Cenni soon found time away from the battlefront irksome for all its attractions and he became restless. By August 1937, he was back again in Spain, flying CR 32s with 153 Squadriaglie. In the meantime the meritorious service he had already achieved in that country was recognised officially and, despite his youth, he was rewarded with a permanent commission in the Regia Aeronautica. In December of the same year, he was also promoted to Pilot Lieutenant in the SPE.

His further service in Spain was mainly in the ground strafing role, but new lessons were being imparted, first by the German Stukas of the Legion Kondor and, second, by the achievements of certain Italian pilots who had started to use dive-bombing for the first time as an effective bombing method. In July 1938, for example, three Breda Ca65 monoplane fighters of 65 Squadriaglie Assalto, based at Puig Moreno, attacked the important bridges spanning the river Ebro at Flix in power dives at angles of 80 degrees and scored devastating hits which destroyed both targets.

This one precision attack had an enormous influence on the outcome of the campaign in that region; but it also provided the occasion for considerable discussion because, ever since the Abyssinian crisis, the ability of the Italians to inflict severe damage on their most dangerous opponent, the British

Mediterranean Fleet, had been occupying the minds of the higher councils in Rome. The proven accuracy of the dive-bomber in Spain seemed to point the way to one answer to the problem, and plans were put in hand for a competition to produce Italy's first specialised dive-bomber. These ideas were to result in the Savoia Marchetti SM 84 types, which proved to be a failure; nonetheless the impact made by the method of attack ensured that much serious thought was now given to it in Italy.

In August 1938, Cenni returned home to Italy once more and took up a new appointment, befitting his hard-won experience, as fighter pilot instructor at the training school (Scuola Caccia di Castiglione del Largo). This gave him the opportunity to press his ambitions in more romantic directions and, early in October 1939, he married Tina Zoratti who, the following year, bore him Raffaella, the first of their two children.

After the honeymoon he joined his new combat unit, 354 Squadriaglie, of 51 Stormo Caccia. This unit was equipped with the Fiat G50 fighter, a fast, low-wing, radial-engined monoplane then entering service. It was highly manoeuvrable and Cenni became an accomplished performer of stunts and displays all over Italy during this time.

It was a tense period, however. Europe was already ablaze with war. Poland was soon defeated, and the dive-bombing Stukas were on everyone's lips. The German and Allied armies stared at each other across static defences as the winter set in and the neutral Americans sneered at the 'phoney war'. Italy was also neutral, much to the delight of the majority of the population, but to Mussolini's chagrin. He wanted to join in the glory, but Italy's desperate economic plight made this impossible. Still he yearned for the opportunity and continued to build up his forces in readiness. Other European powers were also anxiously watching events and developments around them, the middle-European nations especially, sandwiched between the Nazi state and its conquests, and with the rapacious Soviet Union at their backs. They too began desperately to build up their slender forces and turned to their friends and Allies for help. Romania was one of these powers and, with their own government modelled on Italy's Fascist one, they turned to her for aid, both material and technical.

One of the results of this appeal was the dispatch of specialist aircrew and instructors to Romania in April 1940. Among the first contingent thus sent to help in their training programme was Giuseppe Cenni. However this brief period was abruptly cut short when, on 10 June 1940, Italy finally entered the war on Germany's side. Italy was pushed into it as much by the British coal embargo as by Mussolini's own ambitions, in much the same way as the Allied oil embargo made war later inevitable for Japan.

On the declaration of war a hasty recall signal was sent to all available skilled personnel and Cenni found himself back in Italy by July. He was immediately appointed to the proposed new dive-bomber unit which had been hastily devised and set up following the failure of the SM84 project. Cenni was assigned to the new 239 Squadriaglie of the 97 Gruppo Tuffa-tori (Dive-Bomber Group) which was to train in Germany and re-equip with specially purchased Junkers 87B dive-bombers. A special mission had been sent to Germany by General Pricolo, Chief of the Air Staff in Italy, who had closely ex-amined the reports on the home-built dive-bombers and their weaknesses. General Urbani and the Italian Air Attaché in Berlin, Colonel Teucchi, had held long talks with the Luftwaf-fe's leader, Goering, and from this came the decision to purch-ase outright enough Stukas to set up two dive-bomber units with the minimum delay.

To expedite teaching the new skills in this form of flying, picked pilots were to be trained by German instructors at the Stukaschule at Graz, Austria, in specially accelerated courses. Two groups were trained initially, each taking fifteen skilled pilots; the first began that July, the second started the following month. Thus, no sooner had Cenni returned home from his teaching role in Romania than he found himself travelling northward but this time as a pupil. He was already well established as one of Italy's most skilled young pilots. His service in Spain between August and December 1936 had won him the Medaglia d'Argento al VM while his subsequent stint up to April 1937 had been rewarded with a second. Subse-quently he earned a further four of these coveted silver gallan-try awards. True dive-bombing, however, was new to him and for the next period of his career Cenni had to start again from scratch. He was now to become a Stuka pilot with all that that entailed.

During the initial familiarisation programmes, conducted in Germany with the Junkers Ju 87, the German instructors expressed frank admiration for the aerobatic skills of their new trainees. Italian stock was not generally high with the senior Axis partner but, in this field at least, the Italians on the early course more than held their own, and indeed, in some aspects, were admitted to be superior to the normal run of German entrants. This was due to the decision by the Italians to send out hand-picked fighter and ground-strafing aces to train for dive-bombing and could have been anticipated. Cenni's experience on the second course was similar to those encountered by the first group. For a start the course was a hurried one and training was rushed to comply with Mussolini's desire for some operational units to be in the war as soon as possible. The Germans did their best to impart what they could in the short time allowed but it was not a satisfactory training for either instructor or pupil.

Cenni's first flight in a Junkers Ju 87B at Graz lasted for a mere ten minutes. It was to familiarise him with the plane and its controls, and it took place, with Instructor-Pilot Weihranz, on 21 August 1940. Like all those who flew the legendary Stuka (as opposed to Allied 'experts' who misunderstood its slowness) Cenni found it easy to control. It felt at its most natural in an almost vertical dive, but in other respects his comments were that vision was excellent all round, the aircraft highly manoeuvrable, comparable with a fighter save for speed; indeed a Stuka could easily out-turn most modern fighters, as Royal Air Force pilots were then finding out in the Battle of Britain. The most vulnerable moments were at the bottom of the dive, just after bomb-release, and before the pull-up. Defensive armament was slight but the German tactic of forming defensive boxes for mutual protection proved highly efficient in minimising losses once the flight had closed up again. Being of all-metal construction the Stuka did not easily burn under machine-gun attack as did most contemporary Italian bombers.

After his initial flight with his instructor and frequent theory lessons in the classroom, Cenni and his fellow Italians went solo. Cenni practised take-offs, aerobatics and formation flying initially. Using his fighter knowledge Cenni soon mastered his mount and could move on to the prime subject, the vertical dive itself. He was already used to this and to the g forces suffered, and so his adaptation was not as severe as for a complete novice. Nevertheless it was a special experience, he later claimed. Two days of intensive practice dives – 'point-blank' attacks, as he termed them – followed on 2 and 3 September, including attacks on mock-ups of warships, the principal role envisaged by the Regia Aeronautica for their new precision bomber units. Here Cenni differed from Antonio Cumbat who attended the first course. The latter told me that no special training against ship targets had taken place, a fact confirmed to me also by former German Stuka pilots. Indeed Cumbat stated that, even two years later when he flew against the aircraft-carrier *Indomitable* in August 1942, he had never even been shown a model of a warship target. In contrast Cenni developed into an élite ship-buster, scoring most of his successes on small-ship objectives such as destroyers, the most elusive targets of all. Practice bombing was conducted against the outline of a large battleship marked on the ground, and photographic proof of accuracy was available for study after each attempt.

Training continued at a high pitch, but the need to get the dive-bombers into action was even more pressing and Cenni returned to Italy on 22 September to form his new unit. Here, at the main training base at Lonato Pozzolo and also at the front-line airfield of Comiso in Sicily, Cenni continued to put his new Stuka through its paces using the ZC–Zemente-Cilindrisch (cement-filled practice bombs supplied by the Luftwaffe) – against warship target outlines. (Later in the war shortages of bombs resulted in some Stukas actually taking such practice bombs into combat over Malta, much to the puzzlement of their targets and also of some post-war historians!)

The first nucleus of the newly formed 97 Gruppo reached Comiso de Lecce on 11 November 1940, and comprised eight Ju 87s (R and B types) which were ex-96 Gruppo machines. The detachment was made an official unit on 20 November and formed into two Squadriaglia under the command of Captain

Moscatelli. These squadrons were 238, commanded by Tenente Bertuzzi (for internal administration) and Cenni himself as air leader. The total strength of the Gruppo on formation was only 14 aircraft, the remaining machines for the equipping of 239 did not arrive from the German manufacturers until 26 November from Lonate Pozzolo, when the squadron was finally initiated at the Forli air base. Almost at once they were thrown into the fighting in the Mediterranean, later being joined by several squadrons of the newly transferred German Stuka units, including another commanded by a celebrated flyer (discussed in Chapter 6), Walter Enneccerus, with II/StG 2. The Italians were never able to muster anything like the overall strength of the Luftwaffe Stuka formations in the Mediterranean but they nevertheless played their part, and Cenni himself more than just a supporting role. Inevitably they were almost always reported as German planes in Allied accounts of actions, so firmly had the Stuka stamped its place in dive-bomber history and that of the war up to that date.

The very first operational mission conducted by the Italian Stukas took place on 28 November over the Sicilian Channel. The Royal Navy, under Admiral Sir Andrew Cunningham, was, in the aftermath of the Taranto attack and several surface-ship victories, able to exploit fully the weakness of the Italian navy by conducting a whole series of operations throughout the Mediterranean from Gibraltar in the west to Alexandria in the east. In particular the passage of fast convoys of troops and material via Malta was covered by the whole fleet. Following the early sighting of a vast concentration of shipping by Italian aircraft on 26 November the head of the Air Staff (Superaero), General Pricolo, personally intervened and sent an urgent telegram ordering that the nine operational Italian Stukas (the Germans had not yet arrived) should at once join in attacks with Savoia Marchetti SM79 long-range bombers. The dive-bombers were to be armed with 1000-kg bombs and their principal targets were to be two cruisers and an aircraft-carrier accompanying the merchant ships, and smaller warships back eastward after they had relieved Force 'H' which had brought them from Gibraltar.

Six Ju 87R–2s of 239 Squadriaglie and one Ju 87B–2 of 238 Squadriaglie, all armed with SD500 bombs (all that were immediately available for use at such short notice, for the squadrons were not yet worked up or fully operational) took off, and they located the British fleet at 10.55 on 28 November. The units they found to the south of the island of Gozo, near Malta, were subsequently reported to be a cruiser and several destroyers. The Stukas led in line-astern attack at once against the largest ship, catching her gunners by surprise. Anti-aircraft fire was late in starting but it then rapidly increased in density but no Stuka was hit. Further intervention quickly arrived in the form of eight Hurricane or Fulmar fighters which attempted to intercept the Stukas but the Italian fighter escorts of 16 Fiat CR42s of 23 Gruppo counter-attacked successfully and no dive-bombers were lost in this attack, all returning safely to their base at 12.55. Unfortunately for them their target, the cruiser HMS *Glasgow*, was not badly damaged by this attack.

The same afternoon three further Stukas from 239 Squadriaglie, carrying long-range fuel tanks, with an escort of nine CR42s of 23 Gruppo, searched the same waters some 15–20 miles off Malta without sighting any worthwhile targets.

Although the first real mission by 97 Gruppo had brought no great excitement or achievements they had nonetheless now been 'blooded' in their new aircraft, and this experience was invaluable training for the pilots themselves. It certainly helped the hitherto widely diverging range of experience among the various pilots to knit them into a closer relationship under Cenni's leadership and make them into a more mentally compact unit. It also made them familiar with this type of air/sea warfare where vast tracts of ocean had to be combed for elusive targets, a type of warfare none of them had hitherto experienced. It was to become Cenni's main hunting ground in the years ahead, but almost immediately fresh commitments took them off to a completely different type of war altogether.

The outbreak of the Italian–Greek conflict that same month necessitated the early dispatch of the new Gruppo to this new area of war. Its role was to support the Italian army engaged in what was to become a brutal and bruising battle in the mountains of the Epiro and in Macedonia in the harshness of winter. Thus the Sicilian Channel remained temporarily the province of the Luftwaffe, apart from the occasional intervention by Italian Stukas flown in especially from time to time to Lecce-Galatina (on the Italian 'heel'). These emergency shifts proved to be a wasteful drain on slender resources, being demanding on both men and machines for small return, yet at this period of short supply there was little alternative. It was hoped to form further dive-bomber squadrons in the future but at that time the Italians had to spread their resources very thinly.

On 14 December the activities of Cenni's 97 Gruppo became mainly concentrated in the bleak and hostile Pigerasi zone with numerous attacks on Greek strong-points. Cenni himself arrived that evening, with Engineering Captain Fioro as his passenger, to set up operations. The fighting had started on 29 October when the Italian armies crossed the Greek–Albanian frontier after presenting an ultimatum which was scornfully rejected. One Italian column had moved along the coastal plain to outflank Jannina; a second moved towards the sources of the Kalamas river in the direction of Jannina itself; a third force attempted to force the mountain passes of Pindus towards Metsovo; while a fourth column moved out from Koritza towards Florina. By 2 November these columns, meeting little resistance had made some headway to their objectives. On the night of 9–10 November, however, in the bleak mountain passes, the Greeks first ambushed and then counter-attacked the struggling columns and a wholesale rout ensued. Within a week the Italians had been driven pell-mell out of Greece and were still retreating into Albania itself. Such was the pace of this retreat that, for a time, it seemed as if the invaders would be driven back into the Adriatic. The weather grew steadily more severe causing supply problems that were almost insurmountable. Numerous missions were flown by the Italian, Greek and British air forces but the weather conditions restricted their value and little damage was done on either side. The 96 Gruppo of Stukas had seen much hard fighting in these disastrous initial stages of the campaign. In particular, during the fighting for the mountain ranges of Marova on 19 November, dive-bomber attacks were directed continually at Greek strongpoints in an attempt to stop the rout. No less than seven Stukas were claimed destroyed in this fighting and although we now know these figures were exaggerated, the wear and tear of operation in such a climate, plus the occasional loss to Greek fighters or anti-aircraft fire, made the need imperative to replace the 96 Gruppo for rest and refit.

The first missions of Cenni's 97 Gruppo took place on 14 December, two strikes being made with nine and six Stukas respectively against Port Palermo and against Pigerasi on the coast road north of Corfu upon which the Greeks launched fresh attacks. One wartime account admitted that: 'Still further south Greek forces advanced from Santi Quaranta to occupy Porto Palermo on 13 December. After this they met strong resistance from the Italians on the hills above Khimara. The Regia Aeronautica was particularly active in this direction, and the road to Khimara was heavily bombed all the time.'

Despite this the town fell a few days later. The experiences of Cenni's command in this campaign matched exactly that of 96 Gruppo. During the course of the next two months' warfare the dive-bombers were hardly, if ever, threatened by enemy fighters, Greek or British, even though there were two Royal Air Force squadrons, 80 and 112, active in Greece at this time. The same conditions of weather and terrain, in which the rugged little Stuka operated, forced the RAF Commander, D'Albiac, to complain: 'Flying conditions in Greece are more difficult than anywhere in Europe. The weather changes with great rapidity, making accurate forecasts impossible, and the nature of the country does not always allow landings when pilots are unable to regain their bases. Ice formations are another difficulty. Instruments freeze, and air-screws get a covering of ice which makes it difficult to maintain sufficient altitude to clear the mountains. The temperature is never more than 28 degrees, and sometimes goes to minus 50 degrees.'

But these conditions applied to friend and foe alike, and Giuseppe Cenni would agree with D'Albiac's description, but 97 Gruppo kept flying, so desperate was the plight of the Italian army at this stage. The ability of the Stuka, which was a rugged and tough little bomber, to operate from the most primitive of airfields in the most extreme conditions was another quality overlooked by the plane's detractors in Britain. In Albania, as elsewhere, it paid off. In practice therefore, despite some British evaluations of the time, the Italian air force always maintained an advantage over the Allied air forces on this front. Back in Italy, however, there were many problems concerned with the construction and allocation of replacement aircraft, and the capacity of the German manufacturing factories to produce sufficient new Stukas to meet the demands of both the Luftwaffe and the Regia Aeronautica. For now the secret but long-planned invasion of the Soviet Union required large numbers of dive-bombers.

In 1940 611 Stukas were produced but it proved impossible to obtain increased allocations for Italy.

At the start of 1941, 97 Gruppo, with 238 and 239 Squadriaglia, was assigned to the 4 Air Army and was based at Lecce-Galatina. They were continuously employed in small numbers almost exclusively on battlefield objectives, enemy reinforcement columns and enemy ground units and installations. Most of Cenni's attacks were directed at the main battlefields on this front: Kosina, Khimara, Cuciari, Pigerasi, Lukova, Permeti, Borsch, Kilcyre. The opposition remained almost always anti-aircraft artillery and, although the Greek AA-fire was comparatively light compared with Malta's defences, it was usually accurate and precise. The first one of Cenni's squadron to be hit was the Stuka of Tenente Bertuzzi, on 21 January 1941, but he returned safely to his base.

Before leaving Sicily for Albania Cenni had devoted much thought to how best to attack warship targets with his much more limited striking force. The German method of massed Stuka attacks from great heights, with units coming in at diverging angles in a continuous stream to confuse the gunners, was obviously the best. But Cenni would never have at his disposal more than a fraction of the aircraft used by the German, Enneccerus. He therefore developed his own plan, which soon became known as the 'Cenni Method'. Following this plan he would himself lead his small formation down to a very low level for the attack, diving quickly almost to sea-level with all guns firing. Then, for the last short distance of his approach he would fly almost horizontally. When he released his bomb it would strike the surface of the sea with considerable force and its forward momentum would make it bounce, just like a coin when flipped across a pond. The 'skip' would carry the missile into the vulnerable side of the ship where it would detonate. Great accuracy could thus be achieved by this method which was in some aspects almost like torpedo-

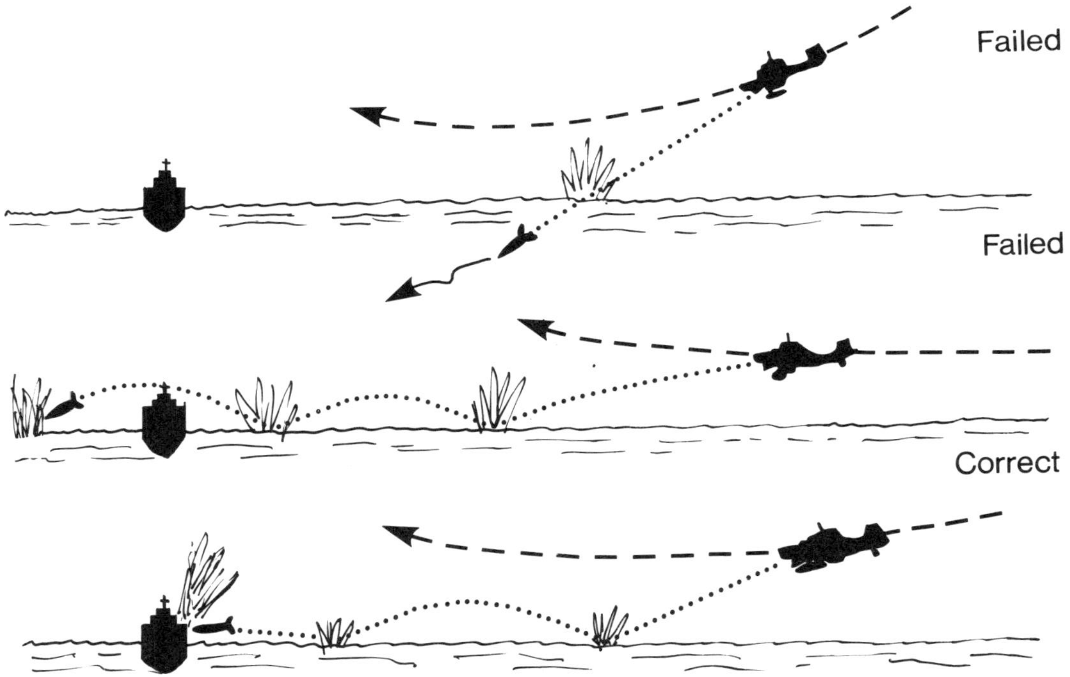

Fig 3 Attack by the 'Cenni Method'. Skip-bombing by Stukas against warships off Tobruk during 1941–2 (*Cesare Gori*)

bombing. The Frenchman, La Burthe, had tried experiments on these lines in the early 1920s; the Americans and Australians were later to develop the technique in the south-west Pacific – they called it 'skip-bombing'; and Britain's Barnes Wallis, with the RAF's 617 Squadron, had applied the same principles on the 'Dambuster' raid; but Cenni was the first to use this technique in combat. Cenni himself led and thus attracted the ships' defensive gunfire away from the following aircraft, leaving them relatively undisturbed for their own attacks. The 'Cenni Method' was to be perfected over the coming months, but it found little scope in Albania until the weather was clearer.

In the early spring came the intervention of Germany in Yugoslavia and Greece, and another demonstration of the blitzkrieg technique. In short order the British were bundled, first out of Greece and then from Crete. On the southern flanks of their assaults the Italians were again able to go forward and thus Cenni's unit was in constant demand at sea as well as on land. Prior to this some topping-up of 97 Gruppo under Captain Larcher had taken place. Two Ju 87s had arrived at the forward airstrips on 6 March (one without a reserve fuel tank) and from 7 to 8 March 1941 there were concentrated at Lecce eight Stukas to reinforce these two and complete Cenni's complement in time for the offensive.

On 4 April they flew sorties against merchant shipping in the Gulf of Deltinico, Corfu, as well as against shore batteries on that fortress island. Cenni himself was able to perform his version of the Spiatielante attack when he effectively carried out at low-level and scored a direct hit on a ship which subsequently sank. Other ships were sunk by the Ju 87s of 239 Squadriaglie the same afternoon. The Greek Admiralty later admitted the loss that day of the 932-ton *Sussana*, but gave the cause as torpedoes not bombs. The photographic evidence of this attack gives the lie, however, to this as it shows Cenni's bombs falling close to this vessel. Evidently a Stuka in a low-level attack fooled the observers. On 4 April also Cenni attacked a small warship and again his bombs were photographed as they scored very close misses alongside the target. She was seen to be towed into port and was later found half-sunk beside the quay when the Italians occupied the island. She proved to be the old gunboat *Proussa*, a former Austrian gunboat of the 'Kyzikos' class (241 tons), built in 1915.

When hostilities were started against Yugoslavia, nine long-range Stukas of 239 Squadriaglie attacked the base at Cattaro and were met by violent anti-aircraft fire, losing one aircraft, that of Sterbini, shot down. On 10 April, 239 Squadriaglie transferred to Jessi for employment in the mid-Adriatic area and completed two missions against the Bay of Sebenico with seven aircraft, sinking and damaging some enemy units. In an attack on 12 April the AA-barrage cost them two Stukas, the aircraft of Acerbi and Bongiovanni. In another mission Ragazzini was obliged to crash-land outside Zara base with engine failure. On 13 April the surviving R–2s returned to Lecce. Again from photographic evidence on 12 April the ships that were attacked and damaged included the seaplane-tender *Zmaj* (1870 tons) which was discovered later moored to the quay near the railway station in damaged condition. On 20 and 21 April 97 Gruppo completed numerous missions in sorties against the retreating enemy troop columns and on merchant ships in the Bay of Corfu, during which the 1102-ton Greek steamer *Ioanna* was sunk by Cenni in another low-level attack.

The final mission of 239 Squadriaglie took place at 16.00 to 18.25 when three Stukas of 209 Squadriaglie and three of 239 Squadriaglie attacked Ktismata roadstead. Almost every aircraft was damaged as it dived vertically into a hurricane of AA-fire, including that of Captain Larcher himself.

The Stuka squadrons were successful in carrying out the many tasks assigned to them in this campaign but they were too small a force to exert a decisive influence on field tactics. Their overall efficiency diminished in direct relation to the lack of replacement aircraft and it was decided, as far back as November, to re-equip them with home-built CR 42s of which there were plenty, starting with 236 Squadriaglie and 239 Squadriaglie, to which Cenni had been posted on 7 May; however, 97 Gruppo continued to be employed at the front being switched from Greece to the Tobruk front in North Africa. Here the Stukas found numerous targets among the defences, the infantry defenders and the warships supplying them.

This switch was decided upon on 15 May 1941. The arrival

of Cenni (now promoted to the rank of Captain) coincided therefore with ample opportunity to put into practice his now perfected 'Cenni Method' attacks against the British warships convoying supplies to the besieged garrison from Alexandria naval base. The first mission in this new theatre of war was against such a formation heading for Tobruk. Cenni took off with seven Picchiatelli escorted by eight CR 42s of 83 Squadriaglie and 10 G50s of 2 Gruppo at 17.20 on 25 March 1941 and attacked a steamer off Marsa Lucch, which he sank. In his own words Cenni described this episode dryly thus: 'Dive-bombed a ship off Marsa Lucch. Vessel hit by three 250-kg bombs and sunk.'

There was rather more to it than that. The petrol tanker *Helka* (3741 tons) had sailed from Alexandria with a vital cargo of petroleum for the Tobruk garrison and was escorted by the sloop *Grimsby* (990 tons) and the trawler *Southern Maid*. At 16.00 on 25 May this convoy was attacked, and both *Helka* and *Grimsby* were sunk some forty miles north-east of Tobruk. *Southern Maid* brought the survivors back to Alexandria, including 11 casualities from *Grimsby*. The official British description at the time was based on garbled and imprecise signals received during the attack. These indicated that the first dive-bombers were sighted at 16.00 and that this attack, Cenni's, resulted in the sinking of the vital tanker, but *Grimsby* was only slightly damaged. However two subsequent attacks by Ju 87s of I/StG 1 finished off the sloop as well.

This day's successful mission was the start of a fruitful partnership between the two Axis dive-bomber units which collaborated fully in frequent attacks on ships, harbour installations and port facilities. Similar attacks took place on 29 May and all through the month of June in an almost daily rhythm, the pounding 'wail' of the Stuka at work.

Protection was usually given by the Falcons of 18 Gruppo and the G50s of 2 Gruppo with Me 110s adding their protection sometimes as well. Ground-fire over Tobruk was heavy and accurate and caused several aircraft to be damaged and also a few losses. On 2 and 8 June the prime targets for dive-bomber attacks were the AA-batteries themselves and other defence positions in the town. Here Daverio and Livio were lost. On 11 June Cenni led the Italian group in a combined attack with both Italian and German Stukas and the CR 42s equipped with bombs, their first use in this role. In a similar attack on 12 June they hit batteries at Fort Perrone and lost Lieutenant Gallo to AA-fire.

On 15 June the British launched their offensive Operation BATTLEAXE with the aim of lifting the siege of Tobruk and much fierce fighting erupted. Counter-attacks by the Axis Stuka forces helped General Rommel defeat this offensive and turn it into a victory which drove the British back still further. Cenni's unit was heavily involved during 16, 17 and 18 June when Ju 87R–5s of 239 Squadriaglie joined I/StG 1 in many dive-bomber attacks in the tank battles around the Sollum area.

With this battle won, Cenni was able to turn his attentions to the convoys again and soon achieved another success. On 29 June the destroyers *Defender* and *Waterhen* (RAN) had sailed from Alexandria on the Tobruk run. As usual they had timed their departure so as to conduct the bulk of their journey during hours of darkness so as to remain undetected. But, as almost always, they were sighted and reported by reconnaissance planes who issued an urgent warning to the Stuka bases. Cenni was immediately airborne from his base at Gambut with seven Ju 87R–5s of 239 Squadriaglie and, at 19.45, off Sollum, they sighted the two ships trailing long wakes in the dusk sea and began their attack dives without further ado. Cenni led down as usual to make a low-level run against the lead ship, *Waterhen* (1090 tons), with SD500 bombs. According to the eyewitness reports of two of the following Stuka pilots, Tarantola and Lastrucci, Cenni scored direct hits amidships on his target. Other explosions were seen close alongside the destroyer which was obviously badly damaged and left dead in the water. After the completion of their attack the Italian dive-bombers circled and then headed back to base leaving the destroyers steering erratic courses which seemed to indicate internal damage. *Defender* escaped unscathed and was circling her sister to give AA-protection against further attacks. According to British official reports it was the near-misses which so damaged *Waterhen* that she lost way and, once the Stukas had departed, *Defender* closed her, took off the bulk of her survivors and prepared to take her in tow. The crippled ship had her engine room and after-cabin flat flooded and the after-boiler room bulkheads were leaking steadily. By 01.50 the following morning the flooding had spread out of control. She capsized and went to the bottom. There were no casualties.

Cenni's unit had meanwhile returned to base, bombed up, and stood ready again. Further reports of concentrations of warships in the same area led to their scrambling again on 30 June, along with I/StG 1. For the protection of the 60 dive-bombers there was provided a strong escort of Me 110s, G50s and the like. Among the German units involved were III/ZG26 and the Me109s of I/JG7 and 7/JG26. Allied fighters attempted to intercept this raid and heavy air battles ensued but the dive-bombers again got through to the targets to deal devastating blows. Once more the 'Cenni Method' was utilised to good effect. Their target was another convoy en route to Tobruk which consisted of two merchant ships, *Aantiklia* and *Miranda*, escorted by the sloop *Flamingo* (1300 tons), the gunboat *Cricket* (625 tons) and the minesweeper *Southern Isle*. The attacks were carried out between 14.20 and sunset in continuing waves, Cenni's target being the gunboat, his companion's the sloop. Both ships were surrounded by near-misses, which resulted in serious damage to both. AA-fire was heavy and 239 Squadriaglie lost Sergeant-Major Tarantola whose Stuka dived into the sea after being hit in its bomb-dive. Near-misses again caused flooding in *Cricket*'s boiler room with serious leaks in others. *Flamingo* had her main engines damaged by a near-miss but was eventually able to get underway again. She took the gunboat in tow and got her to the relative safety of the Mersa Matruh anchorage. She was later towed to Alexandria by the tug *St Issey* and finally paid off on 9 September as a constructive total loss. *Flamingo* was further damaged in subsequent attacks but managed to survive.

After this lesson in control of the seaways Cenni took his Stukas back to Tobruk again. Heavy raids were mounted on 4 and 6 July in conjunction with I/StG 1 and for the last time on 6 July with II/StG 2, with escort again provided by the veteran G50s of Lieutenant-Colonel Baylon.

By this time it was time to rest and reorganise the unit. Thus, on 18 July five R–2s flew back to Benghazi with the faithful groundcrew following aboard their SM81 and a lorry column. Here in Cyrenaica they still found work to do in the unusual role for dive-bombers of coastal convoy protection and anti-submarine patrols and hunts along the convoy route to Benghazi. The sustaining of the Axis offensive depended to a large extent on the supplies reaching them via this route and thus they were conducting a vital task still, albeit, a reserve one. On 30 July they caught the British submarine *Cachalot* on the surface and so damaged her that she could not dive. She was then finished off by being rammed by the escort destroyer *Generale Achille Papa*. This was the second British submarine that they had damaged, for, when *Regent* entered the harbour of Kotor, the Stukas had scored a near-miss which injured several of her crew.

For Cenni there now followed a period back home in Italy with his unit and during this time he was able to spend some time with his young wife and family. He also undertook a period of training and research work which developed the theory of how best to continue making the best use of the limited number of dive-bombers left to the Regia Aeronautica. A special experimental unit was set up on 8 October 1941, under General Capposc, with the newly appointed Commander Cenni as his flying commander to explore all possibilities in this field. With a nucleus of experienced flyers they carried out numerous tests. Cenni himself was later to state their conclusions: 'We found that our dive-bombing specialists, with their intrinsic characteristics of aggressiveness and audacity, are very similar in outlook to our fighter pilots and the German pilots. Thus, as at Graz, former fighter men were consequently able to attain excellent results in dive-bombing in a very short time. To utilise fighter conversions in the dive-bomber role it was necessary for the instructors to communicate all aspects of dive-bombing to them, and it was also essential for themselves first to master the complexities of handling a lively single-seater monoplane. Once they had done this they could transmit their own wartime experience to the detachment which contained large number of purely ex-fighter pilots: this demanded determination . . . It is certain also that a good bomber pilot can, with application, become a good dive-bomber pilot, but the special and indefinable "spirit" of the fighter pilot asserts its own disciplines and ensure that during re-training in their new role there was no "loosening" of attitude.'

These experiments had to come to a temporary halt because of the needs of the war. An all-out effort was called for to stop the convoys reinforcing Malta and to be ready for the planned invasion of that island from the air, Operation HERCULES. For this the precision of the Italian Stuka units was an essential requirement and the best man available was required to lead them. The directive for this originated on 30 April from Super-aero. They had to face the harsh truth that their dive-bomber strength was inadequate for the many tasks required of them. It was thought better, therefore, to concentrate both quantity and quality, to combine the technical skills and war experience of the two operational squadrons. By 1942 losses had reduced these to two main units, 209 Squadriaglie commanded by Captain Stringa and 239 Squadriaglie, now commanded by Lieutenant Tamborra. Altogether they could only muster a total of 18 Picchiatelli. These two Stuka units were concentrated into the newly formed 102 Gruppo of which Cenni was given the command. This was an élite force. Not only were all the crew members volunteers, they were also a mixture of experienced Stuka veterans, many like Cenni himself coming from the NAT (Nucleus Training Fighter and Dive-Bombers), and newly trained men. The similarity of the situation forced upon the Italians and the almost identical situation that the Japanese ace Egusa found himself in needs no further elaboration. The sheer weight and determination of the Allies was already wearing down the skilled professionals of the Axis powers.

The equipping and assembling of the new Gruppo took place between 8 and 14 May 1942. Specialised ammunition and anti-shipping bombs were readied. The reason for this hasty assembly was later revealed to be Intelligence reports which showed large concentrations of warships at Gibraltar. Earlier in the war an audacious bombardment had been made on the north Italian port of Genoa by Force H of the Royal Navy and this new concentration led some quarters to think that a repeat of this operation was on the cards. Cenni and the rest of 102 Gruppo were assembled and quickly transported to Villanova D'Albenga in order to confront the appearance of any such British naval force. These precautions remained operative until 15 May when it was realised that what in fact was happening

was the preparations for the running of a major convoy operation to Malta from the west, Operation HARPOON. At once
another abrupt shift was required from the north back down to
Sicily. Movement by rail of the heavy equipment began at once
and at 09.20 on 29 May Colonel Guido Nobli took off with all
the first-line Stukas to fly down to the central Mediterranean,
where they worked first from Sicily, then l'Egitto at the end of
July until December when they returned to Lonate Pozzolo.

Unfortunately during their flight down the west coast they
ran into bad weather conditions and one aircraft lost contact.
The remainder landed at Cerignola without him and were then
re-routed to Naples. Despite this unwelcome diversion the
Gruppo finally assembled on 25 May with nine Stukas of 209
Squadriaglie and seven of 239 Squadriaglie. There followed a
four-day waiting period then they began to attack Malta again
in nocturnal missions. For the dive-bomber crews the first night
mission was with four aircraft (one of which was forced to
return with engine trouble). They took off at 23.25 on 28 May
carrying FLAM250 bombs. These aircraft were piloted by
Captain Cenni, Lieutenant Tamborra, Marescul Gardi and
Pezzo, all of 239 Squadriaglie. They had to battle against
strong headwinds to conduct this mission. They continued
these attacks on 29 and 30 May in conjunction with sorties by
Cant Z1007 bombers of 33, 50 and 88 Gruppi. They faced the
similar difficulties of night flying and on the latter night
Lieutenant Tamborra failed to return in his Ju 87. After two
days it was assumed that the leader of 239 Squadriaglie had
been lost as a result of headwinds or had been shot down by
enemy night-fighters or flak. During the same mission Sergeant
Convero, while en route to Ta Venezia, received a grave hit,
and all his rudder and undercarriage was badly damaged by
fire from a twin-engined enemy night-fighter. The Stukas
replied with their own guns and by diving to throw the enemy
off their tails. During the following day three seaplanes with an
escort of five RE 2001s scarched in vain for the two crew
members of the lost aircraft.

This activity ceased once word of the sailing of the great
convoy was received and Cenni and his fellow pilots were
placed on stand-by for immediate attack as early as 12 June.
Air attacks, high-level and torpedo-bombing had started on the

morning of 14 June and these sank one transport and damaged a cruiser which had to be towed back to Gibraltar. That day 102 Gruppo were able to join in as the convoy came into range and approached the Sicilian Channel. At dawn nine Stukas of 209 Squadriaglie and 10 of 239 Squadriaglie were ready for action and these 19 aircraft took off at 09.10 to move from Chinisia to Sciacca base on the south-west coast of Sicily. Five were armed with SD1000 bombs and 14 with SD500 bombs. One machine was damaged in pre-take-off taxying and became temporarily out of commission; a second, once airborne, complained of engine trouble and had to abort the mission. In this manner Cenni's main attack force was reduced to 17 Stukas from the outset.

Preceded by Luftwaffe units the Italians were planning to mount further assaults during the evening. The whole attack was to be a combined assault embracing all arms in order to swamp the defences. Under the code-name 'Corali', accompanying the Stukas were to be nine SM84 altitude bombers, four long-range Cant Z1007s and five Savoia Marchetti SM79 torpedo-bombers. All pilots had been briefed on their targets and were instructed to go for the merchantmen if possible and to ignore the escorts for the time being.

The Stukas, now nine of 209 and eight of 239, were led to the convoy by a SM79 'Guide', five armed with the heavy bombs, the rest with 500-kg missiles. For fighter protection there were 19 Folgore fighters of 51 Stormo. This formation, led by Cenni as always, arrived over the convoy intact at 19.15 just after the altitude and torpedo-bombers had begun their attack runs. The convoy was some 50 km north of Bizerta when Cenni led the Stukas in along the lines of merchant ships out of the setting sun. The whole sky above the convoy was patchworked with exploding AA-shells from the huge barrage. From heights ranging from 300 m to 2500 m the Stukas threw themselves boldly into this inferno towards their targets, releasing their bombs at heights that varied between 800 m to 600 m.

Cenni's report later described the fierceness of the barrage which they had to penetrate, but he stressed that, by contrast, the defending fighter planes from the aircraft-carriers hindered them not at all during their attack dives. The importance of their mission had been stressed to them and none flinched from the assault. Attacks were well pressed home on merchant ships in the convoy. This combined assault lasted for twenty minutes off Cape Blanc. The British commander-in-chief, Vice-Admiral Curteis, wrote in his report how the Italian Junkers Ju 87s attacked the left-hand column of the merchantmen, diving from 2000 m to 300 m. He had grave fears for the aircraft-carrier *Eagle* which was stationed on that side of the convoy with only a slender screen of two destroyers of her own. The bulk of the torpedo-bombers had gone for the main heavy AA-artillery group stationed astern, the battleship *Malaya* and the AA-cruiser *Charybdis* among them, but *Eagle* appeared vulnerable to the dive-bombers. The official British historian recorded that, 'Many ships, but especially the carriers, had narrow escapes; but none was hit.'

Harry Rathbone aboard *Eagle* herself had a perfect view of Cenni's Stuka attack on his ship:

'As a signalman my prime duty was to watch for flag and light signals from the fleet and also to report on other incidents. There was no place for me to shelter on the small bridge of the carrier and I could see only too well what was going on and who was likely to be on the receiving end next. I felt very vulnerable.

'I remember the cool way the crew in charge of the multiple pom-pom dealt with the Italian torpedo-bombers and also how our Captain L.D. Mackintosh lay on the deck looking up into the sun watching the on-coming dive-bombers. (I hope his eyesight did not suffer). As they attacked he kept the ship out of trouble by shouting out orders and making emergency turns as late as possible. There were a few very near-misses as the old girl could not shift very quickly and I remember being soaked by one even up on the signal deck which was my action-station. But the Stukas just failed to nail us.

'We had to rely on our ship's gunners to drive off the attackers and in spite of very heavy fire from our pom-pom situated just behind the bridge we had several very near misses as did our chummy carrier, HMS *Argus* (known as "The Ditty Box" because of her shape), which accompanied us on this convoy. The Italian Stukas attacked *Eagle* by approaching from the stern at an angle in line with the sun making them difficult to see but we knew when they were actually into their attack dives by the increased engine noise which rose to a howling screech. I do not recall that they were actually fitted with sirens at this later stage of the war as they had been earlier on.

'Again, at this period of the war, most of our Petty Officers and Chief Petty Officers in charge of our AA-guns were still peacetime-trained naval personnel and their training and discipline stood us in good stead under this attack. We met them with a steady return fire and although we did not actually bring any down we were successful against earlier torpedo-bomber assaults, one of which flew into the sea after being hit and we forced others to sheer off course during their final approach.'

Several near-misses were in fact claimed by the Stuka pilots. Inflated claims were made by the defending fighters of heavy losses inflicted in return, but in truth Italian records clearly show that only one Junkers Ju 87 failed to return from this attack. This was the mount of Lieutenant Vechione and Sergeant Fusco, which joined the formation for the return to base in damaged condition due to a flak hit. But it was the fuel situation which led to their loss. The attack was carried out at extreme range and the journey back to base was hazardous enough, without the additional hazard of damage.

Despite his best efforts to nurse her home Vechione's plane went into the sea some 6 km from the Sicilian coast, close to the island of Favignana. German seaplanes later searched the area for survivors but in vain. Five of the other Stukas of Cenni's command were running just on the smell of their engines by the time they reached home and had to crash-land wherever they could. The remaining 11 Stukas got back to base with less than ten litres of fuel in their tanks. In the de-briefing afterwards they tried to estimate the effect of their attack, but it proved impossible to verify as subsequent Admiralty admissions of losses did not specify times of loss. We now know, however, that they failed to score any hits at all.

The following day some 16 Stukas had reassembled at Gela airbase and, of these, 10 were fully operational for another strike. Accordingly, Cenni led them into the air to seek out the convoy, now approaching Malta on the last stage of its perilous journey. With Cenni leading, and Lieutenant Busetti as second-in-command, this small force, escorted by 25 fighters of 51 Stormo, was directed to a target some 90 km south-east of Pantelleria island, about a couple of hours' total flying time.

They found that the great concourse of ships they had attacked the evening before had dispersed. The big warship group had turned back to the west, the convoy itself with a close escort of cruisers, destroyers and minesweepers had continued onward but they themselves had been attacked by the Italian 7 Cruiser Division and, while some of the escorts defended them in a fierce sea battle, the convoy and other escorts took avoiding action. They had been dive-bombed by the German Stukas earlier when *Cairo* had been hit, and half the convoy, the freighters *Burdwan*, *Chant* and tanker *Kentucky*, also hit so badly they had to be sunk. Following up this assault Cenni's unit found only isolated targets and concentrated on *Cairo*.

All 10 Stukas were armed with SD500 bombs and, at 09.40, they directed their attack against a target identified as a cruiser, attacking again down from 3500 m in the face of heavy AA-fire. Their target was *Cairo* and, as well as the heavy flak from her own guns and the accompanying destroyers, the Stukas had to run the gauntlet of some Spitfires from Malta. A furious mêlée broke out as these tangled with the Italian escorts, and through this the surviving dive-bombers went into their attack dives on *Cairo*, releasing their bombs at a height of 400 m. Again their bravery and determination availed them nothing and near-misses were all that the three Stukas achieved in this attack. The other one who could attack, went for merchant ship targets, again without success. But the attacks by the British fighters was severe, five of the Stukas being damaged before they could start their dives. The only loss was that of a Stuka of 239 Squadriaglie, which was shot into the sea some 50 km south-east of Pantelleria. Both crew members were seen to escape and to be clinging to the tail section of their sinking aircraft. Gilbilterra managed to circle low and throw over his inflatable raft close by in the hope they could reach it, ignoring his own danger. Such gestures between fellow Stuka pilots were normal. But it was in vain. Subsequent air/sea searches with floatplanes and launches combed the area but met with no success.

Meanwhile Cenni and his wingman Fabbri were still over the target taking photographs of the attack for the records, leaving Captain Stringa to guide the others back to base. Both the planes of Stringa and Perozzi returned with serious damage. Boerci's gunner, Sergeant-Major Converso (209 Squadriaglie), was able to avenge him by definitely destroying by return fire one Spitfire which was seen to crash into the sea also. Others managed to avoid damage by heavily jinking and throwing their aircraft around. Thus they survived and came back safely to Gela. Only two ships of the convoy finally reached Malta and on 17 June further air searches were conducted to locate the escorts returning back through the Sicilian Channel to Gibraltar.

The losses of the previous two days had reduced Cenni's command severely and he only had six aircraft for this mission. They took off at 09.00 and directed their attentions to an area to the west of the island of Goletta where *Cairo*, the minelayer *Welshman* and the destroyers *Blankney*, *Ithuriel*, *Marne* and *Middleton* had been reported steering north-west, but although they quartered an area some 600 km wide they found no trace of this squadron. A second sortie was flown by 102 Gruppo at 14.00, another offensive recce patrol seeking the same ships some 50 km north of Cape Bougaroni, Tunisia, but they were again unrewarded and they landed at Cagliari to refuel before returning to base on 18 June via Trapani.

The attacks against Operation HARPOON, though vigorously pressed home, had not resulted in a single success. True, dive-bombers *had* decimated the convoy but these were the Luftwaffe units of the famous StG 3, not Cenni's men. Also this period of intense operation had resulted in the whittling down of the Gruppo to below 12 operational aircraft, less than the 15 or 16 planes required for each of the two squadrons normally. In truth, then, by mid-1942, 102 Gruppo was merely a 'presence', not a force. Although meant to be the equivalent of a German Stukagruppen, it was in fact less than one of their Staffeln. Nonetheless they had fought with valour.

On 24 June the unit moved to Sciacca, then flew to St Pietro airfield, near Rome, for the awarding of medals in recognition of their work. Mussolini decorated them with the Medaglia d'Argento, those so rewarded being Cenni himself and Captain Stringa along with Gamberini, Perozzi, Berretta, Converso, Lanfredi, Fabbri and Campari. A further seven Bronze Medals and various Croci di Guerra were awarded to their crew members also. They then returned to Sicily to continue their missions against Malta. Although the British convoy operations had been mainly failures enough supplies had got through to keep the base functioning, so the relentless war of attrition over the island had to continue. The unit resumed their dusk and night patrols to maintain the blockade.

On the night of 25 June, for example, three of 102 Gruppo's Stukas, led by Cenni, were part of a 19-plane sortie along with six Cant Z1007s and 10 BR20s sent out to hunt down a supply ship reported off Malta. A further 12 Stukas were to remain at base, bombed up and ready to go should she be located. The idea was for the combined unit of 15 aircraft to concentrate and for Cenni to lead them in a massed attack on this ship. However dense fog covered the Straits and the base, and the whole expedition remained grounded. Phone calls to abort the mission failed to reach the advanced Stuka crews, who carried on with the mission. One attacked an AA-battery on the island. The second was shot down by patrolling night-fighters, while Cenni himself returned safely to base.

A similar mission planned for the night of 28 June was also abandoned due to adverse weather conditions.

Cenni's next mission was a straightforward dive-bomber attack on Malta's Hal Far airfield. On the evening of 5 July 1942 11 Stukas took part, with an escort of 13 fighters. They were armed with 250-kg bombs and their objectives were the dispersed fighter aircraft and torpedo-bombers at that base. The mission was accomplished but fighters again intercepted them and Cenni himself was subjected to a fierce attack which lasted for fully ten minutes by a Beaufighter, which he managed eventually to lose before carrying out his bombing. Although it had been planned to drop their bombs from above the 3000 m–1000 m level to avoid the worst of the AA-fire, Cenni himself went down to 300 m to make sure of his target before release. All this was part of the planned softening-up process for the planned invasion of Malta, in support of which 20 Falcon fighter bombers arrived at Gerbini with 5 Stormo. They were to co-ordinate attacks with the Stukas once the paratroops had established themselves.

During this preparation period they still had other tasks, for example to make sure isolated ships did not reach the island. Fast minelayers such as *Welshman* were being used to slip through with essential machinery and food stocks under cover of darkness, and part of Cenni's duties was to try and catch her. On 15 July eight of 102 Gruppo's Stukas caught her south of Sicily and scored several near misses which, in the words of her captain, '. . . exploded under her stern and flung her sideways and forward', but amazingly, she was still able to maintain a good speed and got through safely.

Cenni was enjoying a well-earned leave when the next big Malta convoy was mounted, Operation PEDESTAL. In his absence the unit was led by Cumbat, but Cenni was hastily recalled to command on 20 August and within a few days was once more flying against Malta. His first mission was against a typical Stuka target, the radar station at Carla San Marco. For this, pinpoint accuracy was required and so the Stukas were given the task. Cenni led a small force of just four Ju 87R–2s on the evening of 26 August. They evaded the night-fighter patrols and arrived over their target at 22.15. They started their dives from 2600 m and dropped their 250-kg bombs with considerable skill, causing a large amount of disruption to the station.

Towards the end of this period the launching of the invasion of Malta was first postponed, and then abandoned and 102 Gruppo was withdrawn to refurbish with the new Ju 87D–3 Stukas now being supplied from Germany. These were much-improved aircraft from the old B and R types the Italians had been forced to use, and were similar to those in service with StG 3. To re-equip Cenni took his unit north to Lonate Pozzolo (Varese).

Even so a more satisfactory aircraft was required to specialise in dive-bombing. The Germans were considering switching to the Focke-Wulf FW 190 during the coming year, and in a similar manner Cenni was again involved in discussion and planning work to see if an equivalent Italian fighter could be so adapted to dive-bombing. From December 1942 onward he was testing and planning this transition for 102 Gruppo. The aircraft first chosen was the Reggiane Re 2001 fighter, which Cenni tested thoroughly but which eventually proved unsuitable for its new role, even though several successful attacks were made on Bone from bases in Sardinia early in 1943. Far more satisfactory was another fighter conversion which eventually equipped Cenni's reconstructed 239 Squadriaglie with

102 Gruppo of 5 Stormo. The 2002 Ariete II was a low-wing, radial-engined, single-seater monoplane that had failed to come up to expectations as an interceptor, but it was rugged enough to be utilised in its new role and, fitted with a bomb-crutch and dive-brakes, proved a worthwhile conversion. Powered by a 175 hp Piaggio PXIX RC45 Turbine-B radial engine, and powerfully armed with two 12.7-mm Breda-SAFAT machine-guns and two 7.7-mm guns, it had a maximum speed of some 329 mph which meant it could hold its own with most Allied fighters and engage them on equal terms when required. With the swinging bomb-crutch fitted below its fuselage the Re2002 could carry up to 1433 lb of bombs at high speed into the target with relative immunity compared to the Stuka. She was a much more lively aircraft for Cenni and his young pilots to handle but, with the Allies pressing forward on all fronts, the need for a fast ground-support aircraft was even more vital. Intensive training throughout the spring was followed by re-equipping, and Cenni's unit was fully operational only just in time to meet the Allied invasion of Sicily on 10 June 1943. For the next two months they saw intensive action.

Their priority targets were the great mass of Allied transport lying off the beachhead. This was powerfully protected by hundreds of British and American land-based fighters and British carrier fighters. Against such numbers, plus the huge volume of flak the massed warships were able to throw up, the assaults of Cenni and his few compatriots were like grains of sand against the incoming tide. They knew their task was hopeless but they flew on, doing what they could. From the dawn of Day One low-level attacks on the ships and beaches were maintained. The official historian wrote: 'The very sustained bombing to which the Axis airfields in Sicily had been subjected for several days before the invasion had not prevented the enemy reacting quite strongly. It is furthermore hard to avoid the conclusion that the arrangements made for the fighter protection of the American invasion fleet, and of the beaches in the western assault area, did not prove adequate. As the day progressed and losses to air attacks mounted, the demands for stronger fighter cover grew more insistent.'

In fact the Americans lost the destroyer *Maddox*, the mine-sweeper *Sentinel*, and eight transports totalling 54,306 tons this day. The contribution of 102 Gruppo was the destruction of *Talamba*, an 8018-ton transport (which the Allies stated was being used as a hospital-ship). On 13 July in an attack on the bombarding force off the coast, Cenni's unit claimed a hit on a British battleship. This was, in fact, the monitor *Erebus* (8450 tons) which was bombarding Catania with her 15-in. guns. Although damaged by a direct hit and having her bilges holed by near misses, she was not sunk and was later able to return to the battle. Despite these commendable efforts the Allies finally managed to organise some kind of efficient air cover and further attacks were met with heavy losses. The whole island was quickly overrun. Cenni's unit was pulled back to the mainland to regroup in readiness for the expected further assaults. Further missions continued to be flown throughout August and then, on the last day of the month, huge naval task forces began shelling shore installations to soften them up for Operation BAYTOWN, the Allied invasion of Calabria, at the 'toe' of Italy. 239 Squadriaglie stood by at maximum strength for one last struggle.

The crossing of the Straits of Messina took place on 3 September 1943, the British troops being carried there in almost 300 landing-craft and attacks were directed at their beachheads at Reggio and Villa San Giovanni. Several small attacks were made by Re 2002s during that afternoon and evening. Secret talks were already in progress between the new Italian government and the Allies to prepare for an Armistice but to the fighting men the war was still in progress and they fought on in their hopeless cause. It was a tragic and wasteful misuse of brave young men and those that died in those last days suffered the great irony of war in that they died bravely, but needlessly. The morning of 4 September brought to Cenni only the knowledge that he would be engaged in a desperate fight against odds as so often before. He had always met such difficulties with humour and fortitude before, but the newly promoted major and his companions knew just how desperate Italy's position had become. If he had any premonition of his likely fate that day he did not show it, it was not his way. All the young dive-bomber pilots setting out to face that enormous aerial and naval armada were only too aware that they were living on borrowed time anyway. Each day had to be fought through, and, if they were lucky, lived through.

In order to demonstrate just how great the opposition was at this stage of the war the RAF alone could deploy the following Spitfire units against them:

SPITFIRE SQUADRONS	BASE
43, 72, 93, 111, 243	Gerbini, Sicily
152, 154, 232, 242	Lentini, Sicily
81	Comiso, Sicily
249, 229, 185	Krendi, Malta
1435	Luqa, Malta
126	Safi, Malta

British statements are terse about the day's fighting. 'During the next four days', goes one account, 'the advancing troops were subjected to some small-scale strafing attacks by Re 2002s of 5 Stormo but these were the last offensive sorties of the war for the Regia Aeronautica.' This contempt is shown in other official pronouncements. 'On 4 September 1943, approximately 20 enemy aircraft were intercepted by Spitfires between Augusta and Messina and eight of them were destroyed,' reads another account. Major Cenni's last mission is worthy of more detailed description than these. Even at the height of the Battle of Britain never had 'The Few' faced odds as enormous as ten to one, and those were the odds Cenni and his men now accepted. On this day the true spirit of the Italian dive-bomber pilots is shown when two Re 2002s, piloted by Moglia and Micheli, flew to the Manduria air base from Crotone to join their unit leader and ensure they would take part in the attack at all costs. They arrived before noon and were hastily refuelled and armed. The Commander of 5 Stormo had just finalised details of the last mission which was to be conducted against the numerous landing-craft unloading troops on the beaches between Villa San Giovanni and Reggio Calabria. Secondary targets were allocated as any armoured columns sighted moving inland, and rail communications.

At 11.25 Cenni led the 12 Re 2002s – nine of 101 Gruppo and three of 102 Gruppo (Lieutenant Moglia and Sergeants Melotti and Falvia) – which took off from Manduria and headed towards the beaches, but Melotti had to return with engine trouble. The others pressed home their attacks against intense flak and through a balloon barrage over the ships, escaping unscathed. They had dropped 30 Torpedine 100-kg bombs and fired 6100 rounds of 12.7-mm and 3600 rounds of 7.7-mm into the enemy ships and claimed to have sunk four of the half-laden 350-ton LCFs they hit. In addition they shot up large concentrations of half-tracks and semi-armoured vehicles on rail wagons and on shore and they set on fire some enemy-occupied barracks further inland. Strong enemy fighter formations hit them as they weaved inland after this daring assault, two large Spitfire formations falling on them out of the blue. In the desperate combats which followed they were swamped by the enemy but managed to destroy no less than four of them. However three of the Italian planes failed to return to base, among them that of Major Cenni himself.

The survivors landed at 13.25 at Botricello airfield, effected a hasty replenishment and then flew on to Manduria. Of the pilots shot down, one of them, Sergeant Banfi (who was credited with the destruction of two of the enemy planes on that sortie) managed to bale out. After many adventures he returned to the squadron safe and well two days later. The other two missing pilots, Lieutenant Moglia and Major Cenni never did return. Thus in a few weeks of fighting the command changed leaders rapidly. Just as the death of Colonel Nobili in July had seen Cenni assume command, now, with Cenni in turn gone, the leadership devolved on to Major Rizzi.

The death of their young leader cast a deep gloom over the squadron. Piece by piece during the days which followed more details were put together. Eyewitnesses in the mountains told how they had seen Cenni's aircraft with numerous Spitfires on its tail weaving through the hills in a cloud of machine-gun fire. Others told of the desperate attempts at intervention by the Re 2002 of Sergeant D'Agnino, who tried in vain to draw away the enemy from his leader's crippled plane, but they refused the bait.

Thus passed Giuseppe Cenni in the last action of more than 100 missions undertaken at risk and with skill. He had survived audaciously time after time with miraculous luck. To fall on the very last sortie of all was therefore an especially sad fate for a pilot of his calibre. Later some of his comrades made a diligent search of the area of his last fight and recovered his corpse from its resting place close by the burnt-out wreckage of his aircraft. He was interred in a rough mound while a service was said by Major Suter over the grave. He left behind his widow, Tina, and their two small children.

His loss was the turning point for the unit. One contemporary stated that, 'The waltz of life, into which he had so zestfully thrown himself despite the anguish of war, now took him in one last cruel finale.' This reflected his nickname, the 'Little Waltzer', given him by his companions in affectionate tribute to his skill in the air which they compared to that of a brilliant choreographer. With his death and the loss of both his humour and wise guidance the Gruppo's officers' mess became a sad circle. Not even the announcement of the Armistice could lift their spirits. As a posthumous tribute it was later announced that Cenni had been awarded the coveted Gold Medal for outstanding courage and achievement. Only slowly did this sombre shadow remove itself from the Gruppo, as new pilots joined who had never known him, or been influenced by his charm and knowledge. Between its reformation in May 1942 and 8 September 1943, 102 Gruppo had lost in combat nineteen of its veteran pilots, 10 of them in the bitter days between 10 July and the Armistice. It was a heavy blow to sustain, although gradually the spirit came back to the unit and they fought on in subsequent campaigns, this time on the Allied side.

Gradually Suter was able to rebuild the unit's former pride. As a forty-year-old he had become something of a father figure to the unit, in contrast to the pilots half his age like Cenni, whom he referred to as 'My Boy'. His own sorrow at the loss of his friend was great, and he organised a more lasting memorial to Cenni as soon as he could, and he helped to dedicate it. But he also persevered in trying to bring back to 102 Gruppo some of Cenni's old magic. But in spite of this never again did 102 Gruppo reach the heights of dedication and comradeship that they had when the small, slight figure of Giuseppe Cenni had led them in their own 'Dance of Death' towards the enemy target.

His memorial reflected the feelings of his surviving comrades:

> Skilful fighter and dive-bomber pilot who dedicated his short life to the defence of his country. Always the first into the battle and taking the risks. In two wars his virtue and professionalism always shone through everything he did.

4 Major Richard Partridge

Royal Marines   1910–

It may surprise some readers to learn that it was the British who originally invented dive-bombing. They most certainly used it in direct combat conditions in 1917 with Sopwith Camel and SE fighters on the Western Front. Moreover it was the newly formed Royal Air Force that conducted the first detailed and exhaustive tests into the effectiveness of dive-bombing early in 1918 at the Orfordness testing station. The subsequent abandonment of this form of attack and its constant rejection by that service in the years that followed has tended. to over-shadow other British achievements in this field of bombing development. Although it is true that the dive-bomber as a concept and a viable weapon was proven by the Americans, Japanese, Russians and Germans, the Royal Navy did possess minute numbers of modern dive-bombers at the outbreak of war in 1939, and applied their pre-war lessons and techniques as far as these slender resources permitted.

The aircraft concerned was the Blackburn Skua. This air-craft scored a number of notable firsts. It was the first mono-plane to serve in the Fleet Air Arm. It was also the first aircraft designed from the outset as a dive-bomber to enter service with British forces (earlier dive-bombers had been conversions, while other designs had been converted to Target Tugs by the Royal Air Force and the Skua, despite its reputation, was *always* meant to be a dive-bomber first, and a fighter second, not the other way round). It was the first British aircraft to destroy a German machine in the Second World War, and the first dive-bomber to sink a major naval target. It was the first dive-bomber to attack German battleships, French battleships and German coastal batteries, all in the same year. Thus, even if Britain is more noted for being the victim of dive-bombers she can claim nonetheless, through the Royal Navy and Royal Marines, to have contributed a great deal to the dive-bomber story.

The British contributor to our history who took part in most of these major pre-war and early wartime developments was a flying Marine, Richard 'Birdy' Partridge. One of the 'characters' of that select band that was the much-reduced Royal Marines of the inter-war period, 'Birdy' Partridge was one of forty Royal Marines who flew as pilots in the Second World War and left their mark out of all proportion to their numbers.

'My mother was clever enough to give birth to me on 10 October 1910, and I have always maintained, quite untruly, that it was at 10 minutes past 10 in the morning, so that my real date of birth is 10.10.10.10.10,' he was to write with typical humour. He was born in Hampstead, and moved down to Worthing in Sussex when air raids became a feature of London life in the First World War. His early years were uneventful; however, by the age of seventeen he had set his heart on a naval career and in the summer of 1928 he sat the Civil Service Examination for public-school entry into the Royal Navy or Royal Marines.

These examinations were tough at a time when the Royal Navy had been cut back to the bone as a result of the Washington Treaty when Britain's politicians for the first time cut down the country's naval might to appease foreign governments. Places were scarce to come by and vacancies were few. The examinations lasted four days and included a demanding interview by an Admiral with naval and marine representatives present. Richard failed the hurdle on his first attempt and at first thought about returning to university instead. However he was persuaded to try a second time in December of the same year, this time with great success. Entry into the Royal Marines in those days was different from the other services in that no prior training as a cadet was required. Thus it came about that on 17 December Richard was appointed as Probationary Second Lieutenant in the Royal Marines with orders to report to Royal Naval College, Greenwich, on 2 January 1928. This 'Probationary' period lasted about four years, and during this period any such officer could face instant dismissal from the service at a moment's notice if he failed to come up to expectations. The training involved a rotation around the various naval training establishments to learn the rudiments of all the requirements of the period, Navy, Marine *and* Army. Courses included bayonet training, 15-in. naval gunnery, turret drill, gas warfare, mining, close-order drilling, torpedoes, and *equestrian training*, a delight for students of Royal Marines history.

By 1932, now promoted to Probationary Lieutenant, Richard found himself at the Royal Marines Barracks, Chatham, awaiting his first shipboard posting as a RM subaltern to one of the Marine detachments normally carried by the larger warships, cruisers and battleships. However, when Richard's orders did eventually arrive they were to have a lasting impact on his future career for he was appointed to the aircraft-carrier HMS *Hermes*, then serving on the China Station, and he was to take passage out to the East aboard the training cruiser HMS *Vindictive*. *Vindictive* had been fitted out as a trials ship for shipborne aircraft catapaults and had a larger hangar forward of her bridge instead of the usual 7.5-in. guns. Already the influence of the aircraft was entering the young officer's life, and it was during this commission that Richard decided to try and specialise in a flying career.

The little *Hermes* was one of the first aircraft-carriers built as such from the keel up (the first had been the Japanese *Hosho*) and although she was small and could carry only a few aircraft she provided the navy with much valuable experience. They visited the ports of Formosa, Japan, Philippines and the great ports of the China coast itself, such as Shanghai and Hong Kong, from the leased base of Wei-hai-wei. Between his routine duties aboard Partridge was able to join the 'goofers' that lined the flight-deck to watch the primitive naval aircraft of the day operate – Flycatchers, Fairey IIIFs, and other legendary biplanes that could turn on a sixpence. The contrast between his formal Marine duties and the exhilaration of the young aviator's relative freedom was too much to resist. During the long journey home at the end of this commission Partridge applied, and was accepted as a trainee flyer. He received notice to report to the RAF station at Leuchars, near St Andrews, in Fife in 1933. Unlike the other major navies of that period – the United States, Japan and France – the Royal Navy's aircrew were particularly hamstrung by an extraordinary arrangement whereby the Royal Air Force was responsible for the aircraft designed for the rival service and in charge of the aircrew aboard the ships, along with the maintenance parties, which were made up of roughly equal numbers from each service. Under the burden of an indifferent service the Fleet Air Arm, which in 1918 had led the world, languished and fell far behind in both numbers and modern aircraft. It became an article of faith in the Royal Air Force that shipborne aircraft would have no part to play in any future war which would be won by the heavy bomber, alone and unaided. They also adopted the policy that naval aircraft operating from aircraft-carriers would, of necessity, always be inferior to their shore-based equivalents. As a result, those in the Royal Navy invariably were inferior.

Inevitably the Royal Air Force turned its back on the frequent naval requests to follow the lead of the United States and Japanese navies, both of which were developing the dive-bomber as one of their principal strike components. Having no faith in the technique the Royal Air Force did not apply itself to others with differing ideas, and so dive-bombing in the Fleet Air Arm was conducted with the small fleet fighters equipped with small bombs which, even if accurately placed, would have caused little embarrassment to large naval units.

In 1931 Lieutenant-Commander St J. Prentice of the Royal Navy returned from a visit to the United States full of enthusiasm for the dive-bombing techniques and aircraft he found being developed there. The potential of this method, with its proven accuracy, was ideal for naval requirements over the almost useless high-level methods favoured by the Air Staff, and this was quickly appreciated. But no dive-bombing sight was available and, despite a six-year campaign by the Admiralty, none was ever produced. Nor were the Air Chiefs enthusiastic about producing a specialised dive-bomber aircraft, and the navy had to order the new plane on its own responsibility and combine its new requirements with the incompatible ones of a fighter, a hopeless problem to solve for the builders who, wisely, stuck to the main role, dive-bombing, in producing the Skua.

These parts of the 'grand design' were to affect Partridge in the long-term, but at the time he knew little of service in-fighting, for he was concerned with the more prosaic job of assimilating his new skills. But what the politicians inflicted upon the Fleet Air Arm is clear from Partridge's own words on how his new career influenced his rank and promotion:

> One of the results of this awkward arrangement was that all naval flying personnel had to have a RAF commission, and they were granted a temporary one. Hence, when I started flying, I was a Lieutenant RM and a Flying Officer RAF, and later a Captain RM and Flight-Lieutenant RAF. A squadron embarked in a carrier might be commanded by a Lieutenant-Commander RN or a Squadron-Leader RAF, and the senior aviation officer on board, Wing-Commander Flying, always a Wing-Commander RAF.

All training of non-RAF personnel was conducted at Leuchars and this included Army Co-operation units, very much the poor relation of the RAF in the same way as the Fleet Air Arm, and it was there that Partridge drove on 15 September 1933, along with another Royal Marines contemporary, Lieutenant F.S. 'Tiddler' May. At Leuchars they found themselves in the company of 10 navy officers and three army officers. At the Flying Training squadron there were three flights at varying stages of development: an elementary course of three months; an intermediate course of the same duration; and three months' operational training on contemporary front-line aircraft. The first aircraft Partridge learnt to fly was the basic Avro 504N trainer under the eyes of a RAF commander known as 'Split-Arse Pete'. After 13 hours 45 minutes dual instruction Partridge conducted his first solo flight aboard this docile steed.

By August 1934 Partridge had passed through all three levels of training at Leuchars and, having graduated as an 'above average' pupil, was able to choose fighter aircraft when the options came up for his future specialisation with the Fleet Air Arm. This long course had produced a qualified pilot in all respects save that of actually landing an aircraft on the deck of a carrier. This last hurdle was carried out satisfactorily with Partridge's first operational unit, No 802 Squadron, which was embarked on the aircraft-carrier *Courageous*. Officially described as a FF or 'Fleet Fighter' squadron, 802 Squadron was equipped with the Hawker Nimrod I biplane. This was a 'navalised' version of the Hawker Fury fighter with an increased wingspan but low performance as a consequence of additions such as arrestor-hook and flotation equipment. It was designed to remain the standard fighter in the Royal Navy until the year of Munich, 1938, when it was replaced by the Sea Gladiator which joined the fleet in November of that year.

Richard Partridge was based ashore at Netheravon after his training period for a working-up interval, at the end of which he took part in the fly-over at the Jubilee Review of the Fleet at Spithead on 15 July 1935.

So far all had proceeded at a steady peacetime pace but the dictatorships in Europe were beginning to flex their strength and the first of a steadily increasing crescendo of emergencies upset the Services' stately routine. The first of these was the Italian invasion of Abyssinia, and Partridge's squadron was hastily embarked aboard the aircraft-carrier *Glorious* which was among the many warships dispatched post-haste to the Mediterranean in anticipation of full-scale war. In the event Mussolini called the League of Nations' bluff and was able to proceed on his chosen course while in Britain vacillating politicians huffed-and-puffed but drew back from outright intervention. In the interim *Glorious* remained with the Mediterranean Fleet.

In May 1936, Partridge was transferred to No 803 Squadron which was embarked aboard his old ship *Hermes*, still serving on the China Station, and he eventually caught up with her at the northern Chinese port of Tsingtao three months later, only to learn that she was due to sail back home the following spring. The normal routine of flying from the carrier was continued, including flights with a Hawker Osprey equipped as a float-plane. When *Hermes* finally arrived back at Plymouth on 3 May 1937, the squadron was flown ashore. After a short spell at RAF Gosport Richard again joined 802 Squadron aboard *Glorious* back in the Mediterranean until his five-year Fleet Air Arm detachment period expired and he had to return to the prosaic duties of an orthodox Royal Marines officer in peacetime for a minimum two-year period. This he began at the Royal Marines Barracks in Plymouth in October 1938.

However this was brought to an abrupt termination in May 1939 when Partridge was again recalled to flying duties at the Royal Navy Air Station, Eastleigh. At last the navy had regained control of its own aircraft but time was not on its side and, when war was declared in September 1939, the Fleet Air Arm was still equipped with a miscellaneous collection of makeshift aircraft with more of the same kind in the production schedule, a legacy of RAF neglect. Worse still, the twenty-year hiatus could not easily be overcome with the scramble of priority for new types of aircraft once the nation was at war. But at least in the Blackburn Skua dive-bomber the Royal Navy had one modern weapon.

The Fleet Air Arm also understood the basic techniques of dive-bombing which they had perfected in readiness for a real machine in which to do it, although, as these techniques had been worked out and utilised with the more predictable biplane fighters, many modifications had to be made once they got their hands on the Skuas, soon after the outbreak of war. All Fleet Air Arm pilots had practised 'light' dive-bombing either at shore ranges at Tentasmuir or at the RAF range at Sutton Bridge near the Wash, as well as against towed and radio-controlled targets at sea – old battleships or armoured motor torpedo boats. By the outbreak of hostilities dive-bombing was generally understood in the Fleet even at the highest levels. A dive-bomber sight had been requested from the Air Ministry, but although it had not materialised the art of such attacks was studied.

The methods as practised and put into effect at the time deserve attention and to be remembered. In general, dive-bombing was described as a method of attack where the bombs were released in a dive at a height varying between 3000 and 1000 ft. Unofficially the navy pilots had always pressed in much closer than this to achieve hits. But it must be born in mind that to drop bombs from too low an altitude reduces their penetration effectiveness, which is essential against heavily armoured warships such as battleships and heavy cruisers. The general method of attack fell into four phases: approach, initial dive, aiming dive, and 'get-away'.

The approach was carried out at the best height to take advantage of prevailing weather conditions and the main aim was to achieve surprise by using cloud cover or by approaching from out of the sun. Again it should be remembered that radar was in its infancy at the beginning of the war and so this requirement was still relevant. A good height was also desirable to enable the initial dive to be made outside effective AA-gun range. The target was therefore 'stalked' with great care to eliminate, if possible, interference from either defending fighters or gunfire, especially so in the case of naval targets since much research had been done by most nations between the wars to develop quick-firing guns that would counter such attacks. But speed was essential also to avoid early detection and a balance had to be kept. If the approach was made through cloud the target had to be sighted from time to time but only brief glimpses were necessary in the hope that immunity of detection by the defender could be preserved for as long as possible. The greatest menace was early detection by defending fighters as no dive-bomber was built with much in the way of defensive capacity, it being strictly an *offensive* weapon designed to mete out punishment, not to absorb it. It never fails to puzzle dive-bomber pilots to whom I have spoken, however, when critics write off aircraft of this sort as useless because they fail to stand up to fighter attacks. At the time nobody who designed, planned or flew them *expected* them to do so. Even the heavy bombers, lavishly equipped with defensive guns and carrying huge crews to man them, failed to survive determined fighter attacks. No, it was through avoidance of interception, surprise, speed or their own strong fighter protection, that enabled the dive-bomber to replace its bomb-load precisely on target in the quickest and most accurate way then known.

If no enemy fighters were thought to be about, then the ideal approach of a large unit was determined to be by sub-sections coming in from different areas of the sky above the target in quick succession, both to confuse and split the gun defence. These were the well-known 'Converging Attacks' much practised by the Fleet Air Arm. This was also the standard Luftwaffe and United States navy procedure too, with the vital difference that these organisations had sufficient aircraft to make it viable. The Fleet Air Arm had to make do with 'penny packets' of machines to achieve the same effect and the 'swamping' of a target was never possible to achieve under such limitations.

Approach was also determined by the relative speed and direction of the line of advance of the target of course, and wind direction and funnel haze also played a vital part. When an approach was made from 6000 ft or more then the initial dive was an essential link between the end of the approach and the final attack dive itself, in order to reduce the length of the latter when the aircraft would expect to find itself under heavy fire from its target and other accompanying vessels.

British practice called for a line-astern approach, or sections in line-astern formation should the opportunity arise. If hostile fighters were present then the dive-bombers kept closed-up in the best defensive posture to provide mutual supporting fire for as long as possible, but otherwise a spacing of 500 yds was desirable to reduce the effect of long-range gunfire on such formations. Each section could choose the best position and, in an ideal attack, sections would come in from varying points of the compass to split the defences so that at least one section would, in theory, get through to the target.

In dive-bombing definitions in such conditions, an attacked target was a target hit, whereas altitude bombing rarely achieved any hits at all. There was a natural tendency for pilots to follow closely the aircraft ahead, but it was laid down that individual directions of attack should ideally be sufficiently dispersed to ensure that no aircraft entered the cone of close-range defensive fire directed at another aircraft. Low, broken cloud was considered the ideal weather condition, but con-tinuous cloud cover below 6000 ft was a hazard and the same conditions at 4000 ft might rule out such an attack altogether for it would allow no sight of the target for a sufficient length of time, a fact not always appreciated by those who directed dive-bomber missions but possessed no practical experience of their own.

The 'aiming dive' was begun from a position, generally known as the 'X point', and this was flexible, dependent upon the conditions of bomb-release, and the height, angle of dive and air speed at the moment of release. This had to be considered and constantly updated by the commanding officer of the squadron on the spot. He had to weigh up instantly those factors which would result in the greatest number of hits and the fewest possible aircraft casualties.

After the attack had been delivered came the 'get-away' and here each pilot was allowed considerable discretion to act independently according to three general principles: first, the need to get out of range of the defending guns as fast as he could, taking his own avoiding action as he did so; second, the need to head for the nearest available cloud cover; and finally – most important – if defending fighters were still around, to resume close defensive formation as quickly as possible before they were pounced upon as individual, isolated stragglers. This was often the time when dive-bombers were at their most vulnerable, i.e. *after* the attack, as was shown, for example, by what happened to the Skuas in Norway, and the Stukas during the Battle of Britain. Fighter aircraft of all nations had the greatest difficulty in following attacking dive-bombers down if they failed to head them off initially. Dive-bombers could often out-turn the much faster fighters, but many easy 'kills' were to be had by picking them off afterwards, before they could reform. This did not save the dive-bomber's target, but it could result in spectacular actions and spectacular claims, and could be likened to the fighter pilots imitating the old-time soccer forwards who used to 'goal-hang' in order to pick up easy chances and so gain a reputation.

It was fully recognised that to achieve the optimum 'angle of dive' – the angle which would achieve the best hit/loss ratio – that steep dive-bombing was best. Thus, even in the official guides issued to the Fleet Air Arm in 1940 it is clearly stated that: 'Broadly speaking this angle is the steepest that will allow the control necessary to give accurate aiming . . .'

This varied with different types of aircraft. While the longitudinal control usually remained satisfactory, lateral control often worsened as the speed built up. This resulted in the aircraft becoming 'set' in its dive and meant that it became increasingly more difficult, if not finally impossible, to correct the aim, save by longitudinal direction. With an old biplane such as the Swordfish, this took place at around 160 knots; with the new monoplane Skua with its underwing diving flaps extended, speed could be limited to 240 knots but lateral control was not good. Using a steep dive (by which the British meant 70 degrees although German and American pilots would mean almost vertical) less skill was required to judge the moment of bomb-release as the 'bombing-angle' was smaller and the bomb could be released without appreciable 'pull-out'. This was important, for dive-bombing sights were either primitive or non-existent (and not popular with the pilots anyway). However at such acute angles the need for the pilot to lock on to his target early was essential or else he might find himself committed in vain and unable to change as the target altered course. Further, the committed attacker might find himself 'skidding' or turning to follow such an evasion at the exact moment of bomb-release, thus adding large errors to the already complex factors which affected his accuracy.

By adopting a shallower angle of attack, as favoured by the RAF (when they considered dive-bombing at all), there was less difficulty in keeping a steady course and making aiming adjustments. However it was stated that: 'the aircraft has to be pulled out through a large angle before release, which is difficult to judge, and, also, the target is lost to sight under the nose some time before release.'

The development of a satisfactory automatic gyro-release, associated with a multi-directional dive-bombing sight, would have overcome this disadvantage but the Royal Air Force had failed to push this through before war broke out, although work was being conducted on such a sight by Smith's Instruments in 1940. This 'automatic' dive-bomb sight was based on tachymetric principles which, within certain limits, measured and corrected the aircraft for 'relative wind' and such. Also, pre-war, the Royal Air Force had examined the Swedish dive-bombing sight and had been much impressed by it.

The true dive-bomb, the steep dive, was known to be far less vulnerable to AA-fire than shallow low-level attacks as mounted by the Fairey Battles in their sister-service, despite a lot of talk about dive-bombing presenting gunners with a nil-deflection shoot. Again the official pamphlet states quite clearly that: 'the steeper angle introduces laying and training difficulties (for the defending gunlayers) and also the aircraft is over the vertical from the target slightly sooner. Angles of dive below 50 degrees become increasingly more vulnerable.' The truth of this statement was proven only too well during the attacks on the Maas bridges in 1940.

Failing the fitting of a dive-bomb sight the selection of the 'X point' had naturally to be left to the judgement of the pilot and thus dive-bombing was to always remain an in-built skill rather than a mechanical one. Dive-bomber pilots would be trained but *good* dive-bomber pilots were born. The only practical assistance to help the pilot were the painting of marks on the trailing edges of the wings (as used by the RAF Vengeance dive-bombers in Burma later in the war) or by graticule markings on the perspex cockpits of the aircraft (as favoured by the Stuka flyers in the Luftwaffe at this time and by the Soviet Pe–2 crews later).

Against this infinite variable some general guidelines for attacking warships (the Fleet Air Arm's prime function) could be outlined. Thus it was obvious that against a small, highly manoeuvrable and comparatively lightly armed vessel such as a destroyer the attack could be pressed home much closer (indeed this was essential) than against a battleship target which, deck-armour apart, would be powerfully armed with massed close-range AA-batteries.

The 'slant range of release' factor against a battleship target was the best balance which could be struck between hitting the target and being shot down by the ship's guns, and was estimated to be 1000 yds. In a 45-degree dive this corresponded to a release height of 2120 ft, but defences were improving all the time aboard modern warships, pushing this theoretical height further upward. The prime targets for the Royal Navy's dive-bombers, at least in pre-war exercises, were always considered to be the aircraft-carriers of the opposing (invariably Japanese) fleet which, with their wooden decks, would have made as easy targets for the Skuas as they turned out to be for the SBDs. But with a German or Italian opponent, without aircraft-carriers of their own, then how best to penetrate the thickly armoured decks of battleships and battle-cruisers with only 500-lb bombs became a problem to consider.

Whatever the target, once the 'X point' had been selected according to the pilot's judgement, little latitude would be left. In the case of the Skua, whose speed could be controlled by the flaps, the height of the 'X point' could be varied within considerable limits. The best direction of attack towards the ship target was conditioned by the relative wind rather than the true wind and this had to be allowed for in an 'aim-off' angle. Although all ships, especially high-speed destroyers and the like, would try to throw the attacking aircraft off its aim by taking evasive action it was recorded that: 'Alteration of course by the target ship during the aiming dive and time of fall of the bomb will have little effect, as the time is so short, and such alterations can, therefore, be ignored.'

It is interesting to note how this 1940 evaluation compares with a 1945 study made by the US navy. They found, through detailed analysis of attacks on their own warships by Japanese dive-bombers and later by kamikaze attacks, that it was better for the target ship to maintain a steady course if it was a large ship like a battleship. This gave the ship's own AA-gunners a steady sight of the oncoming aircraft and aided destruction, whereas any turn, however slight, would put the aim of the defenders off and still leave the attacker a large target. In the case of smaller warships, like destroyers, the exact reverse was the case. Such ships were never very accurate gun platforms anyway because of their size and liveliness in the water and thus their best defence against the dive-bomber was their own speed and manoeuvrability.

With relatively small bombs, like the standard 500-lb SAP (semi-armour-piercing) with which the Skua was equipped, the distribution distance was of little consequence as they could carry only one bomb each. Ideally a distribution of at least 20 ft between each bomb-hit on a ship was the ideal against a large ship as the destructive power of the SAP bomb was greatest if each hit burst in a separate compartment, thus effecting a cumulative effect on the hull. Accurate distribution was very hard to achieve in a diving attack and great skill was required to get the correct rate of pull-out during the release. There was also the question of 'lag' to compensate for, that being the distance between the line of flight of the aircraft at the time of release and the actual place the bomb would have hit the ground or sea level. This 'lag' varied with conditions prevailing at the time of release and the ballistics of the bomb itself. With 'no-wind' conditions the actual path of the bomb could be plotted, providing the bomb was assumed to fall away from the direction of flight at the moment of release at a gravity acceleration measured vertically of 30 ft per second. To allow for this the aircraft had to be pulled out through an angle, called the 'bombing' angle, before the bomb was released and this was estimated to be less than the angle between the flight path of the aircraft and a line from the pilot's eye to the top of the engine cowling. However any method of allowing for the 'lag' by 'aiming-off' over the target only introduced further problems, as it involved aiming at an imaginary spot in the sea, and in anything other than a steep dive the target would not be visible at the moment of release, thus making the estimation of the imaginary spot almost impossible.

All these factors could only be overcome by constant practice allied to a natural skill or flair for dive-bombing. According to Richard Partridge: 'The Fleet Air Arm paid a lot of attention to attaining and maintaining efficiency in dive-bombing, in spite of the fact that naval dive-bombing aircraft could not carry a useful bomb-load pre-war. All pilots were trained to use these aircraft as normal fighters and also as dive-bombers. Using them in the latter role, an experienced and skilled pilot could get reasonably accurate results, but the bomb-load carrier was inadequate for attacking enemy warships. The Skua, however, was a very good dive-bomber. It had very large, strong, flaps; and when these were down it could be put into a beautifully controlled 65–70-degree dive and a well-trained pilot could bomb with great accuracy.'

On outbreak of war Partridge found himself at Eastleigh still flying the old Hawker Osprey but, towards the end of October 1939, the first deliveries of the Skua began and the pilots were soon enthusiastically familiarising themselves with it. As well as being a monoplane, it had numerous other revolutionary features that endeared itself to the young Royal Marines airman and his contemporaries after years of flying obsolete machines. It had four Vickers machine-guns in the wings as well as one rearward-firing Browning on a swivel mount for the air-gunner-cum-navigator. Flotation bags in the fuselage and wings could keep it on the surface of the water if it were forced to ditch, and it had an endurance of four and a half hours. The cockpit was all-enclosed, an unheard-of luxury then, and was well equipped by the standards of the day. It was not very fast compared to other fighters but it could carry its payload of one 500-lb bomb and eight 20-lb bombs to the target at a speed of 220 knots. With so many 'new' features to memorise it was almost like learning to fly all over again in many respects. Partridge recalled, for example, how the essential drill for landing and take-off had to be mnemonically learnt as this was the first time he had flown an aircraft with a variable-pitch airscrew or retractable undercarriage. Thus PUF and REPUF helped avoid what could have been a premature end to his flying career. P meant ditch, U stood for undercarriage, F for flaps, R for rudder trim and E for elevator trim.

At the end of October 'Birdy' Partridge received orders to re-join No 803 Squadron. This unit was already equipped with the Skua and, in lieu of sufficient RAF fighters, was being utilised as an interceptor squadron to protect convoys in Scottish waters from the Luftwaffe. Quite how the Skua with a top speed of 220 mph was supposed to catch a Junkers Ju 88 capable of at least 50 mph more was never spelt out by the authorities who ordered such a move.

After a sad farewell to his girlfriend Fay (the outbreak of war had already indefinitely postponed their plans to marry) and a long and tiring train journey from one end of the country to the other, Richard joined his unit early in November 1939. The standing fighter patrols over northern waters were uneventful ones in the main and no sign was ever seen of the enemy while they were protecting either convoys or the Home Fleet. Partridge found himself one of three Royal Marines Skua pilots in this squadron, all three in Red Section which, considering there were less than twenty active Royal Marines pilots in the whole Navy, was unique. They were duly dubbed 'The Thin Red Line' by their companions.

At the end of the month a new FAA squadron was formed and Partridge was appointed its second-in-command. This was No 804 Squadron, which had orders to proceed still further north, to the Royal Naval Air Station, Hatston, in the Orkney Islands. In fact, as the designated CO had not yet arrived, Partridge became acting commander initially of the new unit, their main duties at this stage of the war being still to protect the fleet and the main naval base at Scapa Flow. Earlier in the war Junkers Ju 88s had dive-bombed this anchorage and it was to prevent any repetition of this that No 804 Squadron was kept on hand. The airfield, HMS *Sparrowhawk*, was situated not far from Kirkwall and Partridge's command was at first equipped with six navalised Gloster Gladiator biplane fighters, something of a regression after his new monoplanes but one to which he resigned himself and re-adapted. As before, sight of the

Luftwaffe was minimal, the very rare appearance of a high-flying Heinkel He 111 resulting in a 'no-hope' scramble to chase it away. Tonsilitis caused him to take a short period of leave in December, but for the first three months of 1940 this uneventful routine continued as the last days of the so-called 'phoney war' ticked away.

On 1 April 1940 the prelude to more momentous events was heralded by the arrival of a signal for Captain Partridge to join yet another squadron, this time as its Commanding Officer. This unit was No 800 Squadron which, along with No 803 Squadron commanded by Lieutenant William Lucy RN, had been disembarked from the aircraft-carrier *Ark Royal* at Hatston. They were still there, shore-based, flying routine patrols, when Hitler attacked neutral Denmark and Norway, as a prelude to his major spring offensive against the complaisant Alliance.

One of the German invasion fleets had attacked Bergen harbour on 8 April and succeeded in penetrating its defences easily. However, one of the light cruisers which formed part of the fleet, *Königsberg*, had been slightly damaged by shells from a Norwegian shore battery and, when the rest of her force returned home, she had to be left behind to patch up the holes. In the interim a Coastal Command aircraft had made a brief sortie over Bergen. Among its crew as an Observer on loan (because RAF Observers had great difficulty in differentiating between friendly and enemy warships) was Lieutenant-Commander Geoffrey Hare RN. He identified the Köln class cruiser correctly and, on arrival back at Lossiemouth, quickly hitched passage in a plane to Hatston to report this to *Sparrowhawk*'s CO, Commander C.L. Howe RN. He discussed the matter with Bill Lucy who, in turn, consulted Richard Partridge. Although the hazards involved in such a mission were enormous the two men finally agreed that it was practicable and detailed planning began while clearance was obtained.

There had been little time during the previous six months for the two Skua squadrons to partake of any dive-bombing practice. Mostly their duties concentrated on the fighter aspect of their job, but they were determined to make the most of this opportunity. The distance to the target was the vital factor. As Richard Partridge was later to recall with refreshing honesty, he initially expressed grave doubts about the feasibility of the sortie: 'I pointed out to Bill that Bergen was about two hours' flying each way in still air for Skuas and that our official endurance was only four hours twenty minutes; to which he replied that we both knew that we could stretch this a bit and that if we didn't hang around over the target too long we should be able to make it.'

The fact that the Germans had strong fighter forces based close by at Stavanger was also discounted by Bill Lucy, providing surprise could be achieved. How this was to be done when the target lay some 30–40 miles inland from the enemy-held coast received the answer that they should take off at a time to allow their arrival over the target at dawn. There remained nothing else for it but to prepare themselves and their units accordingly. As navigation was crucial to this operation the most experienced Observer available was embarked by Partridge for this mission, and that proved to be the man who had just come back from the target, Hare himself. 'Birdy' Partridge recorded: 'He was senior to me and vastly experienced and I cannot speak too highly of the support he gave me or of the excellence of his navigation that brought me over the target at exactly the planned time.'

Similar tributes were paid to the other senior Observer, Lieutenant Michael Hanson RN, and to the work of the Air Staff Officer, Lieutenant-Commander Aubrey St John Edwards RN. As it was to be a straightforward 'in-bash-out' operation, with no time for frills, the bomb-load had to be picked with care. *Königsberg* was a light cruiser of some 6600 tons, armed with three triple turrets each of which mounted three 5.9-in. guns and had a total of 14 light AA-weapons. She had no armour to speak of and this was important, her deck protection being almost non-existent, a mere ¾ in. thickness. In short, she was an ideal dive-bomber target, large enough to hit, and vulnerable enough for SAP bombs to stand a chance of doing her serious damage, and with even her sinking a possibility.

The Royal Air Force thought so too, and dispatched a powerful force of their usual Hampden and Wellington heavy bombers which, true to form, failed to score a hit or even a near-miss. This left the Skuas a clear run to show what dive-bombing could achieve. Some 16 Skuas were operationally fit for this mission, 11 of 803 Squadron and five of 800 Squadron, and they operated in two groups under Partridge and Lucy respectively. Final briefing was timed at 04.15 and take-off fixed for half an hour later, but, in the event, this was postponed to 05.10 due to the weather conditions at Hatston. The course taken in and out was the shortest possible route. They were then to climb and at 12,000 ft to cross the Norwegian coast at latitude 60.09 degrees North. Both groups were supposed to remain in visual contact with each other. In the event this did not happen at the end of the operation, but it did not affect the result. Strict radio silence was to be maintained and IFF signals were suppressed. Everything else fell out exactly as planned and all the 16 aircraft crossed the Norwegian coast undetected by the enemy, although one aircraft became detached and carried out a lone attack undaunted. *Königsberg* was spotted alongside the Skoltegrund Mole in the fresh sunlit dawn of 10 April. Attacks began at 07.20, the dive-bombers descending through a thin cloud layer at 8000 ft and into excellent visibility, in single line ahead precisely according to the book. The final aiming dives were begun at 6500 ft but bomb-release varied widely between 3500 ft down to 1500 ft. Likewise the angle of dive varied from 50 degrees to 70 degrees. All the aircraft attacked the target on a run which took them up the target from bows to stern and the hit and near-miss rate was superb in its accuracy, with a mean error average of only 50 yds.

Richard Partridge made a classic attack, leading his unit in a long sweep over the town to the mountains to attack from out of the sun. He concentrated hard on finding the 'X point' to make the work 'easy' for the rest of his formation. Having established this he turned sharply to port, almost at a right-angle so tight did he pull round, and eased the stick back gently, lowering the big, effective dive flaps on the wings to bring his speed down quickly. A further pull back on the joystick, then a half-turn to starboard took him into his final attack dive precisely on target. He found he was following in behind the last aircraft of 803 Squadron in a perfectly co-ordinated strike. No flak came up to meet him save for one semi-automatic weapon which the Germans had manned, so he could concentrate on his work

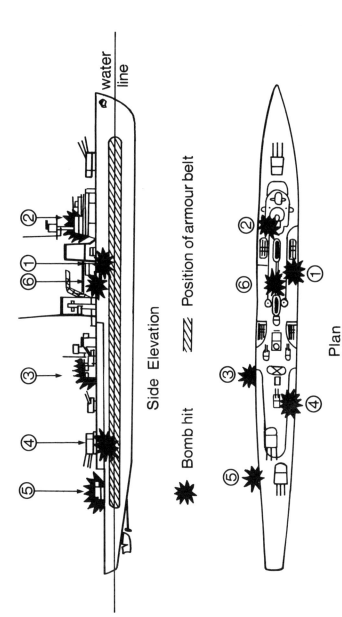

Side Elevation

water line

☒ Position of armour belt

✳ Bomb hit

Plan

Fig 4 From the report of Captain Ruhfus. Hits received by *Königsberg* from British dive-bombers on 10 April 1940

relatively undisturbed, holding the long and slender hull of his target firmly in his ring-and-ball sight. He kept his Skua steady down to 1800 ft, with *Königsberg* now looming enormous before him. He could clearly see the Swastika painted on her fo'c'sle, her bridge and twin funnels and the three big gun-turrets, one forward, two aft. Then he pushed firmly on his bomb-release switch, felt the 500-lb bomb on its cradle swing out and away towards the target, before making a violent turn-away to starboard as he followed the other Skuas weaving their way out of the harbour almost at sea-level. Gazing astern Hare had time to consider the result, a close miss right alongside the ship's starboard bow. *Königsberg* had already been severely hit and near-missed and each Skua was adding its own contribution to her destruction in explosion after explosion.

The official German report is candid and frank on this attack, the cruiser's commanding officer, Captain Ruhfus, admitting that surprise had been achieved by the attackers. Being a professional himself Captain Ruhfus had no reservations on commenting on the methods used to sink his ship and from his report it is clear that he was much impressed. The British reports were, naturally, less well informed, and assessed the result as two hits amidships and one hit on the fo'c'sle, in addition to at least one near-miss. Five more bombs hit the Mole close alongside the ship, of which four went very close indeed. One direct hit was seen to have burst internally, throwing up debris and smoke, while that which struck the forepart of the ship was said to have made a large hole from which belched white smoke and flame. The hit, which the British thought was the fatal blow, was delivered by Captain E.D. McIver and was believed to have struck the target between her funnels.

The German report, however, places a different emphasis on which bombs caused the most damage. In their estimation it was the one, or perhaps two, very near-misses to port which ripped out a large section of the ship's bottom that caused the terminal damage. The amidships hit by McIver, although spectacular, exploded in the ship's torpedo flat and did not directly contribute to her loss. However the cumulative effect of this and other hits was to destroy the ship's capacity both to tackle the many resulting fires and, more critically, to prevent the pumping out of the flooding compartments. The bombs which exploded on the quay itself also contributed in that they destroyed the water mains, similarly cutting off supply and thus effectively hampering efforts to save her. One of the two or three shells from the Norwegian coastal battery which had hit the ship on 9 April had detonated on the waterline abreast of her after-funnel on her starboard side. The two near-misses by Skua bombs were on the same side. One was in line with the after-deckhouse near the sternmost twin 3.5-in. gun mounting, but the other was midway between the funnels, just forward of the patched-up shell damage, and as a result severe flooding soon became uncontrollable. *Königsberg* went down by the bows and within 50 minutes had rolled over and capsized. She was the first major warship to be sunk by bombing alone and showed what could be achieved by using aircraft manned by well-trained crews in the correct manner. This was achieved with the loss of only a single aircraft. All the Skuas had made the rendezvous, but on the way back down towards the sea the aircraft of Red Leader, Lieutenant B.J. Smeeton, suddenly dived into the sea at full speed. It was never established what caused this tragic loss, but he and his Observer, Petty Officer B.M. Seymour, were the only British casualties in this brilliant attack.

Because it had been proven that the Skua was just capable of reaching Bergen with a full bomb-load and returning again under very carefully planned conditions, and at great risk, the Admiralty now assumed it could be done regularly. There has been much comment about how out of touch with reality Whitehall was at this period, with regards to war operations in general and air/sea in particular, and this criticism applies equally to politicians and to senior naval officers. The decision to mount patrols over Bergen as regular offensive reconnaissance runs by single Skuas was just one manifestation of this ignorance and/or complacency. Partridge recalls how he felt at the time that his own CO had been pressured into it from above and, although the advice of the squadron commanders was asked for, and was firmly against these 'posthumous VC' patrols, they were nonetheless initiated. One senses the 'offensive at any cost regardless of reality' touch of the then First Lord of the Admiralty behind this, although there is no direct proof, and it certainly ties in with Churchill's other actions of this period regarding the Fleet and Norway. Partridge himself carried out four of these lonely missions, two of them on 12 and 14 April respectively. Only 15 minutes was left to carry out a survey of Bergen harbour for suitable targets before turning back homeward after dumping the bombs. These all-round four-and-a-half hour trips were abortive. No clear instructions were ever received on whether oil storage tanks ashore, or merchant shipping in the harbour, were to be considered legitimate targets and, as a result, they were left alone.

On the third such mission, which took place on 17 April, the same non-result followed but the next time strong headwinds almost caused 'Birdy's' death. Struggling back towards Orkney from the Norwegian coast used up vital fuel, so Partridge made for the emergency diversion airfield of Sumburgh on Shetland but he was warned off on his approach as it was unserviceable. By now he had been airborne for 4 hours 35 minutes and had no option but to ditch as best he could. The Skua was a write-off but both Partridge and his Observer survived. They were picked up by a Swordfish and ferried back to Hatston where he made a vigorous protest. But the patrols were continued unrelentingly.

Richard Partridge was back over Norway again for the fifth time on 20 April in a brand new Skua. Far from learning from his almost fatal mishap the Admiralty orders for this mission were to attack enemy shipping targets at Larvik, to the southwest of Oslo. Not only did this add a further 80 miles to the journey but they had to pass directly over the main German fighter base near Stavanger to get there. The coastline was crossed at 12,000 ft and a slight detour avoided stirring up any hornet's nest over Stavanger but, on arrival over Larvik, and quite contrary to Admiralty forecasts, no shipping, hostile or otherwise, was to be seen.

In Partridge's own words his decision was 'Let's get the hell out of here while we have the chance.' Their diversion on the homeward leg took them over Skienfjord where a German E-boat was attacked in lieu of a more worthwhile target, but without effect as the bomb missed this small, fast and wildly zigzagging target by 100 yds. It was not the first time Partridge had dive-bombed high-speed power-boat targets. As he told

1 Captain Takashige Egusa (Imperial Japanese Navy) as a young pilot in China, 1939

2 The last photo of Egusa before he left Japan for Guam in 1944

3 Two Aichi D3A 'Vals' being made ready for a sortie. Note bold colour markings

4 Death-throes of the British heavy-
   cruiser *Dorsetshire*, sunk by
   Egusa's dive-bombers in the
   Indian Ocean, April 1942

5 A rare photo of a Yokosuka P1Y
   ('Milky Way') bomber in flight

6 Seen from the deck of the
   American carrier *San Jacinto*, flak
   from the battleship *North Carolina*
   and the carrier *Lexington (II)* hoses
   into the night sky – and Egusa's
   aircraft and those of his squadron
   are destroyed

7 Captain Gerald Mesny (French Navy) in the cockpit of the first Vought V-156F at Bridgeport, Connecticut

8 Mesny at Bridgeport, May 1939

9 Reassembled Voughts lined up at their French base just prior to the Blitzkrieg in 1940

10 Mesny set up, trained and then led AB-1 Squadron of the French Navy's air arm into battle

11 After the bitter fighting of May/June 1940 only three Voughts survived, along with Mesny (*centre*) and a few air and ground crew

12 Major Giuseppe Cenni (Royal Italian Air Force; *foreground, second from right*) and his élite team

13 The gunboat *Cricket* under attack by the 'Cenni Method' off Tobruk

14 Cenni at the wheel of a towing tractor at a Sicilian base

15 A Junkers Ju 87R-2 of 101 Gruppo over Greece in 1941. Note long-range fuel-tanks

16 The normally cheerful Cenni in pensive mood by his Stuka. Note the diving duck emblem on wheel spat

17 Fleet Air Arm Skuas of 800 Squadron at Hatston, Orkney Islands, shortly before taking off to attack *Königsberg*

18 Major Richard Partridge in Royal Marines uniform; only a select few Marines flew with the Fleet Air Arm during the Second World War

19 Skua dive-bombers on the deck of the carrier *Ark Royal* shortly before
their attack on *Scharnhorst* in June 1940

20 The battle-cruiser *Scharnhorst* (*centre*) at anchor in a Norwegian fjord
seen from the attacking Skuas.

21 Major Elmer Glidden (United States Marine Corps) at the controls of his famous 'Slow But Deadly', the Douglas SBD Dauntless

22 Glidden in 1944, nicknamed 'Iron Man' after his surviving more than 100 combat dive-bomber missions

23 Guadalcanal: Henderson Field airstrip and the Glidden-led Dauntless dive-bombers operating from it were the focal-point of the Pacific War in the autumn of 1942

24 Flight briefing in the Marshall Islands: Glidden and his aircrew prepare for another sortie against Japanese bases

25 Glidden (*left*) and his navigator/gunner, Sgt James Boyle, the only man in Glidden's crack squadron to clock up more missions than Glidden himself

26 More bombs for the Japanese: 500-lb bombs on their trolleys ready for loading on the distant SBDs in the Marshall Islands, 1944

27 Wing Commander Walter Enneccerus (German Air Force) being strapped into the cockpit of his Stuka for a mission early in the war

28 The British carrier *Illustrious* under attack by Enneccerus and his Stukas in the Mediterranean, January 1941

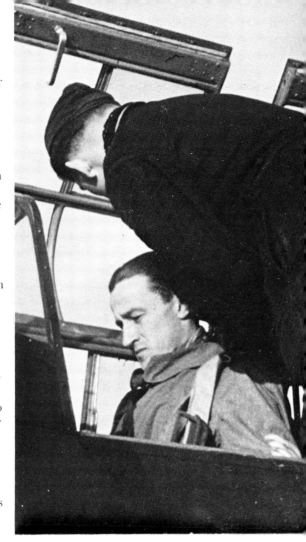

29 Another mass Stuka attack heads towards Tobruk. Enneccerus's squadron was used to spearhead the assaults which led to the fall of the fortress in 1942

30 Enneccerus and his squadron in North Africa during 1942, supporting Rommel's desert offensives

31 Stukas being bombed-up for a Russian Front mission, 1943

32 Major-General Ivan Polbin (Soviet Air Force) in 1944. The poor quality of this photo is matched by its rarity – shortly afterwards Polbin was killed leading his dive-bombers over Germany in 1945

33 Polbin's early war experience was learnt flying the SB-2 bomber against the Japanese in Manchuria and China during 1938–40

34 Aircrew of one of Polbin's Pe-2 dive-bombers in winter garb. Note
paint scheme of the dive-bomber

35 Primitive but effective bomb transportation on the Eastern Front. This photo shows the pilot's hatch underneath the nose of the Pe-2

36 Pe-2s set off from a snowbound forward airstrip on another mission against German troops

me, 'I can remember pre-war bombing targets towed by armoured motor-boats off Singapore for simulated dive-bombing, with similar results.'

Unfortunately, soon after wasting his main bomb-load Partridge came across a really worthwhile target in the shape of a surfaced U-boat making her way up the fjords to Bergen. She at first mistook the Skua for a friendly aircraft and Partridge was able to make a good attacking run at her as she crash-dived. Unfortunately all the ammunition he had to fire at her tough hull were machine-gun bullets from his forward guns, which was like peppering a rhinoceros with an airgun. All the same he gave her a nasty fright.

This was the final such run in which Captain Partridge participated, for by now *Ark Royal* was back from the Mediterranean ready and eager to embark her dive-bombers to work at sea with the fleet. Orders were received for both Hatston-based squadrons to join her at sea. Hasty trials were conducted for many of the Skua pilots who had never yet deck-landed. Nor, for that matter, had their commander . . .

'I kept that fact to myself as I thought it might be bad for morale,' Richard was to write. 'Actually I was not very worried about it because of certain characteristics of the Skua.'

His confidence was not misplaced and all aircraft of both units alighted aboard *Ark Royal* quite safely. At this time the carrier had six full squadrons embarked and could mount quite a punch. As well as 800 and 803 Squadrons, each with a dozen Skuas, she had aboard 801 Squadron with six more Skuas; six Rocs, weird fighter adaptations with a ball-mounted turret like the ill-fated Defiants; and two dozen Fairey Swordfish torpedo-bombers from 10 and 820 Squadrons, plank-winged biplanes from another era. *Ark Royal* operated with the carrier *Glorious*, which had six Skuas, 18 Sea Gladiators and 12 Swordfish of her own. These carriers were protected by the modernised battle-ship *Valiant*, the heavy cruiser *Berwick* and 10 destroyers. This group was, in fact, the very first 'Carrier Task Force' used in combat. Very successful it was too, operating 100 miles offshore and providing air protection (of a kind) for the main fleet, and support for the troops ashore at Andalsnes and Namsos. They also attacked targets ashore and afloat at Trondheim and Vaernes. It was a total mis-use of these valuable ships, in one way, forced on the Royal Navy by the lack of RAF aircraft. Their bombers were totally inefficient and the few Gladiator fighters ashore were vastly outnumbered so that the Royal Navy had to hazard two of its most valuable ships as substitutes. As fighters, the Skuas were totally misapplied and wasted. They were completely outclassed by the single-engined Bf 109s and even the twin-engined Bf 110s; while they were hard put to it to catch, let alone harm, the Heinkel 111s and Junkers Ju 88 bombers that continually bombed their carriers and any other shipping in the area as well as blitzing the Allied troops from the ruins of one small town to the next. However there were some successes and, having made his mark in no uncertain manner as a dive-bomber pilot, Richard Partridge was to take the opportunity of registering his hand as a fighter ace also. This took place on 26 April. Partridge was leading a flight of three Skuas which had taken off from *Ark Royal* at 12.35 and were patrolling in open formation at 11,000 ft over Molde. As they crossed the coast Richard saw flak bursts in the sky ahead and steered towards them. He found that these originated from the sloop *Flamingo* which was resisting a bombing attack by a Heinkel off Andalsnes. Although the Heinkel, having dropped his bombs, had a lead of two miles and a height advantage of 1000 ft, Partridge was determined to attack:

'I guess our speed advantage over the German bomber was only 10 to 15 knots. After ten minutes with throttles jammed wide open I was at the same height as my quarry and gaining slowly but surely on him. Six hundred yards astern of him now and his rear gunner started firing at me, though I was hardly within his range for accurate shooting, but the thought did cross my mind that he might have a lucky shot.'

His wing men were also striving to keep up with him, but Partridge kept going and, after 25 miles, had closed to within 400 yds before firing a long burst with no apparent effect. Another 100 yds was painfully gained, and then Partridge emptied all 600 rounds from each of his machine-guns into the target which left the Heinkel with smoke belching from its starboard wing and under attack from the other Skuas. The enemy was obviously doomed, so Partridge recalled his unit and began to head back to the coast when his engine, obviously hit by return fire, went dead. There was nothing for it but to attempt a crash-landing on one of the frozen Norwegian lakes and, by gliding at 90 knots, he effected such a landing on Lake Breidal. Both Richard Partridge and his Observer, Lieutenant Robin Bostock, walked away from this while their two companions, having followed them down, headed back to *Ark Royal*. After destroying as much of the Skua as they could, the two Britons found refuge in a small hut only to be disturbed a little later by the crew of the Heinkel they had shot down, asking if they could join them in that sanctuary. The Germans had one pistol, the British had nothing but Richard proved a good diplomat and persuaded the three Germans that they were his prisoners. Later they were found by a Norwegian patrol and finally returned to *Ark Royal* after many adventures and hitching a lift aboard the cruiser *Manchester*.

There were two sequels to this extraordinary adventure. Many, many years later, the remains of the Skua were discovered post-war at the bottom of the lake and eventually salvaged to become the only surviving Skua, which is now housed at the Fleet Air Arm Museum at Yeovilton. The other involved one of the German aircrew, Horst Schopis, who read about the salvage, finally contacted Richard Partridge and met him in 1975. They have since become good friends.

Having reported back on board *Ark Royal* at Scapa Flow, Partridge was sent off on some well-earned leave, with orders on his return to collect a new Skua from RNAS Donibristle. By the time they flew back aboard the carrier via Hatston on 25 May much had changed. Norway was no longer the headline news. The steady retreat on all fronts had been overshadowed by the complete defeat and rout of the Dutch, Belgian and French armies and the retreat of the BEF to Dunkirk. It was clear, with such enormous disasters further south, that Norway could not be held and evacuations were in progress from the last Allied bastion in the north, Narvik. To cover this final withdrawal the two aircraft-carriers were once more sent to patrol offshore and provide air protection. On 4 June the Fleet arrived in its operational area off Hinnoy and four days of intensive fighter patrolling followed.

At these latitudes there was little or no darkness at all in the summer, so patrolling was non-stop around the clock. Defensive flights of three Skuas had to be maintained throughout the whole 24-hour period. Once the troops were safely embarked and the convoys started for home, the carriers headed south once more, under intermittent attack by Heinkel bombers, several of which were destroyed. Among these evacuated was a squadron of RAF Hurricanes whose pilots managed somehow to land aboard the carrier *Glorious*. Unfortunately she was detached to return to Scapa Flow independently with only two destroyers as escorts. As is well-known she fell in with the German battle-cruisers *Gneisenau* and *Scharnhorst* and was destroyed by long-range gunfire without launching a counter strike of torpedo-bombers. Her two escorts shared her fate but one of them scored a torpedo hit on the *Scharnhorst* which meant she had to head to the nearest harbour, Trondheim, for repairs before returning to Germany. With grim and bitter thoughts in their hearts for their 'chummy ship' and the hundreds of her crew and aircrew who had been personal friends and who had all been lost with her, it was perhaps natural for *Ark Royal* to make some sort of vengeance strike. And thus it turned out.

The presence at Trondheim of *Scharnhorst*, along with the heavy cruiser *Admiral Hipper* and four destroyers, was confirmed by aerial reconnaissance on 12 June, although she had lain alongside the repair ship *Huaskaran* for six days prior to that. Vice-Admiral L.V. Wells was flying his flag aboard *Ark Royal* when she sailed from Scapa Flow with the battleship *Rodney*, the battle-cruiser *Renown* and destroyers, to attack the German battle-cruiser. Richard Partridge was called into his cabin and told that the plan was to attack the German ships with both Skua squadrons. As at Hatston he was asked his opinion. As before 'Birdy' gave his honest opinion: that *Scharnhorst* with her 4½-in. thick deck armour was no *Königsberg* and that 500-lb bombs would hardly dent her; that there was no question of surprise as there were now 24 hours of daylight; that the target lay 80 miles from German-occupied islands off the coast; that there were ample German fighters on hand at nearby Vaernes airfield. It transpired that the commanding officer of 803 Squadron, Lieutenant-Commander John Casson, who was to lead this attack, had also been interviewed and gave much the same advice, adding that 50 per cent casualties should be expected from such a mission, with only the chance of one hit and one near-miss resulting.

As before, the advice was in vain, and the mission went ahead. There were elaborate paper plans for the RAF to lay on a pre-emptive strike to subdue the Luftwaffe and for long-range fighter escorts to rendezvous before the attack. Co-ordinating such complex movements at such a distance did not seem likely to work at all, given the RAF's record to date, and thus it turned out. The bombing attack was delivered too soon and, instead of grounding the German fighters, it brought them up into the sky in perfect time to intercept the Skuas. The fighter cover failed to put in an appearance until it was all over anyway.

Afterwards, back at Admiralty, the Director of the Naval Air Division was to make a sober assessment of the Skuas' chances which, if anything, read more gloomily than either Partridge's, or Casson's viewpoints. He estimated that, given the circumstances, the most which could be hoped for was one hit, with a 25 per cent chance of a second, with expected losses of 30 per cent from flak and another 30 per cent from fighters. Both estimates proved only too accurate. The two COs and their Observers went ahead with the planning. It was decided that, as no concealment was possible, a straightforward approach at 12,000 ft would be made, the dive-bombers descending to 8000 ft over Trondheim itself and that from there on in the survivors – should there be any – would make individual attacks as best they could and then try to make it back to *Ark Royal*. Several considerations decided on the number of aircraft to be used. First, only 15 of the available aircrew had done dive-bombing in the Skua. This ruled out the remainder. A standing fighter patrol had to be maintained over the fleet in their absence, therefore machines had to be left behind for this. Only light winds were blowing and 15 was the maximum number of heavily laden Skuas that could be ranged on deck at one time. Thus it was decided to use nine aircraft of 803 Squadron and six of 800 Squadron. The aircrew were duly notified in a preliminary briefing at 16.30 that afternoon. It was a long and wearisome wait during the interim before the final briefing at 23.00. None of the chosen had any illusions about their probable fate on this mission. Partridge later admitted that he was apprehensive like the others, but most tried to conceal it. He confessed he considered writing a farewell letter to Fay but then changed his mind as, '. . . this was a bit melodramatic and perhaps even courting disaster by anticipation'. Others had similar forebodings. Lieutenant G.E.D. 'Ned' Finch-Noyes, one of the driving forces behind the ship's concert parties and usually irrepressible, entered the cabin of his close friend Lieutenant Bob Everett and said to him: 'I don't know if I'm going to come back from this one, Bob. I want you to give these personal things to my wife.'

Flying-off was completed by 00.02 on 13 June, each Skua as usual being armed with a single 500-lb SAP bomb. By 01.23 they had crossed the outlying coastal islands heading towards their target under a brilliantly clear sky. At 140 knots in two loose groups they headed on towards the awaiting flak gunners and fighters, Casson timing their arrival over the target for 02.00. Some 25 miles down-fjord from Trondheim the leading Skua began to drop down into the preliminary dive and speed began to increase to 200 knots, then to 240 knots. Their height had come down to 9000 ft and the sky ahead and the fjord below remained crystal-clear, and empty of any sign of opposition. At 01.57 Partridge could make out the distinct shapes of several warships anchored in Strindfjord but there were no signs of the promised British fighters. Immediately the German flak, both ashore and from the host of ships, started firing and at once the empty sky became an angry pockmarked hornets'-nest of shell-bursts. As Casson swung his unit to port Partridge broke to starboard to confuse the gunners.

Even as they did so the first Bf 110 flashed by them intent on the other squadron and within seconds Partridge saw the first Skua falling from the sky in flames. There was still some way to go before they could even begin their attack dive and suddenly his Observer reported a Bf 109 off their port quarter homing in for the kill. Partridge pulled round in the tightest turn possible and the fighter overshot him, but others were lining up awaiting their turn. Another brief cameo he observed was of another Skua making a textbook controlled dive-bombing attack at one of the bigger warships from which the aircraft failed to pull out, smashing into the fjord at full power. For a brief instant no fighter was behind them. It was now or never. Picking the closest battle-cruiser Partridge shoved the nose of his Skua hard down and, as the speed built up to 260 knots, went into his attack dive.

Just below 6000 ft he pulled up to lose speed and then came hard out of a stall turn with his flaps down, going straight into the dive. This attack was started lower than the recommended height but that was unavoidable, since *Scharnhorst* alone mounted some 46 anti-aircraft guns of various calibres and the flak rising to meet Partridge at this point was intense. At 1700 ft he released his bomb, immediately turning hard to port and raising his flaps. Thus he dropped as fast as possible down to sea level and weaved away across the fjord. His Observer, Robin, was able to report that they had achieved a near-miss off the battle-cruiser's bow. He also added the grim news that he had witnessed at least two more Skuas crash into the water.

All-in-all 800 Squadron made shallow attacks in line astern from the north while 803 went in from bows-to-stern in the opposite direction. At the end of the runs most pilots tried to escape from the ambush by the same deck-scraping tactics as Partridge. The bulk of the survivors were in this group. Others pulled back and attempted to fight their way back. Few, if any, of this group made it. They reported, in good faith, and under impossible conditions, that they had scored two direct hits on *Scharnhorst*, two vivid red flashes being observed abaft her funnel, and several close misses. Tragically, German records revealed that only one bomb had in fact hit the giant vessel on her upper deck and this had failed to detonate. It is not certain whether this was because it was a 'dud' bomb or because it had been released from too low a height to be effective. It was a terrible disappointment after the gallantry and the self-sacrifice.

Between the swarming fighters and the flak no less than eight of the 15 Skuas failed to make it back to *Ark Royal*, among them Casson, Finch-Noyes and 'Birdy'. The survivors reported that Partridge's aircraft had last been seen to 'continue his dive and not observed to pull out'. Happily this was not the case. For a brief period Richard Partridge bore a charmed life, evading both flak and fighters by hugging the plate-grey sea, the Skua's own dark grey-green dazzle paint blending well. For a time he thought he was going to make it. Unfortunately he proved over-confident, almost colliding with a German seaplane, on which he opened fire. The German fired a Verey cartridge which brought two Bf 109s hastening to the scene and 'Birdy' and Robin knew they were doomed. They might shake off a single fighter, even though it had at least 80 knots excess speed over the Skua. Indeed, by a series of clever turns and violent use of the versatile dive flaps Partridge managed to out-manoeuvre the enemy for several minutes, but the end was inevitable. Changing their tactics the two German fighters came in from different directions. By avoiding one attacker Partridge must expose his aircraft to the other. There was a last warning from Robin then a heavy bump and a huge chunk of wing came away as a cannon shell ploughed into it. The petrol tank immediately adjacent to Partridge ignited and he was left with no alternative but to bale out. Sadly Robin failed to follow him and the Skua crashed into the sea at the head of Stjornfjord, just south of the coastal village of Stallvik.

Partridge survived but was badly burned about the face. Fishermen from a farm near the little port of Stallvik rescued him after twenty minutes in the water. They cared for him and a Norwegian doctor dressed his wounds, but decided he must have proper treatment. Accordingly the German army was notified and 'Birdy' was handed over to them to start five years as a prisoner-of-war.

This long and dreary period included one successful escape by Partridge tunnelling out of a Dulag Luft near Frankfurt, only to be re-captured after three days on the loose. Further imprisonment included terms at Stalag Luft 1, the infamous Stalag Luft III and Oflag XXIb until his liberation in May 1945 and return to England.

A three-month period of leave followed but, at the end of that, Partridge resumed flying duties again with a refresher course at Lee-on-Solent, learning how to handle modern aircraft such as Fireflies, Seafires and Avengers after which there followed an unhappy period as Commander (Flying) and OIC at the same airfield. On escaping from this Richard Partridge, now a newly promoted Major of the Royal Marines, was sent to RAF Hullavington for an advanced flying course on such diverse aircraft as Lancaster bombers, Hotspur glider and Meteor jet fighters, from which he graduated on 9 November 1946 with a Distinguished Pass. He may have had an incentive, of course. While at Hullavington he managed to obtain a weekend pass and he and Fay were married on the Saturday morning, honeymooned on the Sunday and Monday and then he flew his first jet fighter on the Tuesday. A good start to anybody's week.

Graduation from Hullavington was followed by a three-year stint at Admiralty with the Directorate of Air Organisation and Training. Partridge was responsible for flying training in the Fleet and found it a satisfactory and worthwhile job. Apart from his Royal Marines uniform he was like any other commuter catching the train up to Town from Arundel Station as he had set up home with Fay at the village of Angmering in West Sussex. During this time his two children, a son and a daughter were born, in 1947 and 1948 respectively.

At the end of this idyllic period he was given the option of switching over to the Royal Navy as a Commander (Air) but, after discussion with Fay, Partridge decided to take retirement and left the Service at the age of forty in 1950. They bought a 100-acre dairy farm in East Sussex and he settled down to learn a new trade. Instead of a roaring dive-bomber to control, 'Birdy' now had to contend with the more prosaic problems of 100 Jersey cows and 2000 chickens but he managed to do so with great success for the next eleven years. With his children grown up he finally decided in 1961 to sell up and settle for the less strenuous life of a smallholder at Piltdown, near Uckfield, and there he lives still with his wife in peace and contentment.

Only once was this tranquillity disturbed, and that was when his old Skua was located at the bottom of the Norwegian lake and, amid much publicity, raised, brought back to England and restored. At the Fleet Air Arm Museum at Yeovilton, it is a fitting monument not only to the Fleet Air Arm's only successful dive-bomber, but to the memory of the gallant men, the 'reluctant' (as Partridge insists) heroes of the dive-bomber arm, who flew them with such panache and bravery in those desperate, now almost forgotten, days in the spring of 1940.

5 Colonel Elmer Glidden

United States Marine Corps   1915–

In the history of dive-bombers and dive-bombing the United States Marines has a long and honourable tradition. It was their flyers who were mainly instrumental in rescuing dive-bombing from the post-Great War doldrums into which it had sunk almost without trace, and breathed into it a vital spark which quickly spread across the world. In the 1920s Marine flyers in Haiti and Nicaragua utilised the diving form of attack when aiding hard-pressed Marines isolated by guerrilla forces and, so successful was this tactic, that they embraced it further on return to the States. The American navy picked up the threads and the famous 'Helldiver' units were born. Their accuracy was legendary and had world-wide effects. Not only did they show that carrier aircraft could pack a worthwhile punch, but, by showing that precision attacks on warships were viable, helped to influence flyers in Japan, Germany and Great Britain that dive-bombing was what might in today's world be termed 'cost-effective' in terms of men, machines and economic hit-return against bomb-outlay. If the 'Flying Leathernecks' caught the headlines and stirred Hollywood's passions via the epic films of Errol Flynn and John Wayne, then behind the razzmatazz there was much to recommend it. Marine Corps flyers continued to bring a special expertise to dive-bombing and, on the outbreak of the Pacific War, which was largely decided by the correct use of the dive-bomber on both sides, the Marine Corps produced its own band of heroes and new legends.

It was in line and in keeping with this proud record of innovation and achievement that Colonel Elmer George Glidden jr's combat record emerged as second-to-none in the United States military during the Second World War. Moreover Elmer Glidden was to find himself still flying dive-bomber sorties when most of his contemporaries had long retired to far less demanding roles. As a 'Fighting Marine' or, better yet, a Dive-Bomber Marine, Elmer Glidden became an almost legendary figure in the corps as late as the Vietnam conflict.

Glidden, the second eldest of four children, was born in the small burg of Hyde Park, in the state of Massachusetts, on 1 December 1915. His mother later moved to West Roxbury and then to Scituate, on the coast of the Bay, between Boston and Cape Cod.

'My parents were most supportive during my younger days in any activity I took part in,' Glidden later recalled to me. 'My father was a Certified Public Accountant and a successful businessman, my mother was always a housewife and family raiser. Early on I wasn't the best student in the world, preferring sports activities of all kinds. Our family life was very close and centred on a summerhouse on the beach and school activities. We were neither poor nor well off, but always comfortable with no stresses due to "hard times".'

The young Glidden was educated for eight years at Grammar and then four years at High School, firstly at Mechanic Arts High School until 1933. He initially opted for a Trade School over the objections of his father who wanted him to aim for college. At this time one of Elmer's uncles, who was a US army career officer, influenced the young man a lot with his tales of life in Hawaii and the Philippines and of distant travel to such exotic lands. To meet his father's desire he opted for college but this meant a year at nearby New Hampton Preparatory School to reach a good enough standard, and he worked very hard for the first time to qualify. He set his heart on an engineering career and kept to this when he graduated in 1934.

Glidden jr took his qualifications straight to the Renssellaer Polytechnic Institute at Troy, New York State, for a further four years and worked diligently. He still had his heart set on a military career and he joined the Marine Corps Reserve in April 1936 while still at the Polytechnic, becoming a Platoon Leader of his class at Quantico, Virginia. His steady application to his chosen vocation was rewarded on his graduation from the Institute with a Bachelor of Aeronautical Engineering degree in 1938.

These were the depression years and the only job available was with a firm manufacturing and converting cotton and cotton materials, basically a curtain manufacturer, boring tedious and uninteresting work. After sticking it for a year Glidden had had enough. He took himself back to the Marine Corps and requested flight training. By now the war clouds were gathering over Europe while, in the Pacific, Japan's expansionist plans were more and more encroaching on American tolerance and pacificism. The sinking of the US gunboat *Panay* was just one incident that indicated the way things were developing. In September full-scale war broke out in Europe and the young graduate hesitated no longer. With the qualifications he required and with his heart still set on flying, Elmer, now twenty-two, took the final step. In October 1939, he enlisted in the US Marine Corps. On 15 November, he was sent to the Elimination Base at Squantum, Massachusetts and, on passing the corps' preliminary examination of him, he was appointed as an aviation cadet and, in January 1940, was sent to Pensacola, on the southern coast of Florida facing the Gulf of Mexico, for flight training.

The Naval Aeronautical Station of Pensacola was the world's first such naval air school. It was laid out on the site of an abandoned navy yard and purpose-built for the job as a result of a decision by the Secretary of the Navy as early as 1914. The American navy had always been more air-minded than any other and, by 1940, was at least a decade ahead of the Royal Navy not only in aircraft numbers and application but in its wealth and depth of training. This training was severe. No corners were skimped and no excuses accepted. The failure rate reflected the standards and the standards were of the highest. Flying pupils they might be and future aces of the air perhaps, but the initial work was on the ground and they had to absorb the theory of flight, carburetion and ignition, of navigation, signalling, trigonometry and the special ways of the navy, before they could even touch an aircraft. The lesson periods were from seven in the morning to three in the afternoon, five days a week. Once these painful lessons were absorbed, the examinations taken and the theoretical dunces weeded out, then at last came the chance to get into the sky.

Training was carried out in sedate biplanes even though at

this stage the United States Navy and Marine Corps were almost exclusively equipped with monoplane fighters, scouts, dive- and torpedo-bombers. In dual-control training aircraft they patiently assimilated the delights of take-offs and landings on the broad concrete runways, the intricacies of climbing and stalling, looping and diving, of tight evasive turns and of fatal spins. The standard dive-bomber trainer was the F4B–4 which had a low terminal velocity and thus enabled them to ease their way into the special skills of estimating the correct point at which to start the attack dive, of allowing for wind-drift, and 'lag', to compensate for evasive action, and of holding the target

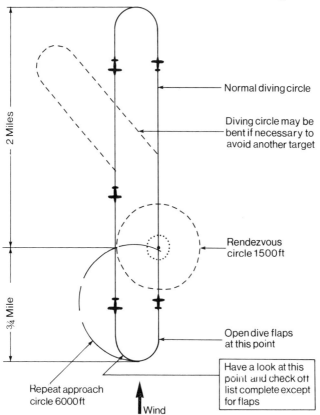

Fig 5 Bombing procedure diagram from lecture at US Naval Air Station, Miami, Supplementary VSB Dive-Bombing Lecture, 1941

steady in telescopic sights. They learned that the legendary 'black-out' at the bottom of a vertical dive was a largely needless infliction brought about more by carelessness than necessity. They learnt control in this, as in all else they did. With control and care, one survived. Those that failed to heed this lesson soon left the course, one way or the other.

'My training was uneventful,' recalled Glidden, 'except for one accident which proved fatal to the instructor and seriously bruised and banged me. Flying was a thrill to me and I really loved all aspects of it. To this day I think that flying that old biplane was my greatest joy, even more than jets.'

Then he graduated to the SBC–3, the last biplane Helldiver for 'advanced' practice sessions. Attacks were made against land targets, a 50-ft bull's-eye on the bombing range, and later, as their proficiency grew, against spars towed by destroyers in the Gulf. The syllabus required at least 50 practice dives, 10 flights each of which had to include at least five dives. Many aspirants were eliminated at this last hurdle, lacking the natural dive-bomber pilot's ability to estimate the correct angle of approach, 'aim-off' required in given weather conditions and the like. Some became almost hypnotised when in a vertical dive by the onrushing land or sea. Such men might be excellent flyers, but not for the dive-bomber arm which was the élite. At this period no fully automatic pull-out devices were in use by US marine or navy flyers. As in most nations one was under development, but even when it eventually appeared it was never popular.

And so the daily grind continued as 1940 slipped by. Gradually the classes were weaned down until only the best remained. But it was not all hell. There was ample time set aside for relaxation and leisure and the navy had made ample provision for the young Officer Cadets to ease up on the strains and trials by providing lavish facilities. There was a gymnasium, a football field, a baseball diamond and a basket-ball court. A stable of riding horses and polo ponies was on hand while a clubhouse at nearby Mustin Beach, with its pure white fine-grained sand, was in the luxury class. Then there were the more pertinent attractions of movies, free dances, fishing in the Gulf and the attractive southern belles from nearby Mobile, Montgomery and Tallahassee, although Cadets were forbidden to marry within four years.

This tough series of courses lasted until September, when Glidden was finally commissioned into the Marine Corps as Second Lieutenant Glidden USMC. In October he was transferred to nearby Miami for further advance training in Marine Corps dive-bombers and in November was designated a naval aviator.

'At San Diego I had hoped for fighter assignments as it seemed more exciting than bombing. I was, however, assigned to the scout/bomber squadron and given additional duties as assistant Material Officer. Training as a squadron was casual, as the aircraft were obsolescent and worn out. Fuel was in short supply too. We flew Curtiss biplane bombers and a Great Lakes biplane called a BG. In addition there was some rumbling about moving to Hawaii after we had picked up our new mounts at the Vought plant in Connecticut. It was a thrill to be selected as one of the team to go back and pick up the first deliveries of the Vindicators, SB2U–3s and ferry them back to California. This SB2U–3 was not really a great aircraft although as a "Scout" plane it had tremendous range – beyond a real good navigational capacity. As a bomber, though, it lacked power and required a long runway to get airborne with a maximum load of fuel. From the rear cockpit aft it was fabric covered which usually split while dive-bombing. It was never a popular plane and was sometimes called the "Wind Indicator" – but it was all we had.'

To meet the special Marine request for range a special batch of 57 SB2Us were constructed with much larger extra fuel stowage built into their fuselage and wings until, in the words of one observer, they became literally flying petrol-bowsers. They had some extra armour as well and, as a result, their performance dropped still further. The range however was vastly extended, by as much as a third again, which, for a single-engined, two-seater dive-bomber, was outstanding. These special adaptations joined the Marine Corps late as the SB2U–3, but they were to make their mark on the war before they were phased out.

Glidden had completed his training in January 1941, his appointment had been to the VMS–2 part of the Second Marine Air Group, at San Diego Naval Air Station on the west coast. Checking out the Voughts, and getting ready for deployment to Hawaii, kept the squadron and entire group VMB–231 busy. But proper training had to go by the board in the interim and Glidden confessed he had not advanced much further than when he had first finished his training. The whole unit finally took passage by carrier, with the Voughts on deck in non-flying status, in May 1941. They were at Hawaii only a few months during which time they not only had to break in their new aircraft properly but train themselves to use them. There were airfields to get ready and a mass of routine jobs. Early in December word came that they were urgently required further west, at Midway Island. The Marine Corps Vindicators were therefore embarked on a carrier with their crews and hustled to sea. Parked on deck as they were they could not fly off by themselves, nor could any of the carrier's aircraft get airborne, but it was still peacetime so this was not thought too important.

However it was while they were still at sea on 7 December that the Japanese carrier force hit Pearl Harbor behind them. While Egusa sought in vain to destroy the carriers, Glidden was parked on the deck on one of those carriers only a few hundred miles behind, but safe from discovery. Orders were at once received to seek out the enemy and destroy them, but, perhaps fortunately, they failed to locate the Japanese striking force and returned to the ruin of the base a few days later. Now the dive-bombers were even more urgently needed in the new front line and, after a short stopover to disembark from the carrier, they set off again.

This time the men and the gear were sent by ship, but the squadron itself flew out as a unit following a PBY patrol plane for long-range guidance. It was a flight for which the Vindicator was ideal and it was conducted without a hitch. At the time it was the longest mass flight of single-engined planes over water. Glidden recalls that he still had enough fuel on landing at Midway for the flight back again. Tension was already high out in the islands and no matter what sanguine expectations were held back in Washington about what was coming, the men in the front line had few illusions about future Japanese intentions. The news of the European war had been one of non-stop victories for the German forces, spearheaded by dive-bombers, and the initial onslaught on Soviet Russia, which began soon after Glidden reached Hawaii, seemed to continue this trend. In any conflict in the Pacific Glidden and his compatriots in VMB–231 seemed destined soon to be part of it. And so it proved.

'Midway before the fight', Glidden stated, 'was a pretty unsettled place. Newer pilots were coming out of training at a great rate. The older Marine squadrons, such as mine, were considered a concentration of old hands. So our squadron was split and amalgamated with a brand new group of pilots, fresh out of training, and we acquired a new skipper, Major Loften Henderson, and picked up also a newer type aircraft, the SBD Dauntless. A scrambled training was conducted but there was no time for anything meaningful. I think the SBD squadron which I was on had only two or three hours in the plane before the fight and the newer pilots had only a few hours in whichever type they were assigned.'

That tiny speck of sand and rock in the middle of the Pacific Ocean appeared an insignificant outpost, lonely, and hopelessly defiant – a few ancient coastal guns, 16 obsolete dive-bombers and 21 Brewster Buffalo fighters of similar vintage. There was nothing to back them up for several thousand miles to their rear but ocean. In front lay the whole Japanese navy just beginning its unprecedented rampage of victory. For the moment, however, Midway Island was beneath their notice. Six months later that had changed.

Apart from the odd shelling from a disgruntled Japanese submarine with nothing else to do, Midway had seen little or nothing of the Japanese despite the fighting that had swirled by them on all sides. Then, on 2 May 1942, things began to alter. On that day Admiral Chester W. Nimitz paid a flying visit to the island, inspected its defences, shook hands with all the Marine aviators and flew off into the blue again. To Marine veterans the implications were obvious, something nasty was coming their way and the top brass wanted to check them out before they vanished into its maw. The island's commanders, Lieutenant-Colonel Shannon and Captain Simard, had taken the opportunity to request modest reinforcements. Hitherto any such requests had fallen on deaf ears but this time, within a short while, a few crumbs from the table began to appear in transports. Included in these reinforcements that arrived on 26

May were 19 of the new SBD bombers and seven Wildcat fighters, along with 21 pilots, 17 of whom were fresh out of training school and even more inexperienced than Glidden himself. This brought the bomber squadrons' strength to 29 officers and 201 enlisted men. Also a notification arrived from the commander-in-chief that the whole Japanese Fleet was at sea and heading their way. Ten battleships, eight aircraft carriers, numerous cruisers and destroyers and an invasion convoy. The Marines' instructions were simple. Hold the island.

Elmer recalled how 'There was a great deal of excitement and pre-planning for the Japanese attack on Midway. We had rendezvous points and codes and many briefings as we waited upon the Japanese approach. No one had been exposed, prior to this, to the shooting war, and although I'm sure we were apprehensive, we were too naive to be frightened. We were a pretty rag-tailed bunch due to the absorption of new pilots, acquisition of new aircraft, and lack of time for meaningful training, but we did our best.'

As Henderson could muster only 29 pilots to man his 34 dive-bombers one of the fighter pilots from VMF–221 was assigned to fly with them, and the best 12 SB2U–3s out of the 17 that still remained operational were selected for operations along with 16 of the 19 Dauntless planes. Long-range reconnaissance sorties were flown continuously from 23 May to 4 June and plans were made on how to attack the Japanese armada when it was eventually sighted. As soon as the enemy were seen all planes were to clear the airstrip, to avoid being caught on the ground, and the dive-bombers sent to rendezvous at a point some 20 miles, bearing 90 degrees true, from Eastern Island and there to await instructions. Their priority targets were of course the Japanese carriers, if located, or else to shadow homeward-bound Japanese bombers in order to find the carriers and then attack at once. Instructions were to be relayed from Midway by radio.

Accidents continued with the old Vindicators as the new intake pilots learned how to operate them on the job knowing that they would have to fly them in earnest at any time. Not surprisingly two were ground-looped on 28 May and placed out of commission leaving 11, but by 31 May one more was made operational again. Not only the novices had to learn, the more experienced pilots, Glidden among them, were assigned to the new Dauntless aircraft and had to re-familiarise themselves after many months flying Voughts. On 2 June they flew escort for a tanker from a distance of 50 miles out from the island. Next day the long-range B17s were out attacking the enemy invasion convoy, to no avail, while Glidden and his companions prepared themselves for their turn.

At 05.20 the Japanese carriers were finally sighted some 180 miles out from the island. The long-awaited moment of truth had come. Within ten minutes all the dive-bomber crews had been alerted and were standing by their planes with their engines turning over. At 05.45 they were inside the elongated 'greenhouse' cockpits, pilot and radio operator/air gunner, with their radios on and engines well warmed up. Another ten minutes and the radar reported numerous 'bogies' closing fast and the Air Raid Red sounded off. At one minute past six all the bombers received the expected radio signal, 'Attack enemy carriers, bearing 320 degrees, distance 180 miles, course 135 degrees, speed 25 knots.' This message was picked up on its first transmission but was not acknowledged by any of the dive-bombers and so was frequently repeated. They need not have bothered, the Marines were on their way. They left behind two grounded SB2U–3s plus three others that had been totally written off and were being used for spares by the others and three non-operational SBDs. The dive-bombers were formed into two distinct divisions. The First Division, led by Major Henderson, had the Dauntless SBDs and were to lead in. The Second Division consisted of the gallant old Vibrators plugging gamely along but falling steadily behind. The organisation of the First Division, with which Glidden was flying, was as follows:

Command Section:
1 HENDERSON, Loften R., Major/REININGER, Lee W., Pfc
2 FLEMING, Richard E., Captain/CARD, Eugene T., Corp
3 STAMPS, Clyde H., TSgt/THOMAS, Horace B., Pfc

First Section
1 GLIDDEN, Elmer G. Jr, Capt/JOHNSON, Meade T., Corp
2 GRATZEK, Thomas J., 2ndLt/RECKE, Charles W., Sgt

Second Section
1 IVERSON, Daniel Jr/REID, Wallace J., Pfc
2 BEAR, Robert J. 'R'., 2ndLt/SIDEBOTTOM, Truell L., Pfc

Third Section:
1 DeLALIO, Armond H., Captain/MOORE, John A., Corp
2 WARD, Maurice A., 2ndLt/RADFORD, Harry M., Pfc

Fourth Section:
1 TWEEDY, Albert W., 2ndLt/RAYMOND, Elza L., Sgt
2 HAGEDORN, Bruno P., 2ndLt/FIRANEO, Joseph T., Pfc

The rendezvous was completed on bearing 90 degrees at a distance of 20 miles by about 06.30 and the approach was started. At about 07.55 the enemy fleet was sighted and seen to contain at least two carriers. Issuing the order 'Attack two enemy CVs on port bow', Major Henderson started a wide losing height circle down from 9000 ft with the intention of beginning a glide-bombing attack on *Akagi* in from an altitude of 4000 ft. It is not certain why this more lengthy method of approach was chosen, unless he felt his aircrew were not yet familiar enough with their new mounts to attempt the faster and more accurate dive attack. Lack of aviation fuel had curtailed somewhat the chance to practise more. Whatever the reason the results were deadly. Almost at once the ten or more defending Zeros were slashing in towards them, cutting swathes through the bombers in attack after attack. Heavy and violent anti-aircraft fire was also opened by all ships in the enemy fleet within range. The first casualty was Henderson himself, attacked by two or three Zero fighters right at the start of his approach. His SBD was soon burning steadily and out of control with the pilot himself obviously badly injured.

'As we approached the Japanese fleet and their carriers it was a beautiful day with scattered broken layers of clouds below us,' Glidden remembered. 'Before we could reach them we were attacked by the shipboard fighters and I was amazed at the ease with which they flew rings around us. Their gunnery wasn't the best though as they could and should have blown us out of the sky. I was in the number three position on the squadron commander's wing and after a few runs both he and the other wingman were gone.'

Glidden now took over the formation. He decided that this slow approach was suicidal under these conditions and committed the surviving SBDs to the attack without further ado. Complying with this, however, was difficult as the sky was alive with Zeros and pockmarked with flak bursts. Glidden sought protection in some cloud cover over one of the Japanese carriers to gain some respite. The rest of the Dauntless bombers dived down into it with him. From this protective layer they emerged at a height of some 200 ft to find two carriers with destroyer escorts immediately below them. 'We headed for the fleet', recalled Glidden to me later, 'in a long let-down rather than a dive and dropped our bombs.'

The enemy carriers were steaming on parallel courses, surrounded by other fleet units and easily identified by the Rising Sun painted on their flight decks. Glidden then led the 10 surviving SBDs into the final attack dives, pushing hard down to release at heights estimated at between 600 ft and 400 ft, and losing two more of their number in the process. Even this ploy failed to throw many of the Japanese fighters off the scent, however, and attacks were unrelenting all the way down, each Dauntless taking one or more Zero fighters down towards the target with it. Moreover these leeches clung to their targets even after bomb-release, drilling the little dive-bombers with a hail of bullets. Glidden himself was under attack for 40 miles from the Japanese fleet before being left in peace. He lost his tail-gunner in the process. The anti-aircraft fire did not relent either, and both light and heavy gunfire was reported to be 'of tremendous volume'. A Japanese eyewitness later recalled how 'Even when half of them had been shot down, the remaining planes bravely held their course and finally released bombs which seemed certain to hit the carrier. But when the bomb splashes and smoke cleared, *Hiryu* was still intact, steaming on as gallantly as ever.'

The Marine flyers reported in good faith that two direct hits were made on the enemy carrier from this attack with at least two very close misses on the same ship. When last seen, as they weaved and dodged away from the death-trap they had entered, the carrier was reported to be burning and a large column of smoke to have been issuing from her stern. Alas for their hopes, they, like all the other land-based attack planes that day, failed to score any hits at all, deserving though they had been. Only near-misses rocked *Hiryu* and she was able to continue operations unhindered. Likewise each tail-gunner claimed at least one Zero destroyed but none was reported lost at this time by the Japanese.

'I don't think we accomplished much,' said Glidden, 'but we did our best and turned to reorganise for return to base. The Jap fighters followed us down and away from the Jap fleet having at us at will. We staggered back to base in bad shape.'

The SBDs had taken a severe mauling. Only half of them made it back to Midway and most were full of holes, one pilot counting no less than 250 in his machine. It had been a gallant effort. But more was to be demanded of them yet. A fully detailed report had to be prepared while the two remaining fit aircraft that could be patched up and re-armed and fuelled ready for another try were seen to. Glidden made several pertinent comments in his report. First and foremost was the fact that glide-bombing was more hazardous than dive-bombing in the absence of protecting fighters ('This has been known for a long time' was scribbled in the margin by his CO). Secondly there was a need for attacks by different units to be co-ordinated whenever possible, another old lesson which the harsh realities of war had brushed aside. As the planes had arrived over the target in dribs and drabs the Japanese countered each wave with relative ease and emerged unscathed. On sighting, the target units should have proceeded directly towards it as rapidly as possible. Again comment in the margin backed up this opinion: 'And no circling'. Although the enemy AA-fire was heavy and accurate it counted for little compared with the fighter opposition. The Japanese fighter tactics were reported as operating on two or three different levels, the Zeros working in pairs with excellent teamwork and their attacks on formation leaders were described as 'heavy and persistent'.

Only a brief period of rest after this traumatic attack was allowed. At 17.00 Glidden was aroused when a fresh signal came in reporting an enemy aircraft-carrier burning some 200 miles distant from Midway following attacks by American carrier units. MAG–22 was instructed immediately to deliver an attack on this crippled ship, '. . . with all available dive-bombers'. At 17.05 Major Benjamin W. Norris, who was now senior flying officer, was ordered to comply with this request. However in view of the odds against another daylight attack faring any better than the first he remonstrated with the CO, arguing that a delay to enable him to make a night attack would minimise the deadly effect of the Japanese fighter opposition, and this request was granted.

At 19.15 this attack duly took off from Midway, again formed in two, now much smaller, groups. Norris led this time with five Vindicators while Captain Tyler followed with six SBDs. The composition of the latter force was as follows:

1 TYLER, Marshall A., Capt./UNDERWOOD, Robert A., Sgt
2 VAUPELL, Robert W., 2nd Lt/HICKMAN, Carl T., Sgt
3 DeLALIO, Armond H., Capt./RAMSEY, Reed T., Pfc
4 GLIDDEN, Elmer G. Jr, Capt./JOHNSON, Arlow A., Pvt
5 BEAR, Robert J. 'R'., 2nd Lt/SIDEBOTTOM, Truell L., Pfc
6 IVERSON, Daniel, Jr, 1st Lt/REID, Wallace J., Pfc

It was a forlorn hope. The night was pitch-black, the target could not be found and only tragedy resulted. Operations of this nature were just not worthwhile at that stage of the war, with primitive equipment and the difficulties of navigating over water at night. Without a horizon, flyers were totally reliant on their instruments and either missed their objective or became lost on the return leg. After casting fruitlessly around in the night the SBDs returned around 22.00 but Norris was lost when he flew into the sea some 40 miles from the island trying to lead his units back through overcast. The others finally made it back, the last one at 01.45 with only 30 minutes' fuel left. The fire from the burning oil-tanks on Sand Island was the beacon that eventually saved them.

Glidden remembers that sortie very well: 'The intelligence was faulty and we were unable to find anything after groping around in the black night. It was a hairy flight and we lost another pilot probably to vertigo before we straggled back to Midway. That flight bothered me more than the attack as I was really worried that the newer pilots could not have carried out an attack, rendezvoused and returned to base with the weather and darkness being what it was. Fortunately we found nothing and our problem was just difficult flying conditions.'

During the night tension was further increased by the shelling of positions by a Japanese submarine, so sleep was hard to come by. Moreover there was still the expectancy of invasion on the morrow. Had they but known it, a squadron of four heavy cruisers bristling with 8-in. guns was on its way to blow them all to kingdom-come but, fortunately for the defenders, the Japanese commander cancelled this operation. More than this, in reversing course two of the heavy cruisers had collided and, thus damaged, were left behind by the rest of the fleet. They were trailing oil, had no air cover and thus, come the dawn, presented the dive-bomber crews with worthwhile targets for their skills. They were not slow to take advantage of the opportunity.

At 05.45 these two cruisers (reported as battleships initially) were reported to be on a bearing 268, distance 140 miles. At 07.00 six SBDs and six SB2U–3s, each armed with 500-lb AP bombs, were airborne to seek out these cripples and destroy them. This time the plan was for the Dauntless unit to make a dive-bombing attack down from 10,000 ft. The composition of the SBD force was as follows:

1 TYLER, Marshall A., Capt/UNDERWOOD, Robert A., Sgt
2 DeLALIO, Armond H., Capt/RAMSAY, Reed T., Pfc
3 VAUPEL, Robert W., 2nd Lt/HICKMAN, Carl T., Sgt
4 GLIDDEN, Elmer G., Capt/JOHNSON, Arlow A., Pvt
5 IVERSON, Daniel, Jr, 1st Lt/REID, Wallace J., Pfc
6 BEAR, Robert J, 'R'., 2nd Lt/SIDEBOTTOM, Truell L., Pvt

The enemy cruisers, *Mogami* and *Mikuma*, were sighted at 08.00 and all the dive-bombers deployed to the attack. Five minutes later the SBDs led in, followed by the Vindicators. As usual they met heavy and accurate AA-fire but pressed on down to the target. Bombs were released at a low level and two direct hits and two near-misses were observed. One of the Vindicators was hit and lost, but all the SBDs returned safely from this mission. After further hits the *Mikuma* finally sank, while her sister ship, little better than a floating wreck, managed to crawl back to base. It had been a great American victory overall and, if the Marine Corps flyers were not themselves personally rewarded with the kudos of a carrier scalp, at least they had led the attacks that had worn down and thus led to the enemy's defeat, and they had struck hard blows at his retiring force right to the very end. To the exhausted survivors of this brief and bloody encounter it was hard to believe it was all over so soon and that they had survived it. Eight SBDs had been lost and five severely damaged from the 19 that had been landed at Midway a few days before. Twenty-three officers and 18 enlisted men had flown to their deaths with the Marines Corps dive-bombers in the two-day battle. For his part in these missions Glidden was awarded a well-deserved Navy Cross.

Glidden and the rest of the survivors stayed at Midway for several more weeks with mixed feelings of mourning for their comrades, elation at the victory achieved, and anti-climax as the two great fleets drew apart and left the tiny speck in the vast ocean to revert to its former anonymity. But if the battle was over and won the war was far from either. To the north the Japanese had seized the Aleutian islands, far to the south they were still pouring into New Guinea and down the Solomon Island chain towards Samoa to sever Australia's last links with the US. They had been stopped at Midway and now they had to be stopped again and again, until sufficient resources were available to drive them back from their huge area of conquests. The Marine Group 22 were eventually relieved in July and took passage back to Ewa. Here they had a brief period of rest but the time was mainly spent in hastily re-equipping with new SBD–3s and assimilating replacement aircrew and groundcrew in readiness for their next hurried shift to where the action was. Glidden was now appointed Executive Officer of VMSB–231 and much of the heavy workload involved in all this fell on him. He shouldered it with resolution and set-to with a will.

His new commanding officer was Major Leo Smith and VMSB–231, sporting the famous 'Ace of Spades' motif proudly on the side of their 12 brand new Dauntless bombers, in the direct tradition of the old De Havilland DH–4s at Haiti in 1919, made ready in conjunction with the Wildcat fighters of VMF–224 to form part of MAG–23. Their ultimate destination was to join with their comrades on another hitherto unknown island that was destined to achieve immortal memory, Guadalcanal.

Their new mounts, the 'dash-3s', had the same dimensions as the earlier marks of Dauntless, but incorporated certain improvements, the most notable of which was a better engine, a

Wright R–1820–52, rated at 1000 hp. Top speed actually dropped slightly, to 250 mph, but the rate of climb, service ceiling and range (1345 miles) were all improved. Another upgrade was the defensive armament, a much-needed modification which saw the .30 calibre machine-guns replaced by .50s. Already a 'dash-4' was on the way but the first of these did not reach the Marines until October. Standard bomb-load remained at 1200 lb in all models. Dives were normally made from around 15,000 ft and, with flaps down, the descent was made at about 275 mph over a period of 40 seconds, the pilot using the ailerons to correct for lateral drift. Bomb-release was normally made between 1500 ft to 2000 ft and the standard 1000-lb GP bomb with varying fuse settings was usually carried.

Their sister unit, VMSB–232, had been operating under the most primitive conditions from a half-completed airstrip the Japanese had been hacking out of the jungle on the northern coast of Guadalcanal. This they had named Henderson Field, in memory of their leader at Midway. Struggle for the control of this one runway was to dominate the war in the Pacific for the next six months and, over that period, battles to gain possession of it, or to halt its operations, were to cost the lives of thousands of men. Truly if ever there was a focal-point of war, it was Henderson Field. And that was the destination of Glidden and his companions as they enshipped from Oahu at the end of the month and steamed steadily southward. On 30 August they first gazed down on the waters of 'The Slot', that narrow stretch of sea between the jungle-clad islands of the Solomons group. They bounced and bumped down on to that primitive runway surrounded by gloomy and dank jungle and entered a world of absolute chaos. Under constant attack from land, sea and air, the aviators and groundcrew lived from one crisis to the next at instant readiness for anything at all.

'The field was a mess', Glidden remembered, 'with no good communications and navigation only dead-reckoning. So far as Marine aviation is concerned the real heroes here were the enlisted maintenance men, ordnance, armourers. How they kept us in the air is really an incredible story. In the evenings the Japanese navy, including battleships, gave us hell, with the airfield being the principal target. There was no rest at night or day, food was atrocious and so on.'

Over the next months the Japanese, who held most of the jungle, made repeated attempts to break the perimeter of the defending Marine infantry. Savage hand-to-hand fighting took place during these offensives, mainly at night. During the day Japanese bombers cruised overhead and deluged the strip with bombs. Periodically Japanese destroyers and submarines appeared off the coastline and fired hundreds of rounds of 3-in. and 5-in. shells into the area. After a while the enemy brought up heavy cruisers with batteries of 8-in. guns to do the same job, and, ultimately, battleships which contributed one-ton 14-in. projectiles to the Marines' discomfiture.

If the Japanese ruled the night, then the Marines, mainly through the SBDs, took over at daybreak. Attempts to run in convoys of troops and supplies to their armies by the Japanese resulted in a whole series of major naval actions offshore to which the Marine flyers were able to contribute with the coming of dawn, by finishing off the cripples or pounding incoming troopships that had been too slow. Eventually losses in merchant ships grew so great that the Japanese turned to high-speed destroyers to do the job. This was inefficient, for destroyers are not built to carry passengers, but it worked. Nonetheless the Dauntless dive-bombers made them pay a heavy price.

The tempo of life at Henderson Field was unlike anything else. Lack of sleep, and continual action, were coupled with a ghastly climate and the many unpleasant tropical illnesses, all of which dragged the men down from their peak performance. But they carried on. Aircraft were patched up, rebuilt, tacked together and then re-patched, anything to keep them in the air. While the SBDs could fly the island would be held – that was their motto and a true one. The casualty rate from all sources was heavy.

'Guadalcanal sticks in my mind,' Glidden said later, 'because it was there I picked up a squadron and it was there that I realised how much I liked my part of the war. On the ground I felt useless and subject to all sorts of indignities and of no particular value. But flying on any mission always seemed more of a "one-on-one" affair and the environment was certainly better. Any apprehension came during briefings for attacks; once you were airborne it was a busy time and you were engrossed with the job at hand. Anti-aircraft fire was never considered a real threat and by constantly changing directions and altitude you could stay ahead of it. Small-arms fire during a committed dive was more troublesome. We soon lost our skipper and then the Exec. I was third in line and after the Exec went I became Squadron CO. We were in bad shape what with our flying and living conditions and were ready for relief. Our relief squadron came in and before getting off the ground lost the three senior people during a Naval bombardment.'

The runway itself was half morass and casualties from accidents during landings and take-offs equalled those in combat or destroyed in the frequent bombardments. Flying conditions were bad also with abrupt tropical storms blowing up and causing serious hazards for lost and lonely SBDs. Many went this way. Bare essentials in the form of food, equipment and basics were run in whenever possible but there was little room for any luxury. The only one Glidden permitted himself were his cigars, which became as much his trademark as Winston Churchill's among his comrades (and, some would add, more deadly in their effects on the Marines than the enemy). Glidden was to experience the special quality of life at Henderson Field from 30 August through to the middle of October, a two-and-a-half-month spell that was like a year anywhere else. When Major Smith was killed in combat early on Glidden had taken over as Commanding Officer and carried out no less than 25 missions in that short period. The targets were diverse enough as would be expected – ground troops and concentrations, landing barges and transports, destroyers and bigger fish. All were grist to VMSB–231's mill and the 'Ace of Spades' flyers caused havoc among them all.

Glidden recalled a typical mission: 'The preparation for attack produced the most apprehension in myself. Others provided Intelligence, targets, co-ordinates, opposition expected, recommended release altitudes, target departure, safety measures to include recovery etc. Then it was up to the squadron to prepare, physically and mentally. Armaments selected for low release point, winding a few turns into the arming propeller, briefing the squadron pilots and gunners. Lots of work and co-ordination to fill one's mind with practical details rather than brooding on possible outcomes. Then the waiting for the attack time, perhaps while undergoing intense shelling by Japanese warships.

'Once the attack take-off time arrived things usually fell into place and the flight to the target was a time to stew over what was coming ahead. Once in the target area one's interest was fully occupied with getting into the best position for all squadron members to do their bit. When I broke over and down into the final attack dive I felt exhilarated as the time had arrived to get on with the real job. The flights to target provided all the time needed for each pilot to check for sights, practice arming of bombs and to test communications. The actual dive was the moment and reason for it all – keep on the target visually over the cowling and aligning direction over attack and also preparing to depart the danger zone and its defences by the shortest, safety route. Check altitude, go to sights, release, close flaps, get out. A feeling of genuine relief when away from the target replaced by immediate concern on safety and rendezvous with others of the squadron.

'The gunners were invaluable here as well as he was free to follow others in their dives and also spot hits and misses for debriefing and analysis. The return to base provided no great emotional feelings unless someone was hit or having plane trouble – or the weather was bad. Debriefing was a bore.'

On 24 September the Marine SBDs caught the destroyers *Kawakaze* and *Umikaze* running one of the 'Tokyo Express' reinforcing missions down 'The Slot' and scored near-misses on both, slightly damaging them. To help in night attacks on Japanese transport off-loading troops and supplies the SBDs flew flare-dropping sorties off Lunga Point, another innovation for this versatile unit. After the battleship bombardment on the night of 14 October only seven of the 39 SBDs remained serviceable, some 40 personnel had been killed also. Much of their fuel had been destroyed and radio communications were out for a period. Nonetheless enough aircraft were got off the battered runway to make fresh attacks on incoming Japanese units but only five SBDs were operational at the end of the day. Reinforcements were flown in from Espiritu Santo but the following night a cruiser bombardment left 19 major shell-holes in the runway and just three Dauntlesses in flyable condition.

By the end of the day they were down to one but superb work by the groundcrews got together enough flyable wrecks to continue mounting sorties until the newcomers arrived and Guadalcanal survived.

By 16 October VMSB–231 had been reduced to just four pilots. Along with the indefatigable Glidden, who had now earned the unasked-for name of 'Iron Man' Glidden, a press tag which stuck despite all his efforts, there were Lieutenant G.B. Loeffel, Staff-Sergeant L.F. Bass, and Staff-Sergeant W.W. Witherspoon. These veterans were finally evacuated out of Henderson Field on 16 October as they had no planes left to fly. This marked the end of MAG–23's involvement in the campaign. For his work at Guadalcanal Glidden was awarded his second Navy Cross and promoted to Major. He was also given some well-earned home leave. This respite was all too brief, however.

Glidden recollected: 'I was able to get back to Massachusetts for a visit with my mother. My father had died while I was on Guadalcanal. I didn't have a girlfriend and had no attachments, for which I was happy as I wouldn't have wanted to have been worrying about somebody worrying about me. I enjoyed home for two weeks and returned to San Diego to pick up my squadron again and move it to a brand new Marine Corps Air Base. Again the job was to re-group and train. The new young pilots joining us this time were well trained, especially in contrast to myself and those who had joined us at Midway. Upon completion of flight training and commissioning they were sent to either fighter or bomber training units for real intensive training and ended up with many good tactical hours in the air. They were well advanced in training and ability, but as the realities of the war were well known by then they were, I believe, less naive than those of us earlier on and, as a result, more apprehensive and especially reluctant to go into dive-bombing. The newer pilots wanted fighter duty (and I don't blame them) as the aircraft were the better F4Us now while there was no real advance in dive-bombers and we still had old reliable SBD Dauntless planes.'

It was in December 1942 that Glidden was back on the job at the United States Marine Corps Air Station of El Toro, California, to begin again the task of rebuilding the 'Ace of Spades' squadron, almost from scratch. The task was to take six months. The rebuilding of VMSB–231 was complicated by the great inrush of new recruits, as the war expansion programme got underway, and the need to impart to these raw newcomers as much as possible of the unique expertise and experience of combat veterans such as Glidden. The re-equipping of Marine units with the new 'dash-4' Dauntless also took place in this period. El Toro was also something of a staging-post as the constant demands for Marine flyers out in the Solomons and elsewhere delayed a full build-up for some time. It was not until July 1943 that the unit found itself again on the move into the war zone and nobody could have been more surprised than Glidden to find out its ultimate destination: Midway Island.

'We shipped out in July and for a while were at Midway for further training and awaiting further assignment. This time Midway was fun as the living conditions had improved and we had the time and fuel for good intensive tactical training. Before we left for the Marshall Islands the squadron was truly capable and I wished that I could have had it as such for the Battle of Midway and Guadalcanal. What a job we could have done.'

All the fighting had long since passed Midway by and it was a period of relative idleness for the crack squadron. It lasted until December 1943. Much had happened far to the south of them during this long period. The holding of Guadalcanal had marked the turning-point and, from 1943 onward, the Japanese were gradually pushed back up the chain of islands towards their main base at Rabaul in New Britain. By January 1944, this base was under constant attack from the air and was neutralised. However in the Central Pacific the re-built US Fleet was ready for its own offensives and, with the capture of the first outposts, the Gilbert Islands, the Marines were called upon to move up in support. A special unit, Marine Air Wing 4, was formed under Brigadier-General Louis Woods USMC out of two Air Groups and was eventually based at Tarawa, making strikes on the Japanese-held Marshall islands with four squadrons of SBDs at the end of the 1943. By the beginning of 1944 VMSB–231 ceased to be a static spectator of these great events and moved back to take its rightful place in the front line once more. With the invasion of Eniwetok and Engebi the Japanese garrisons in that area had been by-passed and left to wither on the vine by the carrier Task Forces. The isolated Japanese garrisons lacked any aircraft but they were well dug in on several of the islands and well stocked with supplies and anti-aircraft weapons. The runways on the islands of Jaluit, Maloelap, Mili and Wotje were still intact and, should the enemy choose to fly in aircraft, a potential threat to the rear of the American advance. The islands therefore had to be kept neutralised, and the Marine flyers were given the less than glamorous, but very essential, chore of grinding them down with constant air attacks. It was very much a war of attrition, with little positive result to show for a great deal of effort and no little risk. It was a far different war to that on Midway or Guadalcanal but, after the enforced idleness of the previous six months, the squadron was eager to get stuck into some worthwhile operations and accepted their opportunity with some relish.

The squadron moved into the palm-fringed Majuro Lagoon on the western fringes of the Marshalls, soon after its unopposed capture, and turned it into a major fleet base at the beginning of February 1944. From the airstrip on Majuro itself, beginning in March, VMSB–231 started its long period of pounding the Japanese strongholds. With his new partner and gunner, Master Technical Sergeant James A. Boyle jr, from Chicago, Glidden now began to rack up an impressive total of dive-bomber sorties.

'There was no pressure as the Japanese couldn't protect these islands now and their garrisons were by-passed,' he recalled. 'Our mission was to pound them into submission by repeated attacks from the air. This we attempted and flew countless missions against miniscule targets such as gun emplacements and bunkers. Our tactics changed as the urgency of the attacks diminished – instead of a release point of about 1200 ft we raised it for safety's sake. Accuracy suffered but we usually could lay them in. There was occasional AA-fire but not much as their supply was limited and there was no re-supply. Small-arms fire was heavy and accurate and holes in aircraft were frequently received. I lost my Executive officer to small-AA. I had, up to that point of the war, lost many acquaintances but this time it was personal as we had become very close friends.'

As the year wore on mission followed mission against pinpoint targets in the islands, the flak faced him day after day but the precision never faltered. Leading from the front was always Elmer Glidden's way and he fiercely fought attempts to shunt him behind a desk. He was at his best tipping the nose of his SBD down towards the coral islets. Already he was something of a legend although he shunned the publicity. Of all those who had flown with him at Midway and Guadalcanal less than ten still remained in similar operational flying. About half of them had been killed in action, in contrast to his own charmed life. Although his own aircraft had been hit many times it was never seriously damaged and Glidden had not received so much as a scratch. Of the remaining veterans, some were behind desks already, others victims of war neurosis and grounded. But to someone like Glidden, who had flown missions at Guadalcanal 250 miles out from his base while suffering the after-effects of malaria and dysentery, such a future held an absolute horror for him. So he held out against the inevitable as long as he could. In six months of operations Glidden clocked up another 73 dive-bomber missions and, although he had not kept count himself, others had. By August they found out that not only had he spent some 800 hours' flying time in combat zones and flown countless patrol missions, but his latest sortie would mark his 100th dive-bomber attack. They invited the press to take note, feeling, quite correctly, that the lonely war of the Marine dive-bomber crews had received scant publicity back home. First-Lieutenant Louis Olszyk, formerly a reporter on the *Milwaukee Journal*, was therefore on hand as a passenger in another patrol plane when Glidden led his unit in what was to be his centenary mission.

Olszyk duly wrote it up in typical press style: 'Layers of cloud formations enveloped him on the downward journey. Then he pulled out and levelled off. He left his mark below – his one 500-lb and two 100-lb bombs sending up a geyser of debris, smoke and dust from the Jap atoll.

'Back on the ground at his home field, the scene was typical of the Major's own New England reserve. There was no fanfare and, at first, only an occasional congratulatory handshake. Glidden had kept the number of his missions a secret, with only First-Lieutenant Lytton (Bud) Blass of Garretsville, Ohio, who had served with him on Guadalcanal, and members of the flight office knowing the score.

'When others learned of his 100th dive and expressed awe at
the number, Glidden dismissed them with: "If you keep flying
long enough, the number just automatically piles up. You don't
have much else to do or say about it except to keep nosing over
and dropping those bombs." On his own immunity Elmer
replied wryly, "I guess my mother must do a lot of praying for
me." On his future he was quoted as saying, "I was in on
practically the beginning of the war and I want to stay on for
the kill." '

He kept on flying but his long fight against being grounded
was almost at an end. Another four dive-bomber missions
followed. This, a record for a US aviator, was marked with the
award of a third decoration, the Air Medal. The Gold Star was
pinned on Elmer Glidden with due ceremony by Brigadier-
General Woods himself. The accompanying citation, signed by
Vice-Admiral J.H. Hoover, commander, forward area, Central
Pacific, read: 'For meritorious acts in aerial flight as commanding officer of a Marine Scout Bombing Squadron during the
Central Pacific campaign. During the period March 1944 to
10 August 1944 he flew numerous reconnaissance missions
over Japanese-occupied atolls in the Marshall Islands area,
conducted frequent anti-submarine patrols, and led dive-
bombing attacks through enemy anti-aircraft fire against
enemy surface craft and vital ground installations, inflicting
severe damage and destruction to his targets. His great courage, outstanding leadership ability and devotion to duty are in
keeping with the highest traditions of the United States Naval
Service.'

Along with the medal, the citation and the praise, however,
came the sting in the tail as far as Glidden was concerned. It
was a bitter-sweet moment in his career. Along with all these he
also received a promotion: to Lieutenant-Colonel, and with this
new rank came a new job, of the sort he had so dreaded,
deskbound. It was not all bad however, he did not have to leave
the war zone or be relegated to Washington. His new appointment came as Assistant Operations Officer, Fourth Marine Air
Wing (MAW), and he was to be based at Kwajalein atoll, 150
miles to the north-east, headquarters of the MAW. Glidden
held this post for the next nine months which saw the war in the

Pacific move far away from the Marshalls and on towards Japan itself. By the following spring, when his tour of duty expired, Glidden had a combat total of 41 out of 48 months – a great achievement. In May 1945 that period was finally brought to an end and Glidden returned home to New England for a long rest period. This ended in July by which time the war was all but won. For a fighting Marine the prospects looked daunting, but there was still much work to be done, even if not at the helm of his much-loved SBDs. His next appointment was at the Division of Aviation Headquarters at Washington DC. They finally had the elusive flyer nailed down. Or so they thought. In one respect though the young officer with no commitments *was* nailed, though quite willingly: 'In 1945, while on duty at Marine Corps HQ in Washington, I met my future wife, Phyllis, on a visit to Boston. We were married in 1946 and were soon a typical service family. We had two children, a son Elmer (Gray) in 1948 and a daughter Gail in 1950, and fortunately my wife and children enjoyed our service life too.'

In the immediate post-war period there was a large run-down in the armed forces of the West and the old wartime Alliance was allowed to wane. However the Soviet Union busily re-armed itself in strict contrast and began to move west, fermenting revolutions and uprisings as well as subtle take-overs in central Europe. By the time the American people awoke to the danger Hungary, Romania, Poland, Albania, Yugoslavia and Czechoslovakia had become Communist states, Greece was threatened and the weakened powers of Western Europe had hastily formed the Western Union Defence Organisation, in the grave fear that the Soviets would move in at any time. This period, the forerunner of the founding of the NATO Alliance when the USA again joined herself with the European democracies, was a period of great upheaval in the Armed Forces.

The dramatic and horrifying introduction of the atomic bomb seemed to render all the wartime lessons obsolete. However some held firm that conventional warfare was far from dead and indeed many decades of armed strife since then have proved them right. The need for strong naval and naval air forces has been shown time and time again, as well as the flexibility of sea/air strength. However finally only the USA and France had the wisdom to hold on to that unique power while the Soviet Union adopted it at the same time as an impoverished Britain rejected it. Elmer Glidden was fortunate to be the right man in the right place to be at the forefront of such new developments in the United States. His stint at Washington was followed by two periods with the Amphibious Warfare School at Quantico in 1948 and again in 1954. The need for strong air cover in any such eventuality was one lesson on which Elmer could speak with some authority. The Korean conflict, with the landings at Inchon, certainly gave dramatic proof of these ideas.

Glidden returned to his first love, flying operations, in December 1955 when he joined Marine Air Group 32, part of Second MAW, as Combined Operations and Executive Officer. Here was a job tailor-made for him and he threw himself into it with renewed zest. It was a Service Group however and he spent most of his time in Japan.

This was followed in July 1957, with an eighteen-month stint with the Marine Air Division at Memphis, Tennessee as Commanding Officer, including a period at the Special Weapon Command at Albuquerque. In July 1958 he was promoted to full Colonel, and, in January 1959, found himself once more at El Toro, MCAS, as Assistant Chief of Staff. This lasted until January 1961 and although it is said you cannot teach an old dog new tricks Colonel Glidden became a Student at the National War College in Washington DC between July 1961 and January 1962 in readiness for joining the Joint Chiefs of Staff at the Pentagon as Action Officer in the Pacific Division. This was the period when the Vietnam War loomed large in American life. The need for close air support in the old Marine traditions of the Second World War was found to be totally relevant in the post-hydrogen bomb and missile age. Once again the GIs on the ground in the jungle, fighting a largely unseen enemy, needed the instant and accurate response that only a deliver-or-linger dive-bomber could provide, despite the much-publicised views of the strategic bomber and jet fighter-bomber lobby. Luckily there was such an aircraft still in service with the US Navy and Marines, that old workhorse the Douglas AD Skyraider. The 'Able-Dog' had taken on the same burden in Korea. Now, as the AH–1, modified versions of this veteran provided the backbone to a whole series of squadrons that took up the close-support mantle laid down by Glidden and his compatriots and covered themselves in new glory.

Between September 1964 and July 1965, much to his delight, Glidden himself was back in the saddle, serving as AC/S G–5 and G–3 at the Headquarters of the Third Marine Air Wing in that combat zone, and he followed this up with a year with III/MAF as Deputy Chief of Staff and Assistant Chief of Staff with G–6. 'I flew only staff missions, non-combat, during Korea and Vietnam. During Korea I was Commanding Officer of the Service Squadron, providing the combat groups with higher echelon services than they were able to perform themselves. In Vietnam I was Deputy Chief of Staff. My duties were 100 per cent staff and paper work. Not much excitement!' What his wife Phyllis and his son and daughter thought of it all one can only guess. Happily he survived all his missions over South-East Asia and reluctantly, in September 1966, moved on to a new appointment, as Chief of Staff, COMCABWEST. He became Commanding Officer of the Marine Barracks at Panama. This was to prove his last service appointment and on 1 January 1970 he took his retirement from the Corps.

He returned to Massachusetts to start his own firm as owner/operator of a print business, but he sold this in 1976 and retired for the second and final time. Now living contentedly with his wife in Canton, Massachusetts, Colonel Glidden can look back on one of the most distinguished Marine careers of all time. During that long period he was awarded, in addition to his two Navy Crosses, the Legion of Merit/Combat Distinguishing Device, three Distinguished Flying Crosses and no less than a dozen Air Medals. Elmer Glidden summed it all up to me by saying, 'I will always miss not being on duty in the Corps and being a part of something good.'

6 Brigadier-General Walter Enneccerus
German Air Force 1911–71

As was perhaps fitting for the Air Force which, at the beginning of the Second World War, was the foremost in its close co-operation with troops on the ground, many of the Luftwaffe's officers of all ranks came originally from the Army. The very strong military traditions helped mould the German Air Force into the formidable weapon it was. Blitzkrieg, in retrospect, seems so obvious that it is taken for granted and yet none of the other major powers involved in that war achieved anything remotely close to the German efficiency in co-operation until much later in the conflict and with infinitely greater resources. Indeed most of the Air Leaders of the Western nations openly scorned such a policy, and were wedded to Trenchard's vision of unaided air power achieving total victory.

Steeped in the German military tradition, through his family and his early career, was one of Germany's leading Stuka pilots, Walter Rudolf Enneccerus. Enneccerus was born on 21 November 1911, at Trier/Mosel, in Rheinland. This was an historic birthplace, the town of Trier (Treves) nestling just below the confluence of the Kyil and Mosel rivers and bounded further down by the joining of the Sauer and the Saar rivers. This important wedge, hard by the Luxembourg borders, had deep roots as the strategic road of conquest on Germany's western boundaries with her traditional enemy, France. Walter was the third child, and second son, of the then Königlich-Preussischer Hauptmann of the 10 Rheinisches Infanterieregiment 161, Willhelm Viktor Enneccerus, and his wife Elisabeth, née Hillmar. His father was a stern military man, as Walter's daughter Bärbel Wilke has explained: 'His father was Königlich-Preussischer Major which was much more than just a profession, it was a *Weltanschauung* (world-philosophy). Part of this was his deep affinity to the German monarchy which is best transcribed by the term *Kaisertreu*. To do precisely one's duty even without surveillance, to be truthful, honest and straightforward, to do more than just appear to do one's duty ("mehr sein als scheinen . . ."). These were the almost mystic qualities that Walter's father had been educated to and which he, in his turn, expected of his own children. My father's father must have been a rather strict parent; on the other hand, he was a very patient and good grandfather, as far as I can remember. When I was born on 27 January, which also was the Kaiser's birthday, my grandfather had the brilliant idea that I should be christened Wilhelmine or Wilhelma. I am still grateful that my father refused this suggestion . . .'

Enneccerus had an elder brother and an elder sister and all three children held a deep affection for their parents, although this did not mean that they slavishly followed their stern teaching. Walter grew up in this rigid but benevolent atmosphere as any normal boy. He attended the Oberrealschule at Hamburg-Eimsbüttel from the autumn of 1917 until the autumn of 1921 and then went on to the Oberrealschule at Hamburg-Eppendorf. Walter was apparently a particularly bright and outstanding pupil at both schools, especially in mathematics and the natural sciences, and he was one of the leaders in the final examinations. He later commented that this was not due to his own brilliance so much as the dullness of his companions. From the tales that he frequently, and with relish, related to his own children many years later Walter was not a particularly adventurous lad, being the more studious type rather than a daring innovator, no doubt due to his strict upbringing. He was particularly interested in sport, as so many of the dive-bomber pilots were when young. If true dive-bomber pilots are made, rather than taught, then it is clear that precise co-ordination, as is essential in most sports, helped to foster this natural talent to a high degree. Walter was particularly fond as a boy of gymnastics and tennis. A childhood friend from those days recalls that, even then, he was rather reserved in his manner, although he always participated in the undertakings and jokes of his particular 'gang', a group of a dozen boys and girls from the school and neighbourhood. Walter passed his final exams (Abitur) on 13 September 1929, and

followed by attending Hamburg University where he sub-
scribed to a course of mathematics lectures in the winter term
1929/30. This was but a preliminary to his chosen career,
however, and, on 1 April 1930, he followed his father's footsteps
and joined the Reichswehr as an officer candidate in the
6 (Preussische) Nachrichtenabteilung at Hanover.

This was the period when Germany was at her lowest ebb.
The inflation of the 1920s had gutted the defeated people, and
the Great Depression which followed took further toll on
national pride and will. Little wonder then that the hope and
promise of Adolf Hitler and his new party seemed to many like
a breath of fresh air. Enneccerus did not take part in any
political agitation, preferring to concentrate on his chosen life.
Although Germany had been strictly forbidden by the Versailles Treaty from developing military aviation, behind the scenes
much was being done at this time to ensure that a nucleus or
kernel of aviation-minded youths was given basic training in
readiness for the future. Thus it was that Enneccerus's first
military training, from 1 April 1930 to 31 May 1931, was in fact
pilot training with the Deutsche Verkehrsfliegerschule at
Schleibheim. He was listed as a DVS Starter Entrant, with
costs paid by the Reich. It was now that his comrades began to
call him 'Ennec' because they could not wrap their tongues
round his full name, and 'Ennec' stuck for the rest of his career.

On completion of this year-long introduction course he was
sent secretly to the Soviet Russian airfield at Lipezk. This secret
German base had been set up in 1924. Located some 250 miles
south-southwest of Moscow a continuing turn-round of young
cadet officers achieved their initial training far from the prying
eyes of the Allied Occupation supervisors. By this period some
300 German staff were based there along with Russian personnel. Specialised courses in all aspects of pilot training lasted
some twenty weeks. Here, between 1 April and 30 September
1931, Ennec was instructed in the skills of a fighter pilot.

On his return to Germany he was assigned as an ordinary
recruit in 12 Infantry Regiment Halberstadt Gefreiter for
training as a wireless operator and in night-flying transferring,
on 1 January 1932, to Gefreiter (Army signalman 1st Class) in
the 3rd (Prussian) Nachrichtenabteilung again this time at
Potsdam. This tough course lasted until the end of March but

Ennec came through it well enough and, on 1 April, qualified as an Unteroffizier (Corporal) and was sent to join his operational unit at Hanover. A further promotion followed in August to Fahnenjunker-Unteroffizier (Flag Cadet entrant) and, on 1 October of the same year, he was sent to the Infantry School at Dresden where he remained until the end of May 1933, before emerging from his examinations and practical work as a Fähnrich (Cadet Sergeant). Having qualified as a flyer and a navigator there was only one other specialist subject left and Ennec duly joined the Artillery School at Jüterbog on 1 June 1933 for further night-flying skills. He completed his course here at the end of January 1933 and emerged as an Oberfähnrich (Senior Cadet Sergeant) on 25 January. On 15 May 1933 the Luftschutzamt (Air Defence Office) of the Weimar Republic had become the Luftkommandoamt (Office of Air Command) under Goering and the expansion of the air arm as a separate force got underway, still partially of course in secret. One significant move was made on 1 October 1933 when the setting up of the first dive-bomber group was ordered, the Fighter Group 132 being assigned the job of providing initial dive-bomber training using the first Heinkel He 50 biplanes for the task.

Ennec's first official job on completion of his training was as Kompanie-und Rekrutenoffizier with his old regiment, again at Hanover, in which capacity he served until the end of August, being promoted to Leutnant (Pilot Officer) on 2 March backdated to 1 August 1933. He continued as Kompanieoffizier in Nachrichtenausbildungs-und versuchskommando Jüterbog-Altes Lager during September of 1934 and in the same post between October and the end of the year at Halle/Saale.

This marked the end of his army career but it also marked the beginning of something much more permanent, his marriage, for it was at Halle/Saale that he first met his future wife. One of the sports in which the young officer aviator partook at this time was horse riding and while following what we now call 'show-jumping' and similar pursuits Ennec met Hella Seydel, the second daughter of the lawyer and solicitor Dr Max Seydel and his wife Hedwig. The attraction of the young officer and Hella proved mutual.

As Bärbel Wilke recalled: 'She was deeply involved in horse

riding and participated until her marriage frequently and successfully in national riding competitions. She had become a professional riding teacher although she did not have to live on this because her father was well-to-do and owned a large house, participating in the social life of Halle. Later I learned to know him as the best and most patient grandfather I can imagine, although he had more-or-less lost his earlier position after the war.

'My father and my mother's father were not at all of the same character, which led to occasional outbursts on my father's side followed by my grandfather's offended silence. However they treated each other with respect in regard to their own particular talents.'

Despite this the young couple's courtship flourished, blotting out to some extent for them the great social changes that were now taking place in Germany, with Hitler firmly at the helm and Goering given full rein to build up the new Luftwaffe in the shortest possible time. Ennec, with all other air-trained young officers, was compulsorily transferred into the Air Force on 1 January 1935. He became a fighter pilot instructor in the Fliegergruppe Schleibheim, a post which he held until March 1936, being given the rank of Oberleutnant (Flying Officer) on 1 October 1935. At this time he became Adjutant of the same fighter group, a position he held until January 1936. In March he moved to Kitzingen to take up a new post with the erstwhile Fighter Group 165 which was in the process of refitting as a dive-bomber unit. This was only a temporary transfer as a fighter pilot, therefore, before Ennec finally took up what was to be his main lifetime's task. On 1 April 1936 he became Staffeloffizier zbV of the 2 Staffel in I/StukaGeschwader 165 dive-bomber unit, and began to perfect the special skills which dive-bombing entailed. Ennec was fully engrossed with this new task from then until the end of March 1939.

Perhaps 'fully engrossed' is not quite correct, on 19 March 1937, he and Hella were married and moved into a little flat inside the newly built officers' mess at Schweinfurt airbase. This was to be their home for the next few turbulent years. Their first-born, one of three daughters, was born on 27 January 1939. Bärbel recalls family life in the immediate pre-war and early wartime years: 'Looking at the dates of my father's posts before and during the war it is obvious that he had only limited opportunity to play his proper role as a father. My mother, like many mothers in those days, stayed at home waiting for him, first in Schweinfurt, later, when air attacks against Schweinfurt became heavier and heavier, in a small village not far from Halle. We visited my grandparents in Halle very often.'

Ennec's dive-bomber unit, I/Sturzkampfgeschwader 165 was one of the new units which took part in operations connected with the remilitarisation of the Rhineland on 7 March 1936, Hitler's first successful act of calling the Allies' bluff. It must have been an occasion of special significance to Ennec when his Staffel, with one other, moved from Kitzingen to Frankfurt/Main airfield ready to back up the troops if the French reacted violently. Amazingly, the French did not react and the British merely stated that the Germans were moving into their own backyard. It was just as well, as Ennec's crews had only been together for a short time and their skills were extremely rudimentary. On 18 August Ennec was appointed Leader of the Horstkompanie I/165 and, on 9 October, Leader of the 2 Staffel. On 1 March 1937, he became Staffelkapitän of the 4 Staffel of II/StG165 when it was set up first at Schweinfurt, then at Wetheim.

Although Ennec himself did not go to Spain, practical experience of dive-bombing and ground-support was being obtained there. One of the first groups of Heinkel He51 fighters was sent out with the Legion Kondor to take part in the Civil War in November 1936. This unit was 3 Staffel of Jagdgruppe 88 under Oberleutnant Pitcairn, 14 He 51s being shipped out from the German Baltic ports and joining their commander, Major-General Sperrle, at the front. It was soon found that the He 51 was no match as a fighter for the Russian Rata or the American Curtiss fighters used by the Republican forces and so they were utilised instead to great effect in the ground-attack role. This experience was put to immediate practical use and a special staff force Fliegerführer zbV was set up for special evaluation duties with a team of experts under Adolf Galland. They worked out detailed guidelines on the organisation, training and operation of ground-attack forces. The original He 50 and He 51 aircraft were replaced at first by Hs 123s as an interim measure but, by 1938, there were a large number of Stukagruppen being formed and they were refitting as soon as possible with a new monoplane dive-bomber designed for the job. This was the Junkers Ju 87A (Anton), the famous Stuka. Between 1 and 10 October 1938, these took part in Operation GREEN, the occupation of the Sudetenland close to Ennec's family home. Early in the following year II/StG 165 became StG 51.

The future of the dive-bomber in the Luftwaffe was set out in some detail with the drawing-up of the 'Concentrated Aircraft Procurement Programme' on 7 November 1938. In this document it was laid down that the Sturzkampfgeschwader were to be expanded to a total of eight. These were to be equipped with the new Junkers Ju 87–B (Bertha), then about to enter front-line service to replace the Anton but it was next planned that these would, in their turn, be phased out with the anticipated introduction of the Messerschmitt Me 210 twin-engined dive-bomber, then still in planning stage. This statement is interesting for it clearly shows that the Me 210 was all along intended as a dive-bomber replacement whereas British statements both during the war and after, have insisted that this aircraft was a replacement for the long-range Me 110 fighter aircraft.

This programme was initiated at once with the original units forming the basis for several new formations as the overall numbers of squadrons mushroomed. A considerable amount of re-numbering followed as this expansion continued, typically II/StG 77 was formed from the StG 51 on 1 May 1939 at Breslau-Schöngarten. By 1 July 1939, a total of 27 dive-bomber squadrons had been formed giving the Luftwaffe an establishment strength of 366 Junkers Ju 87–Bs, each Gruppe having a paper strength of 40 aircraft. Ennec was at this time serving on the Stab (Staff) of StG 77 which he had joined on 1 July 1939 after three months at the Höhere Luftwaffenschule in Gatow. It was with the establishment of this new unit that he was serving on the eve of the Polish campaign. His commander was Hauptmann Graf Clemens von Schönborn, while in overall command of the whole of StG 77 was Günter Schwartzkopff, the famous 'Stuka Father' who, like Ennec, had an army background.

War operations started on 1 September 1939, with II/StG 77 working initially in the northern area of Poland as part of

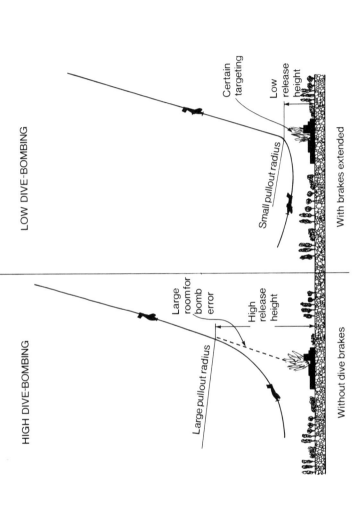

Fig 6 From the 1941 edition of the German magazine *Flugsport*. Showing the effectiveness of the slatted dive-brakes as fitted to the Junkers Ju 87

Luftflotte 1 commanded by General Kesselring, supporting 4 Army. Preliminary strikes were often delayed by the fog and overcast weather conditions and thus insufficient strikes were made against Polish airfields and similar targets on Day One to ensure the complete eradication of aerial opposition. Indeed many Stuka strikes were re-directed to other targets following some confusion earlier. Once the Polish air force had been eliminated, however, the Stukas were unleashed in what was to become the classic Blitzkrieg, co-ordinating their attacks closely with the forward units of the army to an extent unthought-of in the West. Every available aircraft was used to smash opposition and wipe out hard centres of enemy resistance as the fast-moving Panzer armies struck deep through static defences in great enveloping movements. Here it was that the dive-bomber, with its inherent bonus of reliable accuracy, came firmly into its own and targets like rail and road bridges, marshalling yards, crossroads, arms depots, barracks, gun emplacements, fortresses, HQ posts and even, on one occasion, an armoured train, were quickly eliminated. The exponents of strategical bombing saw the long-range bomber winning the war by smashing distant targets far behind the front line. But with the dive-bomber there was no need to smash tank and aircraft factories because they could be occupied by the ground forces intact and used by one's own side, a far swifter and more economical use of forces in the long run.

The cumulative effect caused the maximum disruption to Polish communications in the immediate rear area, and was widely anticipated (indeed the whole Blitzkrieg concept had been widely discussed before the war and dismissed as impracticable by Western experts other than those who followed Liddell-Hart). What was not widely expected, however, was the paralysing effect that the Stuka in a near-vertical dive would have on unseasoned troops to whom such accurate bombing was a revelation. The psychological effect was very unnerving as the aircraft made a lot of noise on the way down. Once it was realised just how demoralising this was, the Stuka units were fitted with small sirens to emphasise this demoralising scream still more.

But if the exponents of strategic bombing were amazed by the dive-bomber's success, so were the equally vociferous advocates of 'back-area' bombing, like von Richthofen, the nephew of the First World War ace, who originally believed that this was all the Stuka was capable of. They too were rapidly confounded. The dive-bombers took a direct part in the actual land battles, hitting troops disembarking from trains or in the process of forming up for assaults, cutting swathes through cavalry units with fragmentation-bombs and machine-gun fire, hemming in whole armies and blasting them into submission. Finally they also participated in massed air attacks on defensive positions in Warsaw itself, proving that they were just as capable of urban target selection also. Thus they earned the title and laurel of 'Flying Artillery'.

For the loss of a mere 31 of the more than 300 Stukas employed, the dive-bomber units were the outstanding factor in the quick defeat of Poland. Ennec's squadron, II/StG 77, had earlier moved up to Neudorf, their operational airfield to the west of Oppelnon on the afternoon of 25 August. On the original projected 'Day One' they had stood to take part in the initial operations, co-operating closely with the 1st and 4th Armoured Divisions of Major-General Hoepner's XVI Army Corps, but so dense was the fog over much of the region that Ennec's unit remained grounded throughout the whole morning. Not until noon did the haze lift sufficiently for the Stukas to get into the air. At once reports started to be received of strong Polish resistance being given by large concentrations of cavalry at Wielun and Dzialozyn. Strong Stuka attacks were mounted against these formations by I/StG 1 and I/StG 77 and the Poles were annihilated or dispersed. Dive-bombers against cavalry: this was the action that set the keynote of that fateful campaign. As one German historian was to write: 'Without his Panzers on the ground and his Stukas in the air, Hitler's blitz campaign at the beginning of the Second World War would have been unthinkable. Again and again it was the Ju 87–B dive-bomber that struck the mortal blow. Above all it was the Stuka that cleared the way for the German armour and infantry, and made rapid victory possible.'

StG 77 matched these words with deeds. On 2 September they were continually in action with precision attacks on troop concentrations in the Radomsko strongpoint, allowing the two armoured columns to penetrate through them and wheel northward towards Warsaw itself. They crossed the river Warte and, at the Battle of Ilza on 9 September 1939, the Stukas were thrown in en masse to tip the scales.

In the words of the Staffelkapitän himself: 'With their white crosses on their backs, the tanks showed us the way. Wherever they went, we came across throngs of Polish troops, against which our 100-lb fragmentation-bombs were deadly. After that we went almost down to the deck firing our machine-guns. The confusion was indescribable.'

With the crumbling of their armies in the field the final stand by the Poles was scheduled to take place around their capital city, Warsaw, and nearby Modlin. By 24 September the German armies had closed in and prepared for bitter street-by-street battles with the entrenched garrison, 100,000 strong. In order to save such bloodshed on both sides in what was known to be a hopeless cause, Goering ordered von Richthofen to mount a series of massive air attacks to persuade the Polish garrison to surrender. These were duly initiated on 25 September. All eight Stukagruppen were employed in this task, with a total of 240 dive-bombers, a few long-range bombers (for the bulk had been withdrawn to face the inert Western Front) and a group of old Junkers Ju 52 transports laden with incendiaries, about 400 planes in all. Ennec's unit, like the other dive-bombers, had to make up to three sorties in one day to maintain a steady stream of aircraft over the western part of the city. Starting at first light, by the time he was over the city for the second time in mid-morning Ennec had great difficulty in making out his particular target because of the huge pall of smoke from the burning flour mills which rose up above the stricken city to a height of some 10,000 ft masking everything. The German artillery commanders with the besieging 8 Army also complained that the smoke was making their task equally difficult but, at Hitler's express order, the attacks continued unabated.

Next day Ennec's dive-bombers were switched to attack targets at Modlin to the north in a similar manner. Here, at the confluence of the rivers Vistula and Bug, the Polish General Przedrzmirski held out with what was left of the Polish 8 and 20 Infantry Divisions and the Mazow and Nowogrod Cavalry Brigades. Two days of intensive operations by the German dive-bombers followed. Both Warsaw and Modlin surrendered on 28 September 1939, and the Polish campaign was over. A whole nation had been conquered in three weeks, as a result of the Stukas. Next day Ennec was awarded the Knight's Cross, 2nd Class, for his work.

As the very bad weather of the winter of 1939/40 caused repeated delays to the expected German offensive in the west, operational flying by Luftwaffe units was deliberately kept low and the squadrons refitted and refurbished. Ennec was able to spend a good deal of time with his family although training and preparations continued at a high level of activity. Many vital lessons had been learnt and these were duly absorbed in readiness for the more severe test to come. The new B–2 mark of Stuka was now operational and, in the general re-organising that followed, Ennec, still a Hauptmann, was given command of the whole of II/StG 2. On 15 October 1939, he officially became the first proper Gruppenkommandeur of this unit.

Ennec's dive-bombers were a part of Luftflotte 2 assigned to assist Army Group B in forcing the line of the Maas and the Albert Canal, by destroying or capturing the strong line of Belgian fortresses that barred the way across the Flanders plain. Heavy siege guns had torn the old forts asunder in 1914, but in 1940 new ideas were to be put into practice. To take their place, the modern successor, the airborne assault parties and the Stukas, used precision and speed instead of brute force and battering power.

The great attack went in at first light on 10 May 1940, with the Dutch, Belgian and advanced French and British airfields as the main targets. Vital bridges were seized intact at Vroenhoven and Velwezelt and were held by the assault parties against fierce counter-attacks. To help the assault parties resist, Ennec's Stukas were heavily committed in striking at Belgian troop concentrations around the village of Eben Emael itself where Belgian reserve troops were forming up for an attack, and they also took part in precision raids on Liège fortresses. Targets in the following days were similar, including other forts and strong-points both in Belgium and at the northern end of the Maginot Line. All of these were subjected to pin-point bombing which helped neutralise them.

Ennec said of one typical attack, 'When, near to Namur, a

fortification could not be taken by the ground troops despite every effort, we got the command to attack the enemy Command Bunker itself with bombs. For this operation I called up our reserve squadron from Lippstadt so that our pilots who had not yet been in combat could have a try. After twenty bombs we saw a white flag, and it all ended very quickly after an exchange between the 'Top Brass" of both sides, and our corps gave permission for the French Captain to leave wearing his sword. He said that his troops had to surrender for they could not stand any more of the shock waves caused by our bombs.'

In the wake of II/StG 2's attack on one such strong-point the grateful Infantry Division Commander signalled directly by radio to Ennec's headquarters, 'Thanks to your Stuka attack we took Fort Battiste without a single casualty.'

Other such targets struck were forts near Luttich, at Mauberg, and at Givet. The Maginot Line forts hit were near Weisenburg and the Kaiserstuhl which left them open to direct storming by the infantry. Missions were being flown at an intense sortie rate per day and, once the front line had been overrun, the Stukas were moved up quickly, their operational airstrips changing almost daily to keep up with the pell-mell advance of the racing Panzer columns. It was again weary work in the hot May and June days but, although they were sometimes flying nine sorties per day in direct support missions and were dog-tired, morale was very high. As in Poland they could see the direct result of their intervention everywhere and the collapse of the four Allied armies under their hammer blows was a revelation even to themselves. Losses were even lighter in this campaign. Only 14 Stukas were destroyed in the first four days' fighting on the Western Front against the cream of the Allied fighter forces.

Once more Ennec's targets included columns of advancing and retreating troops, concentrations of infantry, and gun batteries whenever the enemy tried to make a stand. As they plunged on across France and Flanders II/StG 2 was also called in for the first time against a new target, Allied tanks. This action took place during one of the rare French counter-attacks, when Colonel Charles de Gaulle led his tank force out from Bruyères on 17 May and set out towards Montcornet in the hope of severing the Panzer columns' corridor. He did not get far before Ennec's dive-bombers found him and so the Stukas tried their luck against the lumbering French tanks. Many near-misses were in fact achieved and the French were forced to withdraw, but afterwards it was found that no tanks had actually been destroyed by this method, although several were put out of action by having their tracks torn off by the blast. Machine-gunning their vulnerable engine spaces at the rear was more effective in bringing them to a halt. Thus a second French thrust was halted in short order by the same methods. In a citation received at the time for his work in France it was stated that: 'In the counter-attacks by French tanks near Philippeville the Stuka attacks of his group dispersed them near Evreux railway station.'

Very soon they were just within range of the English Channel and began to turn their attention to the harbours, docks and the ships operating outside. Ennec personally led many such attacks, learning all the time. In dive-bombing missions against ship targets at Dunkirk, Le Havre and La Rochelle during that frenetic period, he was credited with the sinking of four vessels and of hitting and causing heavy damage to another eight. His reputation as a ship-buster was firmly established and was soon to be enhanced. No pre-war training had been undertaken by the normal Stuka crews against such targets, notoriously the most difficult to hit, but Ennec rapidly began to build up his own unique techniques and tactics.

With the fall of France the bulk of the Luftwaffe was granted a brief respite to prepare themselves for the final mission, the invasion of Britain. The principal tasks for the dive-bombers, once the army had got ashore, were to remain those of close support but, until that time, they had to be allocated secondary tasks. Their limited range marked them down for precision attacks on radar stations, harbours and coastal convoys in the interim period leading up to what was to become known as the Battle of Britain. The elimination of the RAF airfields along the south coast of England was to follow; meanwhile, the convoys plodding up and down the Channel gave them the chance to contribute to the blockade and the elimination of the anti-invasion destroyer forces of the Royal Navy. Concentrated at St Omer and St Trond airfields Ennec had II/StG 2 built up to full strength of 43 aircraft once more, including his own Stab Staffel of three aircraft. For most of the convoy battles and the Battle of Britain period Ennec's command operated closely with StG 3.

Meanwhile, on 28 May 1940, Ennec was awarded the Knight's Cross, 1st Class, for his work and on 25 July his promotion to Major (Squadron Leader) was accompanied by the award of the coveted Ritterkreuz. After the award ceremony he took the opportunity to spend a brief leave with his family. The initial fighting in the west had taken place almost in their backyard, but now the front was the coast and far away.

His chances of seeing his family were to become more and more rare as the struggle, at the time thought by many in Germany to be almost over, became more grim and widespread. From 19 July 1940, it was as Major Enneccerus that he led II/StG 2 into its severest tests so far. The unit, based at its airfields in Normandy, found that they were in easy range of the whole south coast of England. They were part of von Richthofen's VIII Fliegerkorps and, at full strength, found themselves ready to take part in the initial assaults on the valuable convoys sailing past their doorstep to the Thames and the port of London. In effect Britain's lifelines had become the new battleground. The opening moves, leading to the Battle of Britain, were getting under way.

On 4 July StG 2 hit a large convoy outward-bound into the Atlantic and heading down-Channel. The devastation they caused to this convoy, OA178, caused a political and inter-service row in Britain with wide repercussions. Four ships were sent to the bottom totalling 15,856 tons, while a further nine, totalling 40,236 tons, were badly damaged. Attacks on the Portland naval base at the same time sank the brand new 5582-ton naval AA-ship *Foylebank* which bristled with long- and short-range guns. It was a major victory. There had been no standing patrol of fighters overhead to protect this convoy, nor were any scrambled to help them until it was too late.

Admiral Sir Max Horton wrote at the time, expressing the Royal Navy's feelings: 'The disgraceful episode of Convoy 178 is a blatant indication of the complete absence of co-operation by Air Force and the perils of divided responsibility – this convoy coming down Channel was attacked by relays of bombers off Portland between 1 and 2 pm – six at a time for two hours – some ten ships were sunk, fired or damaged . . . no fighters and no escort worth talking about.'

The Royal Navy's ire was compounded by a statement by a Fighter representative who said that their role was the defence of Britain and not the defence of our ships. Such was the anger this attitude aroused that the Premier, Winston Churchill, had personally to intervene and directly order a standing patrol of six fighters over convoys during the hours of daylight; but no such big ships were used again, instead only the small coasting-type vessels were risked in the English Channel. Ennec's first mission had been a significant success.

On 11 July Portland harbour was the objective of another Stuka attack by both StG 2 and StG 77 which this time the RAF managed to intercept. Nonetheless the dive-bombers sank the cargo ship *Eleanor Brooke* (1037 tons), the patrol ship *Warrior II* and damaged the merchant ships *City of Melbourne* (6630 tons), *Kylemount* (704 tons) and *Peru* (6971 tons). This set the pattern for Ennec's unit as July passed into August. They gradually became more and more proficient at hitting these elusive targets and developed techniques which were to stand them in good stead later. On 8 August the Stukas were sent in to finish off convoy CW9 which had been decimated by E-boat attack the night before. Again the Royal Air Force intercepted them and claimed 31 German aircraft for the loss of 20 of their own, but that did not save the merchantmen, *Coquetdale* (1597 tons) and *Empire Crusader* (1042 tons) which were sent to the bottom, while hits were made on *Balmaha* (1428 tons), *John M* (500 tons) and *Scheldt* (497 tons). The Allied ships *Surte*, *Omlandia*, *Veeneburgh* and *Tres* were all hit and had to be towed in, the last-named sinking.

With the start of Adlertag (Eagle Day) on 13 August the tempo increased and now the targets were airfields and radar stations along the defensive coastal area of southern England, as well as naval bases and shipping, in the first stage of the softening-up process preceding the planned invasion. On this day Ennec's unit took off to attack the RAF fighter base of Middle Wallop in Hampshire. Protecting Spitfires intercepted some of them on their return from this attack and, in Ennec's own words, 'ripped our backs open to the collar'. One of his Staffeln was caught over Lyme Bay and lost six out of nine aircraft. It was not all one-sided, however; in another incident when 59 Fighter Squadron RAF swooped down on one Gruppe the Stukas had already formed up on their defensive formation and their rear-gunners gave the British a ruefully acknowledged mauling instead.

On 15 August a heavy attack was made by II/StG 2 on Lympne. They devastated the airfield, putting it out of action for two days in one of the most successful German attacks of the whole battle. On the afternoon of 16 August a heavy dive-bomber assault was mounted against RAF Tangmere by StG 2. This was both accurate and heavy, and the airfield installations and command posts were destroyed. Much damage was inflicted including several Hurricanes and six Blenheims destroyed on the ground by Stukas. Again RAF fighters appeared and nine Ju 87s were shot down and three damaged. This day, however, total British losses were 50 against the German 38. There was a lull on 17 August but next day battle was renewed in earnest. Ennec's unit was one of four Gruppen dispatched by VIII Fliegerkorps and they hit the airfield at Warmwell. Other groups suffered heavily at the hands of the defending fighters and had to be withdrawn from the fight.

In readiness for the next phase of the battle, which was moving further inland and out of Stuka range, Ennec's unit, with others, were now re-grouped to prepare for their true role of Army support for the invasion. On 7 September II/StG 2 had a total strength of 27 aircraft, of which 22 were serviceable. They now came under command of II Fliegerkorps in the Pas de Calais area and were in a tactical position for army support in the expected invasion operations. Reports of dive-bombers concentrating across the Straits were taken by many in Britain as sure indication that the invasion was imminent; that invasion never came but their presence during the waiting period was a constant menace. This period was one of recuperation for Ennec and his young aircrew, but behind-the-scenes steps were already being taken that were to lead to their next assignment.

The entry of Italy into the war on 10 June meant that the Mediterranean Sea was a fresh battleground and the dominance of the Royal Navy in those waters over the Italian fleet, superior in numbers though it was, gave the British a series of naval victories which offset somewhat their land defeats in

Europe. This was emphasised by the attack on Taranto naval base by torpedo-bombers from the aircraft-carrier *Illustrious* in November. Stung by this and by endless Italian reverses in the North African desert Hitler, busy preparing for his reckoning with Stalin, was forced to send crack units south to bail out his floundering ally. These movements were encompassed in Directive Number 18 issued on 12 November 1940. Gibraltar was to be taken and, the Straits thus closed, the Royal Navy would be driven from the Western Mediterranean. In order to accomplish this, 'Dive-bomber units, in particular, are to be transferred to Spain to engage naval targets and to support the attack on the Rock.' These duties would require special ship-busting skills from the Stukas and Ennec's unit, among others, had already built up an enviable record in this respect so there was little doubt that II/StG 2 would be among the dive-bomber units employed in Operation FELIX. But again it was not to be. Franco's refusal to commit his nation led to the abandonment of this idea on 10 December, and new plans were laid instead.

On the same date the transfer of X Fliegerkorps under command of General Hans Ferdinand Geisler, with Oberst Harlinghausen, the anti-shipping expert, as his Chief-of-Staff, was ordered. By January 1941 this had been built up to a strength of 120 long-range bombers, 40 fighters, 20 reconnaissance machines and, the tip of the spear that was to drive the Royal Navy from the Mediterranean, 150 Stukas, among them Ennec's command. Top of their priorities was one task. '*Illustrious muss sinken.*' This they assiduously prepared to do. While Geisler and his staff set up their headquarters in a hotel at Taormina the Stukas moved into specially readied airfields in Sicily, Comisio, Catania and, for II/StG 2 and Captain Werner Hozzel's I/StG 1, Trapani. Here under the baking Mediterranean sun they camouflaged their Stukas in the new pattern of black and grey mottling on the upper surfaces and half black and white below to match their new surroundings. They also set about preparing to close the Straits of Sicily to the parade of convoys of reinforcements that had been flooding through to Malta and Egypt almost at will under the protection of the fleets of Cunningham and Somerville from east and west respectively. A floating mock-up of their principal target, the armoured-decked aircraft-carrier *Illustrious*, was anchored off the island and practice formations and bomb-load groupings were tried out and evaluated.

Illustrious was no easy target. Unlike American and Japanese aircraft-carriers (and the older British ones such as *Ark Royal*) the main flying deck, although presenting a large oblong aiming area some 620 ft by 95 ft in area, was known to be protected. Beneath this was a single vulnerable hangar of 458 ft by 45 ft filled with aircraft and 50,000 gallons of fuel oil. The flight deck itself had 3-in. armour protection, puny compared to a battleship's, but thought, at the time she was built, to be capable of stopping 500-lb bombs from penetrating. It was pierced fore and aft by two large lifts, which were not armoured. Below these again were the vital engine and boiler rooms. For defence she had 16 of the new 4.5-in. AA-guns and a host of smaller weapons, as well as the protective gunfire of two battleships and many lesser vessels. She carried Fairey Fulmar fighters, themselves made-over compromises from an aborted pre-war dive-bomber concept which had then been adapted as a three-seater fighter/recce aircraft. The German experts studied reports on the great aircraft-carrier and estimated that four direct hits would be sufficient to sink her. First the fighter patrol would be lured away; this was to be done by a preliminary torpedo-bomber assault by the Italians. Then the first Stukas would go for the escorting battleships, drawing away their heavy flak protection in a similar manner. This would leave *Illustrious* to her own defences. The majority of the Junkers Ju 87s would then strike her in a series of diverging attacks in two waves. The first wave would hit her with 550-lb fragmentation bombs with direct action fuses set to decimate her own anti-aircraft gunners, then, all her defences breached, the latter wave, also of Ennec's II/StG 2, would finish her off with 1000-lb bombs with delayed-action fuses which would easily punch through her deck armour.

The Stukas lacked the range to seek her out in the distant base of Alexandria in Egypt, but Admiral Andrew Cunningham, having swept the Italian Navy from that area and outfaced the Regia Aeronautica likewise, scorned the Luftwaffe also and brought his great ships right into the Sicilian Channel in defence of an important convoy. The British knew of the arrival of the Stukas in Sicily but the Chief Air Marshal,

Tedder, had but recently assured Cunningham that dive-bombers were harmless, 'our fighter pilots weep for joy when they see them', he boasted. Cunningham was a sailor not an airman, so he took his fellow professional's judgement as being correct and sailed on. Not all the British officers in the fleet believed the RAF's estimation of their foe, however. Both Admiral Lyster and *Illustrious*'s Commander, Captain Boyd, repeatedly advised that there was no necessity for *Illustrious* to steam so close to the convoy as her fighters could protect it from a safer distance, but this advice was overruled. Thus it fell out that, just after midday on 10 January, *Illustrious* presented Enneccerus and his companions with the opportunity they had been waiting for. The plan worked perfectly and the Stukas were able to concentrate over their target despite being picked up at 28 miles range by the radar of their victim. This was at 12.28. At once the Fighter Direction Officer issued a hasty recall signal to his fighters which were busy chasing the Italians at sea-level, and ordered more fighters to be brought up on deck and catapulted off. The ship had to turn into wind to do this, breaking defensive formation, and, as she did so at 12.35, the Stukas were sighted visually off her port bow at about 12,000 ft in a 'large loose formation estimated at 30–40'. The Fulmars were being flown off as the guns opened up in a desperate long-range barrage a minute later.

Seeing the fighters speeding off the decks and the first flak bursts blackening the sky, Ennec knew that he had to make his attack right away while conditions were entirely favourable. He had caught the British fleet flat-footed but he still had to act fast. He ordered the first unit into position to execute their attack dives immediately and carry the first part of the plan, while he took the rest of this formation in a wide sweep astern of the fleet. As so often practised, each formation constantly changed height as well as relative position to confuse the flak sight-setters, thus making the AA-fire relatively ineffective. Hozzel's men then started the ball rolling, pushing over from about 12,000 ft in the first dive, checking at about 7000 ft average and then going into their final aiming attack dives, with release at an average of 1000 ft, though varying widely according to the bomb-load carried. In order to disorientate the gunners further many continued down below this height, some almost to flight-deck level, to machine-gun the ship's deck as diversions to assist their comrades following them down.

In the conventional Stuka style, which many in the Mediterranean Fleet were seeing for the first time, the three waves hit in turn with each wave consisting of two ketten of three aircraft, each carrying simultaneous attacks from different bearings, the majority coming in from astern or off the ship's quarter. This meant that, at any given time, at least six dive-bombers were diving on the ship, further splitting the defensive fire. Each wave took about one minute with a half-minute pause before the next. The diving angle was varied also, from 60 degrees up to 80 degrees. In spite of themselves the British sailors were impressed. Their first sight of Stukas at work did not match Tedder's disparaging estimate in the least. 'Severe and brilliantly executed', was how one report read, while Cunningham himself later wrote that it was clear they were watching 'complete professionals'. The British Admiral's flagship, the battleship *Warspite*, was hit a glancing blow by one Stuka bomb, the other battleship, *Valiant*, blew one of her attackers to pieces at close range by her massed AA-weapons, but this diversion had done its job. AA-gunners on *Illustrious* herself claimed three victims while the Fulmars, once they had panted their way into the sky, claimed to have destroyed two more 'certains' as they chased them back over Sicily. Despite these claims Walter's men did their job and did it well. Far from the four hits required they registered no less than six direct hits and three near-misses on the carrier.

All her after-guns, 4.5-in. and pompoms were put out of action by the initial hits and big fires were started by the latter ones which punched through her decks and went down her lift wells causing carnage and inferno inside her hangar decks. Luckily for the carrier no bomb got through to her engine rooms and so she was able to steer a shaky course for Malta dockyard to effect temporary repairs. There was a three-hour lull before the second attack came in at 16.40 with just 15 Stukas. Again they attacked in two groups, the first scoring two near misses, the second hitting the carrier again on the after-lift and scoring two very close misses alongside. Now little more than a floating wreck, *Illustrious* was saved by darkness and she managed to reach Valletta harbour.

Despite this notable victory Ennec's men were early astir the next day, led by a Heinkel 111, seeking the carrier which was thought to be heading eastward for safety. In fact she was so badly damaged that she had to remain at Malta for a considerable time being patched up, but that early morning sortie was not without results of an equally spectacular type. Instead of the carrier Ennec and his men happened upon a formation of warships speeding eastward some 300 miles east of Sicily. The British sailors thought that they were safe here from Stuka attack and many were at 'rest' positions. These vessels were the 10,000-ton cruisers *Gloucester* and *Southampton* with the escorting destroyers *Defender* and *Diamond*. None of the ships was equipped with radar and, despite the events of the previous day, and the fact that *Southampton* had faced Stukas fitted with long-range fuel-tanks off Norway a few months earlier, surprise was again complete.

Splitting his 12 Stukas between the two bigger ships Ennec led the attack from out of the sun. No guns opened fire until after the attack was completed and no losses were suffered by the German dive-bombers. The results were impressive. *Gloucester* was struck by one bomb, thought to be Ennec's, which burst inside her armoured Director Control Tower and wrecked her bridge, killing nine men and wounding a further 14 there. It failed to explode, otherwise the devastation would have been infinitely greater than it was. *Southampton* was far less fortunate. There were two, possibly three, direct hits with 250-kg delayed-action fused bombs which had incendiaries attached. One or more of these bombs perforated 'X' gundeck, the wardroom and gunroom flat and burst in the main W/T office. It caused extensive internal damage and all the watertight doors near the detonation points were shattered. Intense fires broke out involving the whole of the after-superstructure and the wardroom flats and a large number of off-duty officers and petty officers were killed outright.

'Y' magazine was flooded but as the flooding arrangements to the 4-in. and 'X' magazine were wrecked these spaces could not be flooded. The bomb which hit here entered the port seaplane hangar, perforated the ERA's pantry and exploded on the protective deck above 'A' boiler room. Again it caused enormous internal damage and the protective deck split open, the superheater pipe was blown off from the boiler and the compartment abandoned. Many important engine-room staff were killed. Damage and casualties to these important personnel prevented any effective damage control measures being taken. The fire raging aft was being fought with some success until 'A' boiler room was abandoned and in turn caught fire. All the water supply and power was lost and after that both fires raged uncontrolled throughout the inside of the cruiser. She was abandoned and *Gloucester* put one torpedo into her while the cruiser *Orion*, which had in the interim come to her aid, added four more before she finally sank. She was the largest warship sunk by bombing alone up to that date, and her loss and the damage to *Illustrious* and *Gloucester* had a profound effect on future naval strategy in the central Mediterranean. Henceforth all large warships were banned and special 'Stuka sanctuaries' were defined by the navy outside effective dive-bomber range into which ships would flee at the approach of daylight. Thus, in two days, Ennec and his young pilots had achieved what no other enemy had done before, driven the Royal Navy from the central Mediterranean. It was a striking victory and the lessons Enneccerus had imparted were to be driven home again and again in the months that followed.

From 13 February until 18 October 1941 Ennec's unit was fully employed as the spearhead of the newly formed Fliegerführer Afrika on the North African mainland, supporting General Rommel's audacious thrusts that pushed the hitherto victorious British Army back to Egypt and isolated Tobruk. After the comparative civilisation of being based in France and Italy the desert was something new to Ennec. As well as the high tempo at which the campaign was waged, with the Stukas in constant demand in a very fluid situation and for siege work pounding the Tobruk garrison, the environment was hardly ideal. On one occasion Ennec was bitten by a scorpion that had taken refuge in his hand luggage. He survived that and the numerous missions leading his dive-bombers against such diverse targets as AA-sites, tank columns, supply units and dug-in artillery positions as well as constant sorties in company with Giuseppe Cenni's Stukas to harass the warships supplying Tobruk along the coastal route. Early on in this period, however, at the end of March, Ennec took his group back to Graz in

Austria for replenshing and re-equipping with the new 'tropicalised' Stukas before returning to the desert. While there he
became involved in the Battle for Crete.

He was on patrol over the eastern Mediterranean on 25 May,
with his 20 Stukas, searching for troop transports heading for
Tobruk. At around 13.00 he was on the point of turning back to
the extreme limit of their range, between Bardia and Mersa
Matruh, when they sighted elements of the British Fleet returning from an attack on Scarpanto airfield. At once Ennec
ordered his dive-bombers into the attack. Their targets included the battleships *Queen Elizabeth* and *Barham*, the aircraft-
carrier *Formidable* and eight destroyers. At 13.20 Ennec un-
hesitatingly led in against the prime target, *Formidable*, sister
ship of *Illustrious*. He was followed down by his section leaders
Oberleutnant Eyer, Hamester and Jakob. Again the carrier
was caught off-guard and again she was still desperately trying
to fly off her Fulmar fighters as the first bombs arrived. One
direct hit smashed into her starboard side and the resultant
explosion ripped her open between 17 and 24 bulkheads, starting a fire. Another bomb crashed into one of the 4.5-in. gun
positions, 'X' turret, causing further havoc. Several of the
Stukas, seeing the carrier hard hit and on fire, directed their
attacks at the escorting ships. The destroyer *Nubian* took one
Stuka's main bomb full square on her after-gun deck, 'Y'
mounting, which was wiped out and with it her depth-charges
ignited blowing off her entire stern section. Serious fires broke
out which were contained only with great difficulty. Although
her entire stern and rudder had gone her propellers and shafts
somehow survived and she managed to stagger back to Alexandria. Both ships were put out of action for over a year.

Constant missions were flown against Tobruk to wear down
the defenders, some 60 attacks were mounted that summer with
up to 30 or 40 dive-bombers at a time. At this period Ennec's
unit, based near Dernia, then moved forward with the flow of
the battle. Towards the end of the year they were withdrawn to
refit. On 13 January 1942, Ennec was assigned as Komman-
deur of III/StG 3 when II/StG 2 was so re-designated and
merged. Ennec's Stab with 7 and 8 Staffeln was based at San
Pancrazio with 9 Staffel at San Pietro and over the next three
months undertook many missions during the savage blitz

against the island fortress of Malta.

The new mark of Stuka, the D–1 (Doras), were now joining service which enabled much larger bomb-loads to be carried and these were delivered with good effect into Valletta dockyard. Many ships were sunk there in the almost non-stop attacks of this period and others badly damaged until at last the warship striking forces were driven from the island. Among Ennec's victims were the destroyers *Lance* and *Gallant* bombed in dock on 9 April, *Kingston* bombed in dock on 11 April, submarines *P39*, on 26 March, *P36* and *Pandora* on 1 April, and the minesweeper *Abingdon* on 5 April. The blitz was to continue in order to assist the planned occupation of the island, Operation HERCULES, but, as with Operation SEA LION, continual postponements eventually led to its abandonment. On 10 May they made their final attack and then they returned to the desert campaigns once more, settling into their new base of Bir el Hania by 20 May. Their dive-bombers had to be 'tropicalised', that is, fitted with sand filters for the engine intakes and they themselves were also equipped with special desert survival packs. Ennec had been appointed Fliegerführer Afrika on 1 May 1942, but this post he held for only a very brief period until Major Bernhard Hamester relieved him on 13 May.

After a short stopover in transit through Germany, Ennec joined the desperate battles of the Eastern Front. Initially he joined the operations staff of the Generalkommando des Luftgau at Rostov and served in this position until 18 November. After the death of Major Alfons Orthofer, Ennec was appointed Kommodore of StG 77, heart of the so-called 'Fire Brigade' on the southern section of the front, at Beloretschenskaya. This position he held until 13 February 1943. On that date he was transferred to the so-called Frontflieger-Sammelgruppe, a collection of all available units desperately trying to stem the onrushing Soviet tide after Stalingrad, and on 27 February he was with the Staff of IX Fliegerkorps. These were anxious days but by an outstanding feat of improvisation StG 77 managed to block gap after gap and steady the front to prevent an even greater disaster overtaking them. The Germans no longer had air superiority and the advancing Soviet ground forces often pressed the retreating Germans hard, sometimes threatening to overrun the Stukas at the forward bases. In this connection

Ennec later related a story of how he had very hastily to take full cover during a Russian artillery attack in a countryside lavatory. As he later recalled, he was extremely fortunate in that *everything* was frozen solid!

By 1 March Ennec was Kommodore of the whole Geschwader but he was abruptly dismissed from this position when he refused point-blank to send his unit on a mission which he considered certain suicide. There was some embarrassment at this forthrightness and many secretly agreed with his decision. He risked total dismissal, even a charge of dereliction of duty or worse, but such was his reputation for honesty and endeavour that the whole matter was blamed on stress and ill-health and he was sent back to Germany on extended leave. This marked the end of his Stuka career. He had flown in excess of 200 missions, most of them in the West, and had established himself as one of the leading dive-bomber pilots of his time.

Back at home on 'sick' leave, he took the opportunity to take his family on a winter holiday at Kitzbühel, the first long period they had spent together since the war began. Two other profound events took place this year, 1943, a turning point for Germany and for Ennec himself. His father died, and his second daughter, Heidi, was born on 22 November.

In the increasingly desperate circumstances facing Germany a man of Ennec's calibre was soon forgiven. On 1 April he joined Luftflotte 3 in France on the staff of Generalkommando IX Fliegerkorps and later, from 1 September 1943, he joined the General Staff of the Luftwaffe. On 1 October 1943, he was promoted to Oberstleutnant (Wing Commander). Between 1 March and 18 July 1944 Ennec served with Fliegerführer West placed under Luftflotte 3 in France, before he was again transferred east to Germany's wavering ally, Hungary. Here he found considerable turmoil, with the Russians fast approaching their borders, and Ennec attempted to put some stiffening into Hungary's resistance. Between 29 July and 31 August he served as Liaison Officer with the Hungarian Air Force (under Luftflotte 6) then, from 1 September until 15 March 1945, he saw out the final desperate months of the war in the position of Liaison Officer at Heersgruppe Nord in east Prussia before that also fell to the advancing Soviet army.

Another switch, this time south, took him to perform the

same task at Heeresgruppe Mitte Czechoslovakia where he was taken prisoner by advancing American troops on 9 May. After a short period as a POW he was handed over to the British authorities on 1 June. After cross-examination they found his political past clean and he was discharged, as a Wing Commander, on 6 September 1945.

In the chaos of post-war Germany, divided between the four Great Powers and ruled by Military Governors, there seemed to be only contempt for those fighting men who had bravely performed their duty, and no charity to spare. Like millions of others the Enneccerus family found itself separated, with Ennec in the north and his wife and two daughters still at Halle. As soon as she learned her husband had been released from the POW camp Hella determined to join him in Hamburg. Halle itself was Russian-occupied, and the Russians would have given a great deal to get their hands on one of the much-hated Stuka flyers. Hella's father strongly advised her against taking such risks, for it meant crossing the newly established British–Russian demarcation line, which millions were desperately trying to do. Hella was strong-willed and determined and insisted. Taking Bärbel and Heidi with her she took the risk. Bärbel later described this desperate, illegal journey as 'a frightful flight which I still partly recall', but the brave young wife succeeded, despite the odds.

Reunited with his loved ones Enneccerus gained new strength after the depression which had overtaken him. 'My father confessed later that, had my mother not come, he would have not made any effort to overcome the disaster of his post-war situation.' He took the first job that came his way, and, on 1 October, became a construction worker with the Rathjens company in Hamburg in the British zone, a pitifully inadequate job for his talents and skills but one that at least kept his home and family together through that very hard period. He stoically got on with his work and on 15 October was promoted to timekeeper at the same company's Kiel works, moving as a bookkeeper to the firm of Trümmerverwertungs-Gmbh in May 1951. From September 1952, he held the position of Attorney.

Altogether this was a harsh period for Enneccerus and his family, as his eldest daughter recalls: 'We lived in a small village near Schleswig where my father initially worked as an ordinary construction worker. Later he became a timekeeper which usually kept him away from home during the week. This was a time in which I sometimes did not get on with him very well. He was very strict with me and my sister and got impatient quickly, so I enjoyed the time when he was away rather than the weekends when he was at home. My grandfather once accused him that he treated his children as he had treated his recruits in the old days. Although this was an exaggeration it contained some truth. His behaviour can be explained by his lack of experience of what children are like and by his constantly being reminded that a former officer in the General Staff in many people's eyes had to take the blame for the oppressing consequences of the lost war. There was much that needed to be balanced by my mother's good natured and patient character.

'Things gradually improved after we managed, with my grandfather's support, to move into a larger (and yet still very small) flat in Kiel. My father obtained a somewhat better position in the firm and he could come home every day after work so he was able to devote more time to his three daughters, the youngest of whom, Inge, was born in 1947. He made us all join Kiel gymnastics club and took much interest in our (relatively modest) achievements. I also can recall with much pleasure many bicycle-outings into the beautiful surroundings of Kiel which he organised perfectly. In general he was still very demanding upon his children, often beyond our capabilities, but I am sure he was very fond of his family and treated each of us children with equal justice and growing understanding.'

With the re-emergence of West Germany as a growing power in her own right, the fear of the Soviet Union gradually overcame the Western Allies' hatred of their old enemy. Unwilling to raise powerful enough forces to defend themselves they looked again to Germany to provide a bulwark of men and expertise. The reforming of the German forces included the new Air Force in the Bundeswehr and they sought out men with the expertise and talent to get things started again.

It was like the 1930s all over again in that respect and Ennec had seen it all before. He was invited to return, but hesitated a great deal before he accepted. He finally decided that the Air

Force was the only right and proper profession for which he had full training and experience, and he knew it would certainly give him far more satisfaction than a bookkeeper's job. Initially he spent some time in Ütersen, but then took up the post of Deputy Commander of the Air Force Training Command at Fürstenfeldbruck. In December 1957, he moved his family from the small flat in Kiel and into a large house with a garden near his work. Although this was a heavy new commitment to start upon, the next six years were fruitful ones for his family as a whole. 'I really learned to know and to like my father,' Bärbel recalls. 'He took the time at home to have long discussions with us about nearly every subject and was open to all my questions. I took advantage of his knowledge of maths which he still remembered better than I had understood it at school. We also had a lot of fun with our father and most of his subordinates would not have believed their eyes had they seen how cheerful and relaxed he was at home. His family was his only resort from the growing demands of his new position, he spent all his off-duty time at home. As my mother was content to have the garden, he was happy not to have to travel somewhere during the holidays although he encouraged his daughters to do so in order to widen their horizons. He did not himself buy a car although by then he could have afforded one, partly because he did not see the need, partly he was afraid of the risks of car driving for his family. He conceded, with some reluctance, that my mother took up riding again and paid our riding lessons but could not be persuaded to refresh his own riding, let alone buy a horse of our own.'

This is hardly the portrait one expects of a Stuka leader, but it should not surprise us. Enneccerus, like most professionals, did his duty well and to great effect in the war. Because he was good at his job he was lumped together by wartime propaganda and post-war hysteria with all other German servicemen almost as criminals. They were no more so than Allied officers of any of the services. Enneccerus himself had modest requirements and lived a quiet life. He esteemed good Cognac and certain cigars but did not spend much money on himself. As long as he was comfortable and could educate his children he was not much concerned with money matters. Even when his children left home he kept contact but was particularly careful not to interfere in their affairs but always was ready with advice and support when required. As a leader he had a reputation as an aloof and hard-driving man. This is certainly attributable to his early upbringing in his father's image and his dedication to duty which he expected always of everyone. He always aimed at fulfilling his orders with no respect for his own wishes and welfare, and his subordinates were likewise expected to place their obligations above their personal interests. Not surprisingly, many of a different temperament resented his continual driving.

His daughter remembers: 'He could be frightfully cross with people he found not acting as he expected but he also took considerable effort to help his men out when necessary. He liked to make ironic quips and occasionally shocked people with uncamouflaged sarcastic remarks. When he was asked to be particularly polite to someone (a mistake his mother-in-law sometimes committed) he would often do the exact opposite. Nor did he try very hard to disguise his feelings about people he did not like.'

He was always eager to drive things forward and was resolute in his decisions, but he would spare the time to listen to arguments if they were presented in a competent and precise manner. It was certainly not his way to await events with patience or to stand back and let things take their course. On the other hand it is said that he could be very faithful to people he was fond of, to a degree that made him vulnerable to deep disappointments.

His daughter put this point thus: 'I remember my mother reminding him to be careful in expressing his views at certain high-level meetings. This warning was not unjustified because he used to say always the full truth and to fight vigorously for a matter once he had made it his own. As a man of strong principles and of strict unselfishness he could not be made to accept improper compromises. This did not make him friends in the Luftwaffe and later, post-war, almost certainly contributed to his premature retirement in 1967.'

His last Air Force job was as Deputy Commander and Chief of Staff of German Air Forces at Portz/Wahn, now a suburb of Cologne. He was finally pensioned with the rank of Brigadier-General. Sadly his beloved Hella passed away on the last day of

1970. Such an early parting was one battle Ennec could not overcome. Within a few months he became ill and died. Both he and Hella are buried at Troisdorf.

His career was long and impressive, his achievements as a dive-bomber pilot and leader were legendary. His most fitting epitaph applies equally to all his many facets, as a pilot, as a leader and as a father: 'I could safely rely on him to the end of his life.'

7 Major-General Ivan Polbin

Soviet Air Force   1905–45

In the vast and sprawling empire of Czarist Russia 1905 was a momentous year. The country was already racked by the rumblings and outburst of discontent and rumour of a people harshly treated by an autocratic ruler and held down by secret police. It was also the year that the disastrous war against Japan was lost. For the very first time a major European power had been defeated, and comprehensively defeated at that, by an Asiatic power. The Czarist forces were humiliated. It was little wonder, then, that the stirrings which were taking place were of even greater moment than those that had preceded them over the previous century.

In January 1905 there was revolt in the capital of St Petersburg and in October a similar uprising in Sebastopol. Everywhere there was resentment and ferment, fateful foretastes of the vengeance to come twelve years later. On 6 August some concessions were made by the creation of the first Duma Council of State, but this was seen merely as a sop to the populace and, as a political measure, too little too late.

Also in that year on 27 January (or 14 January by the old Russian calendar). Far away from the seething discontent and upheaval in the great centres of population, there was born in the tiny village of Rtishchevo-Kamenka a male child, later named Ivan Semyonovich Polbin. The village was in Simbirsk Province, now in Maina Raion, Ul'ianovsk Oblast, deep in the heart of the Barabinskaya Steppe, where the Sibirskaya Nizmennost plain rises up towards the great Atlai Mountains which guard northern Mongolia. It was the forgotten meeting place of Europe and Asia, a remote and lonely place, but, lying between the rivers of Ob and Irtysh, a relatively fertile place. It is hard to conceive of the vastness of that mighty land, but Ivan

Polbin's birthplace lay half as far again from Moscow as does Piccadilly Circus. Life there was primitive even by the standards of the day, but the young boy's parents had brought into the world a child destined for a brilliant future and one who was to serve Mother Russia well.

When the revolution came in 1917 it was followed by much fierce fighting between the Red and White Russian forces, in which during 1918–19 the former Allies intervened, somewhat ineffectually. Along the Trans-Siberian railway there was much movement of rival armies, including a large Czech force and even elements of the Royal Navy thousands of miles from salt water at distant Vladivostok. Admiral Alexander V. Kolchak was the leader of the White Russian forces and he became virtual dictator at Omsk in November 1918, but was defeated there a year later when the Red Forces were finally victorious. There was widespread famine as a result of all this turmoil, but in the remote south-eastern corner of the Central Russian Plain much of this turbulence passed by Ivan's small village, despite the fact that it was near a rail link across northern Kazakhskaya. Nonetheless for the growing youth it was a bewildering period.

The power struggle between Stalin and Trotsky followed the death of Lenin in 1924 but, by the time Ivan was twenty years old and a man, all this was resolved and the harsh Communist dictatorship was in place. Ivan therefore knew little else politically, like most of his generation. His education, discipline and whole life became dominated by the then Communist ideal as the Russification of the population took place against a ruthless programme of internal genocide. Ivan Polbin may be seen therefore as one of the first products of the new Soviet youth. To his semi-Asiatic stoicism was added the creed of the new fanatical idealism and nationalism dominated by the State and personified by the ruthless and cynical ruler in the Kremlin who postured as a benign saviour while eliminating whole populations.

At the age of twenty-one Ivan took the two vital steps which were to mould his future career and life. He joined the Communist Party of the Soviet Union as a full-time member and he joined the Red Army, his ambition being a flying career. He was sent to one of the new colleges at Orenburg, west of the

Urals, to learn his new profession.

Under the Communists, air power had at first been neglected, but, during the Civil War, the need for military aviation had become obvious and the remnant of the 2500 machines inherited from the old Czarist forces were re-organised as the Red Air Fleet. But by the early 1920s little was left, some 300 machines only, of doubtful usefulness. Drastic measures were taken to rectify this situation by re-opening manufacturing plant and purchasing military aircraft from overseas, but the building of the new Red Air Fleet was complicated by the power struggle. On Trotsky's exile, his man, A.P. Rozenol, was replaced by Pyotr Baranov as the new head of the GU–VVSRKKA (Military Air Forces of the Workers' and Peasants' Red Army). Under his leadership, until his death in a plane crash in 1933, the slogan was 'self-sufficiency'. A policy of indoctrination of the populace with the importance of air power to the Soviet Union was adopted and drew many an aspiring youngster like Ivan into its orbit. A Society of Friends of the Air Fleet (ODVF) was formed and, together with its successor Osoaviakhim, it did much to foster this natural pride and participation. Ivan became one of the 1½ million members. He read the pages of its magazine *Aeroplane* as avidly as any young man in Milwaukee, Frankfurt or Guildford was doing in the west.

As in later years in Hitler's Germany, this national pride and emphasis on youth was fostered with care and dedication. Glider Clubs were established, competitions run and much publicity given to the new form of transport in the State-controlled media. The formation and growth of the Air Force Scientific Research Committee under Serge Il'Yushin and the Central Aero and Hydrodynamics Institute, initially under Nikolai Zhukovski, 'Father of Russian Aviation', were manifestations of the new outlook. But providing the aircraft and ideas was one thing, providing sufficient trained aircrew was another, and here too the Bolsheviks had to start almost from scratch. This was done by the massed transfer to air units of Red Army personnel, many of whom were neither eager to embrace the new skills nor capable mentally of doing so. In 1926 some 40 per cent of Soviet Air Force Officers had come from infantry units. This was a necessary but unsatisfactory position, and it was one that affected the Germans and other nations at this period. The establishment of military flying schools was quickly undertaken and Orenburg was one of the first to be set up. Like Ivan himself many of the new entrants, aged between eighteen and twenty-five, had no, or only very limited, basic education and so this was the first requirement. After a period of elementary educational study Ivan was put through an intensive eighteen-month flying course.

Polbin graduated from this course at the Orenburg Military School for Pilots in 1931 (or 1932, the accounts vary) with a high reputation. In the next five years he held various posts with Air Force units, always with distinction, and, by 1938, was a noted bomber pilot commanding his own squadron (Eskadrilya) at the age of thirty-two. The organisation of the Voyenno-Vozdushnyye Sily (Air Force-VVS) had also undergone radical alteration. At this time each light bomber squadron contained two Zven'ya (Flights) of some 18 aircraft plus reserves. These in turn were organised into dedicated Air Brigades (Aviabrigada). Every one of the seven Military Districts of the Soviet Union commanded its own air units for tactical control, with overall control resting with the Red Army Command.

The effectiveness of the home-produced aircraft failed to come up to expectations and, along with his other purges, Stalin had many of the leading designers incarcerated for their inability to match developments elsewhere with the rapidity he demanded. Typical of the light bomber planes being flown by Ivan in the late 1930s was the Arkhangel'ski SB (Skorostnoi bombardirovshchik or high-speed bomber). The original requirement had been for a twin-engined tactical bomber whose main defence would be its speed. Under the overall guidance of A.N. Tupolev, Aleksandr Arkhangel'ski produced a sleek, all-metal, mid-wing monoplane to fit the bill.

This aircraft included many features that were innovations for the Soviet aircraft industry and it was hailed as a great advance. Its slender fuselage was of monocoque frame construction, and, along with the wings, was Duralumin-covered. Prototypes were powered by the Wright Cyclone SGR 1820–F3 radial or the Hispano–Suiza 12Ybis inline engines and the bomber first flew in October 1934. It attained the then impressive speed of 420 k/h and could carry a 500-kg bomb for 1250 km. Testing continued into 1935, not always with satisfactory results however, and the chief test pilot, Konstantin Minder, had frequent (and unfortunately public) differences of opinion with the designer. It was finally put into full-scale production, reaching 13 machines a day at one period, and joined squadron service in 1936. In theory it was a winner but, like all military aircraft, it required the hard testing ground of actual combat to see if it really measured up to the standard.

The concept of the Schnellbomber was a universally popular one at this time, ultimately resulting in the Junkers Ju 88, the De Havilland Mosquito and suchlike, but the state of the art in the mid-1930s was not up to it, least of all in Soviet Russia. Too much was changing too fast in the aeronautical field and, although the SB could show a clean pair of heels to most fighters in 1936, two years later in Spain its limitations were severely shown up by the Bf 109 fighter. But in addition to Spain the SB was to undergo the final test of combat against another potential enemy – the old rival, Imperial Japan – and Polbin himself was to participate in this limbering-up for the Second World War.

Japanese expansionism through Korea into Manchuria and China, including the setting up of a puppet state in the latter, was watched with increasing uneasiness by the Soviet Union. Hitherto their defences in the Far East had been left at a very low ebb but, in the early 1930s, reinforcements were sent out, including aircraft, and 'volunteers' were also sent to fight the Japanese in China as they were fighting against the Nationalists in Spain. The heightened tension soon led to more direct armed conflicts that were, in fact, small undeclared wars between the two powers. The first of these was the so-called Changkufeng Incident.

In May 1938, during Stalin's purges, the existing head of the VVS in the Far Eastern area, General P.I. Pumpur, was arrested along with other high-ranking officers. The command of ODVA (Otdel'naya daln'no-vostochnaya armiya – Independent Far Eastern Army) was then split up into three smaller units. The Japanese chose this moment of apparent Russian difficulty and disarray to make their move.

On the north-western coast of the Sea of Japan is the large

bay, Zaliv Petra Velikoga, on which stands the important Soviet port and naval base of Vladivostok. To the west of this bay is an inlet, Posyeta Bay, and here the Russians proposed constructing a new submarine base. This was, naturally, not to Japan's taste at all. Just beyond this inlet the borders of Korea, Manchuria and the USSR all met close to the headland of Tumen.These borders were at that time not too clearly defined and Japanese ambitions on the area led to the seizure of the strategically important hill of Changkufeng. Their aim was to construct an artillery observation post on top of this hill which, in time of war, would serve the same purpose as at Port Arthur in 1905 when their guns had sunk the Russian fleet at their moorings. The Soviets, equally aware of the importance of denying this hill to the Japanese, moved in their own troops on 9 July, and clashes between frontier guards and border posts rapidly developed into a limited, but very active, conflict which spread rapidly up the frontier towards Lake Khasan on the Tumen river. Hostilities intensified on 29 July and fighting lasted twelve days into August. The Soviets had 180 bombers at their disposal including Polbin's squadron and from 6 August these flew continuous sorties against varying opposition (some sources state that the Soviet planes were 'unchallenged', others that the Japanese fought 'bitterly') until the fighting died out on 11 August when the Japanese finally withdrew from the ridge.

This was but a temporary lull, however, for Japanese ambitions were by no means diminished by this reverse. They surfaced again the following spring, this time on the equally remote border between Manchuria (or Manchukuo as the Japanese had renamed it) and Mongolia. Outer Mongolia had been a Chinese province as late as 1921 but became a People's Republic in 1924 and signed a Mutual Assistance Treaty with the USSR. When Japanese penetration up through Inner Mongolia threatened to isolate the Soviet defences another trivial incident rapidly escalated. This was a far more serious affair, for this time the Japanese had considerable aircraft and pilots, already blooded during the China campaign, on hand to support their troops on the ground. This vicious little war was known as the Nomonhan incident.

In the salient formed by the Buyr Nur and Hulun Chih lakes

west of Hailar on the strategic rail link up from Harbin there
was a natural point of contention along the Halhin (Khalkhin)
Gol river, a tributary of the Amur, which again the Japanese
tried to exploit in order to outflank Soviet forces dug in further
north and east. By this time Polbin himself was in command of
150 Regiment flying SB bombers, one of three such units
involved – the others being 32 and 38 Bomber Regiments –
under the overall command of General Aleksandr I. Gunsev.

The first clashes took place on 11 May 1939 and, with an
estimated 500 Japanese machines in Manchuria to draw on,
the air battles were far more serious than before. As the fighting
grew in intensity from 20 May onward, on land as well as in the
air, the Soviets hastily flew in extra aircraft to a peak of some
600 planes. General of Aviation Ya V. Smushkevic, already a
hero of the Soviet Union after his activities in Spain, took over
direction of these operations. Polbin flew his first missions on 26
May, the SB–2s being committed in strengths of up to sixty
aircraft at a time, heavily escorted by I15bis and later I153 and
Polikarpov I16 fighters. They were intercepted by Japanese
Nakajima Ki27 Type 97 fighters, there being five such squadrons (Sentais) in the region, that is, 1, 11, 24, 59 and 64 Sentai,
and these were thrown into the battle regardless of loss. Fierce
clashes took place and casualties were heavy on both sides
although, as in most air battles, equally wildly over-estimated
by each.

The Type 97 fighter (later to be code-named Nate or Abdul
by the USA) was a single-engined low-winged monoplane with
a fixed undercarriage and it had a best speed of some 740 k/h at
a height of 3500 m. It could therefore outpace the high-speed'
SB and, to avoid the worst effects of this, Polbin led his bombers
into the attack at heights in exccess of 6000 m, at which height
the performance of the Ki27 fell off dramatically. Despite this
the loss rate was in excess of that anticipated, but, on the other
hand, the attrition of their most skilled pilots was a nasty shock
to the Japanese. On 20 August Polbin participated in the
full-scale offensive launched by General G.K. Zhukov. About
200 bombers, escorted by half as many again fighters, were
thrown into the battle in two waves, thus swamping the
Japanese defenders. This marked the turning point and,
although the fighting continued until 16 September, once more

the Japanese were thwarted. The Soviet need to grab their half of defeated Poland led to an abandonment of further fighting on any large scale after this, and full losses were never completely determined, but one estimate is that some 200 Soviet and 160 Japanese aircraft were lost in this campaign.

The lessons were painful to both sides. The Japanese became obsessed with Soviet Air Power and planned for the ultimate conflict on land and in the air in this region, basing all their subsequent army thinking on this (which explains why the bulk of the fighting in the Pacific War had to be done by the navy). On the Russian side this experience of the costliness of close support of the army by aviation, and of repelling surprise attack by an enemy, should have been absorbed in time to meet Hitler's blitzkrieg two years later, but they were not. In fact the lessons learnt were misinterpreted. It was concluded from the Manchurian Incident that the VVS had to be organised in tightly organised sections: for close-support of the troops, Army Aviation; for overall air strategy according to each front's needs, Frontal Aviation. While these lessons might have held good for limited conflicts they were soon to be exposed as inadequate for a major conflict.

But if the overall strategy proved unsound, at lower levels the application of the available air strength to influence the land battles were absorbed well enough. Indeed the principal task of the VVS was seen to be ground-support. By October 1940, the four main Military District Commanders were being ordered to draft detailed instructions for such co-ordination between air and ground forces. In the Workers' and Peasants' Red Army (Raboche-Krest' yanskaya Krasnaya Armiya – RKKA) Field Manual for that year it was stressed that: 'Aviation is linked strategically and tactically to the ground forces.'

In the corresponding year's Bomber Manuals (BUBA–40) it was clearly written that one of the major aims was for 'frontal VVS actions in annihilating major enemy mechanised formations penetrating deep into our dispositions'.

But to sketch out a policy or even to fill in the detail was one thing, to implement it was another and to do this the VVS needed two things. The first was experienced aircrew to develop specific techniques and to apply them. This in turn depended on those specialists having the correct aircraft with which to perform those tasks. In Ivan Polbin and a few of his contemporaries they were certainly to find the former, but it needed a superior plane to the now discredited SB to achieve the latter.

What was required, of course, was accuracy. To make up for the fact that its speed was no longer its protection the SB–2 regiments had to fly high, thus losing much of what accuracy they originally possessed. But in Poland there had been a chilling demonstration of a technique that provided accuracy in abundance combined with economical cost. The answer was dive-bombing and the Junkers Ju 87 had made a deep impression on Soviet observers for its ability to hit pinpoint targets with ease and relative immunity due to the short time of the dive approach. It required mastery of the air above the attack zone, of course, but it gradually became apparent from the war in Western Europe that such a requirement applied equally to all other forms of bombing.

The need for a dive-bomber of their own was evident, but where to obtain one at short notice? That was the problem facing them as indeed it faced Italy and Great Britain at the same period. The former turned to Germany, the latter to the USA, but as Russia had no friends able to supply her needs in this field, she had to look after herself. Hitherto the VVS had paid scant attention to the dive-bomber. It was a specialised aircraft that needed strength and other particular attributes and features. The RAF, which invented dive-bombing, had treated it with the same disdain as the VVS between 1920 and the 1930s but, when they were pressed to re-adopt it, their experts were resolute in maintaining that with modern high-speed bombers (by which they meant their equivalents of the SB, the Battle and Blenheim light bombers), it could not be done due to their aerodynamic cleanness. Initially, early Soviet experience would seem to have borne out their gloomy forecasts but, whereas the RAF abandoned all attempts at overcoming such difficulties (even though in the Hawker Henley they had superb dive-bomber potential), the Russians were more persistent.

One brilliant man came up with the answer to the 'insoluble' problem, and not only did he produce a high-speed, accurate dive-bomber, he did it at his first attempt with little or no experience to guide him. The aircraft came on the scene just in time. The man who was to perfect the technique for it was Ivan Polbin. Both factors were to come together at just the right moment under the harsh lash of the German Blitzkrieg.

Short-term solutions to the dive-bomber problem varied in Russia from the sublime to the ridiculous. Starting at the latter end of that spectrum one might cite the case of the design engineer Vladimir Vakhmistrov's idea of a 'piggy-back' composite. Originally the concept was for two short-range fighters to be carried by a heavy bomber and launched from it to fend off attacking interceptors. This idea was adapted in 1940 to the concept of dive-bombers being carried instead, the idea being that they could thus be taken over long distances by their 'mother-ship' before being released near their target to carry out their dive attacks. An aerial aircraft-carrier, in fact. Each TB3 heavy bomber was therefore adapted to carry two of the tiny I16 fighters, themselves converted into dive-bombers as the I16–SPBs. A special dive-bomber unit, 92 Fighter Regiment, was formed with six TB3s and 12 I16–SPBs, and was based at Yevpatoria in the Crimea where they underwent stringent training in this novel concept. Nor was the idea confined to theory or practice, the squadron actually completed several war missions, supervised by Vakhmistrov himself specially released from arrest. About 30 missions were flown by these daring pilots against targets in Romania during the late summer of 1941, including dive attacks on the Danube bridge at Chernovoda, the oil refineries at Ploesti, Constanza naval base and railway bridges across the river Dnieper.

A more orthodox remedy was the conversion of the standard SB2 light bomber into a pikiruyushchi bombardirovochny (dive-bomber) at the direct behest of Stalin himself. Tupolev fitted 200 of his M105R-engined bombers with dive-brakes as a three-seater dive-bomber re-designated the SB–RK (or Arkhangelsky Ar21). Not surprisingly it failed to perform in this role with any great satisfaction. They saw some limited action in the early part of the war but were then replaced.

A third approach in 1938 was seen with the new twin-engined bomber under design by Andrei Tupolev himself, the Samolet 103 (Tu2). Again it was a large machine, a four-seater with a capacious bomb-bay. It was an impressive aircraft which first flew in January 1941. Its basic requirements were altered to incorporate the ability to dive-bomb with what, until then, had been another high-speed medium bomber. It was therefore fitted with electrically-operated dive-brakes. The need to simplify it for production purposes during the war meant, in fact, that its dive-bombing capability largely went by the board although dive-brakes were fitted on some machines under the outer wing panels. Despite these, like most such conversions, it was not an effective dive-bomber.

The fourth concept proved to be the sublime one and from it came the dive-bomber par excellence of the Second World War, the famous Pe2.

The designer Vladimir Petlyakov, yet another internee, was working on an entirely different concept, that of a two-seater high-altitude fighter with a pressurised cabin, the VI100. In 1939 this specification was changed to that of a three-seater high-altitude bomber but, before much progress had been made, this too was halted. Instead the NII–VVS (Nauchno-Ispytatelnyi Institut-VVS – Air Force Technical Test Centre) instructed Petlyakov to concentrate his efforts on producing a high-speed, high-performance, twin-engine monoplane dive-bomber. While experts in Britain had constantly maintained that this was an 'impossible' combination and refused to consider it, the young Russian designer went ahead and de-signed it. As his 'reward' Petlyakov was transferred from the TsKB–29 prison inside Factory 156 and sent with his design team to the notorious Menzhinskii Factory No 39. Production was started at GAZ 39 (Gosudarstvenny aviatsionny zavod – State Aircraft Factory) and at GAZ 22, but the German invasion forced the evacuation of production lines eastward. The Pe2 line was set up at Kazan, far to the rear of Moscow and Gorky, on the east bank of the northern Volga, where 13 Pe2s a day were eventually produced.

As the PB100, the first prototype appeared early in 1940 with the glazed underside nose and a heightened cockpit to give the all-round vision so necessary for dive-bombing. The pilot and navigator/bomb-aimer sat in tandem here while the rear gun-ner lay prone in the constricted after-fuselage space. Under-wing dive brakes of the Venetian blind type were fitted out-board of the twin M105R liquid-cooled engines. These latter were twelve-cylinder Vee engines fitted with two-speed super-chargers and rated at 1100 hp enclosed in slim nacelles which ran back to each wing's trailing edges. They were fitted with the three-bladed metal propeller. To improve the aircraft's lateral stability the twin fins tail-plane was given a notable 8-degree dihedral which became a recognition feature. Otherwise, save for the abandoning of the turbo-superchargers and fighter armament, little was changed. Heavy armour protection was a feature with extra side armour for the pilot. Defensive arm-ament on early models consisted of two fixed machine-guns in the nose, another on a flexible mounting at the rear of the cockpit, and a fourth downward-firing aft on a swing mounting fitted with a periscopic sight. The internal bomb-bay could carry six 100-kg bombs but extra bombs could be carried under each wing's centre-section and in the rear of each engine nacelle.

Speed was exceptional in a dive-bomber which, in other nations, always seemed fated to be a slow aircraft. Not so the PB100 or Pe2 as it was designated: 335 mph at 16,000 ft made it as fast as many single-engined fighters. In the dive, with brakes fully extended, the maximum permissible speed was 373 mph, although speeds of 450 mph had been reached with no ill effects. (One test pilot found his dive-brakes had failed to work but walked away from a dive in which he logged about 500 mph). Its only fault, which was never completely eradicated, was a tendency to 'bounce' on landings. In its designed role this superlative performance did not in any way detract from its ability to dive-bomb accurately. Quite the contrary: with a 1323-lb bomb-load the Pe2 was rock-steady in a 70-degree dive and great accuracy was achieved by experienced pilots. But here was the rub – having little or no previous experience of the art there were very few bomber pilots in the VVS who could take advantage of the Pe2's outstanding merits. Initially it was handled relatively timidly and mis-used in low-level or altitude bombing. It needed the catalyst of an individual who would take the peshka (chess pawn), as it became christened, for the superb dive-bomber that it was and work out how best to use it against the enemy. That man was Ivan Polbin.

The Pe2 was immediately put into full-scale production (a German inspection team viewed the assembly lines at GAZ 22 as late as April 1941, when the two nations were still Allies) but it needed time to get it into service and time was fast running out for the Soviets. When the Luftwaffe heralded the start of Operation BARBAROSSA on 22 June 1941, few of the bomber units of the VVS had received, let alone established and adjusted to, the new aircraft.

From a varying amount of statistical data the following figures give a general indication of this and how important the dive-bomber was held in the VVS by its subsequent mass-production. According to TsGASA (the Central State Archives of the Soviet Army) only two production peshki were delivered in 1940. Up to the date of the German invasion a further 458 had rolled off the assembly lines to give a total of 460. A.G. Fyodorov's book *Aviatsiya v bitve pod Moskvoi* (*The Air War for Moscow*) states that of these, only 42 Pe2s were actually operational on 22 June 1941. Between that date and the end of the year a further 1405 peshki were produced. At first, however, the VVS had to hold with what it had. In one way this was fortunate for the initial German onslaught, which left destroyed a staggering total of 1800 Soviet aircraft on the first day alone, largely passed by the Pe2 units. The standard medium bomber was still the SB and they flew to their destruction against German fighters and flak in their hundreds flying in steady, level formations. They were cut to pieces wholesale, much as were the RAF's Fairey Battles the year before. Loss of the SBs was less serious than the loss of skilled aircrew on such a vast scale. Soon the operational strengths of squadrons had to be cut by half just to keep going. Bombing straight and level from 3000 m was ineffectual; low-level strikes proved to be suicide. The need for the dive-bomber was proven to the hilt.

Polbin, now a Lieutenant-Colonel, was still in command of his old unit from Manchurian days, 150 Bomber Aviation Regiment. Within a short time he was leading this unit against the thrusting German Panzer columns during the battles of the Desna bend. The Germans had taken Smolensk on 16 July, having advanced 440 miles in 25 days. Moscow lay only half that distance ahead of them. By 20 July they had forced the defences at Yelna on the Dnieper river, 47 miles further on. Here the Soviets stood and fought hard to bar further advance, then counter-attacked. For five weeks fierce fighting continued unabated around this German salient holding the high ground and the road junction. Under the Soviet Marshal Semyon Timoshenko fresh reserve armies were launched. Nine Soviet divisions were thrown in to eject the four German divisions dug in there. At the same time the Soviet 13 Army under Lieutenant-General V.F. Gerasimenko, boxed-in at Mogilov, attempted to break out to meet them. Heavy air support was thrown in to support these continual assaults.

By this time the VVS had come to the conclusion that the bulky 60–plane formations of the air regiments were too unwieldy for combat use. They made for easy targets and restricted accurate co-ordination of assaults. Accordingly the Stavka decided to re-organise the air regiments with 32 aircraft and the air division to two regiments each. In the case of the Pikiruyushchi Bombardirovochny regiments such as Polbin's, the lack of aircraft made this inevitable anyway. Moreover dive-bombing was more easily co-ordinated in smaller formations like this. The basic staffing of 150 Regiment at this time would be about 100 aircrew, a third of which were pilots and another third navigators. In support ground personnel, mechanics, fitters and armourers, would be another hundred men. Aircraft establishment was set at two squadrons per regiment, each squadron of nine Pe2s, with two assigned for regimental HQ and a further five reserve machines. In the air the standard formations were the three-plane zveno, three of which formed the squadron or Devyathka. But basic bomber formations no longer applied once the Pe2s began to be used in their proper role. Polbin began to experiment with various approaches and tactical groupings designed to give his regiment the maximum surprise and accuracy combined with the minimum losses from the ever-deadly German flak gunners.

Operations in the Smolensk-Yartsevo pocket were intense. Between 26 and 28 July, for example, 100 aircraft from I Bomber Corps, 120 from II and III Bomber Corps, and 100 bombers and 150 fighters allocated from the Reserve Front were all thrown into the 'cauldron'. Polbin's targets were main tank formations and troop concentrations, and the peshka was blooded in no uncertain manner, flying an average of three or four sorties a day. Over the whole operation the VVS claimed to have flown 20,000 sorties. Unlike the majority of these bombing attacks, which were highly inaccurate, the Pe2s were able to pinpoint such targets and achieve definite results, with far fewer casualties.

At the controls of his peshka Polbin sat offset to the left-hand side of the cockpit which he and his navigator had to reach via a trap door in the underside of the fuselage. The seat itself swung back against the port bulkhead for access. Polbin would lock this seat, which was positioned well forward of the cockpit for visibility. All round his view was good and excellent ahead, for this was not at all restricted by the finely tapering nose. Good vision downward was obtained by the perspex window on which a red line was painted for him to line up the horizon. For protection of his head and torso Polbin had 9-cm thick armour plate. His navigator sat behind him, offset to starboard, and was responsible for the top gun and emergency undercarriage system. The main radio operator was separate from the other two crew members and responsible for the ventral gun position. As well as piloting the plane Polbin was responsible for the bomb-release himself, and he could also operate the radio equipment in part, if necessary, by means of a four-position switch at his left elbow. With his main instrument panel ahead of him Polbin also had a consol running laterally along his right-hand side with rows of toggle switches positioned for easy access. The control column was light of touch and of tubular construction. The only discomfiture in the whole operation would be the harshness of the taxying as the 'bumper' made its way along the primitive runway.

Take-off was made quite simply with the use of 15–20 degrees of flap. The climb rate was exceptional for a bomber and the handling in the air was light and not tiring. Although the Pe2 tended to be unstable longitudinally it was stable and docile directionally and laterally. It was also fitted with a fully-automatic dive recovery system which featured the lighting of a red lamp on the dashboard should acceleration during the recovery exceed 7 g. Once the target was lined up, the method Polbin would use to go into his attack would be for him to ease gently back on the throttle and extend the dive brakes by means of a selector switch on the right-hand panel. As these very efficient slatted brakes quickly extended they automatically cut out the normal trimmers and made the aircraft nose-heavy. These were electrically operated and functioned at between 50-degree and 70-degree dive angles.

Polbin would have experienced little or no changes in trim and vibration during the dive. The controls would remain light, although as the speed built up to the 350 mph mark they would grow stiffer. Once the bombs were released the trimmer was automatically returned to normal, or it could be manually controlled by means of a small white push button on the right-hand shelf. Recovery to level flight would be attained within 800 ft and 950 ft. In normal flight the Pe2 was easily handled except for a nasty tendency to spin to the right if handled slackly. Apart from that it was pleasant to fly, although it required constant alertness, especially on one engine. Strict instructions were issued to combat pilots concerning this tendency to spin and it was forbidden to roll the aircraft.

However Polbin was a believer in testing his units to their fullest limit. When word was brought to him that one of his subordinates was to be disciplined for disobeying this order his reaction was typical. He had the pilot brought before him, but, instead of giving him a full dressing-down for not obeying standing instructions, he quizzed him closely about the peshka's reactions. What he learned was that the pilot had adopted Polbin's own methods. He had sat down deliberately beforehand and mapped out what he was going to attempt. Much impressed, Polbin got himself immediately airborne to put his own plane through the same test pattern, ending up with a succession of continuous rolls to see just how far the Pe2 could be pushed in that respect. What he learnt from his subordinate and his own rule-breaking all went into the melting pot in his head in which future dive-bombing tactics were being steadily evolved. It only awaited the chance to prove his theories in practice. In many respects the Pe2 was a great advance over earlier Soviet aircraft in terms of electrical installations carried. Six 2kw 3v electrically driven motors were carried for the radiators, five for the trim tabs, four for the engine propellers and superchargers and one each for the undercarriage, flaps, and dive-brakes. Some simplification would be made as the war went on due to the overriding need for production but it would still remain a relatively sophisticated aircraft by VVS standards.

A further series of intensive operations followed, with the Pe2s striking hard at Guderian's Panzer forces in the region of Pochep, Shostka and Starodub as in late August the Germans moved on Bryansk. The orders from the Supreme Command were concise: 'The enemy columns must be hit constantly, wave after wave, all day from morning till night to keep the enemy from enjoying a breathing spell or regaining his senses in general.'

In compliance with this directive Polbin led 150 Regiment into continuous strikes against the German tank columns from 29 August onward. On 30 and 31 August, for instance, the Pe2 regiments were again maintaining three or four sorties per day which forced the German 3 Tank Division and 10 Motorised Division to a temporary halt. One hundred tanks, 800 soft-skinned and twenty armoured vehicles were claimed destroyed in these two days for the loss of 42 aircraft.

With the termination of the Smolensk pocket battles caused by the ultimately disastrous German decision to leave Moscow and drive on first to the south, Polbin could assess the lessons of these early combat missions and garner his ideas on improvements. At top level also further changes in the system were being ordered which, it was hoped, would be assimilated by the time the planned Russian winter offensive was launched. Meanwhile desperate measures had to be taken to stem the German advance on Moscow itself, which had now resumed. On 7 October Corps Commissar P.S. Stepanov was dispatched to the front to stiffen the Western front's commander, I.S. Konev, and organised mass air strikes with all available aviation units subordinated to that role, including an extra Pe2 regiment, 46, from the Reserve. In a nine days' offensive 2850 sorties were flown. The defensive battle lasted until early December, with the Germans finally halted in the Moscow suburbs by the weather as much as by the defenders. Now was the opportunity for the counter-blow.

This took place on the Kalinin Front on 5 December, 1000 aircraft being concentrated to support it, the Pe2s alone flying some 800 missions in the opening three days. During the following six weeks, before the Soviets ran out of steam, at least half the 16,000 combat sorties flown on this front were close-support missions. The Germans were pushed back for a considerable distance and Moscow was saved.

During the spring of 1942 the lessons learnt from these operations were studied and new dispositions made. A new deputy commander was appointed that February, General Aleksandr Novikov. The following month new guidelines were issued, the most important of which from Polbin's viewpoint was the setting up of 10 special Assault groups (UAG-Udarnaya aviatsionnaya gruppa). Their strength varied like their models, the German Fliegerkorps. The first one to be set up contained two Pe2 regiments, two I12 Shturmovik regiments, two fighter regiments and two heavy bomber regiments. This proved to be a short-lived experiment and lasted only until June. Then another formation, the Air Army (Vozdushnaya Armiya) came into being. The mission of the Pe units was now laid down as 'to destroy the enemy's tank and motorised columns, annihilate his manpower, and thus support our troops'.

But re-organisation did not end there. At the behest of Stalin, élite units were set up by the GKO (Gosudarstvenny komitet oborony – State Committee for Defence) with picked squadrons, to be held in reserve and thrown in where the fight was most critical. Thus 'Special Group No 1' came into being based around Polbin's 150 Bomber Aviation Regiment and two fighter regiments. Greater encouragement was offered to the front-line commanders to initiate new tactics in these units. This Polbin was in a good position to do, but the lack of adequate and reliable reconnaissance was a big handicap in planning such fast-moving tactics. There was still only experimental close liaison between ground forces and dive-bombers with direct radio links. This had been pioneered by the Russians but not developed. It was left for the Luftwaffe to utilise it and by this time it had been perfected by the Stukas.

Polbin had not only trained his young flyers to master the basic dive-bomber techniques, but he had now fully worked out his own variant in an attempt to overcome the very strong mobile flak defences which were such a feature of German land operations. This technique became famous as the Vertushka ('dipping wheel') method. The squadron still approached the target in the standard formation of vee-of-vees. To ensure the bombers' protection against defending fighter aircraft, Polbin

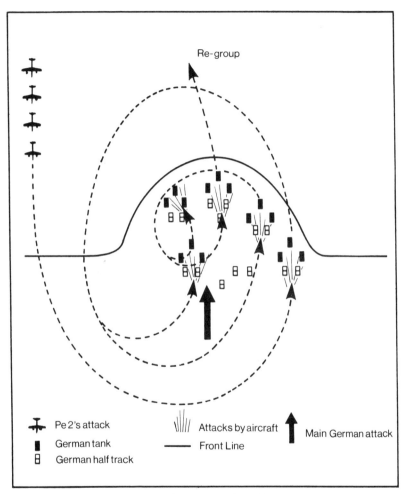

Fig 7 Polbin's Vertushka ('Dipping Wheel') dive-bombing tactic designed to keep the enemy flak defences off-balance during a sustained dive-bomber attack

worked out a technique for the Soviet fighter escorts also. This involved splitting them into sections, one for high cover to prevent surprise and to 'mix it' with the enemy interceptors. This left a smaller section of fighters free to keep close formation on the dive-bombers, even, on occasion, diving with them, to keep in touch should they be 'jumped' by other German planes. With their backs covered, the dive-bombers were free to concentrate on doing their job but, before precision attacks could be made on the objectives, the German AA-gunners had to be suppressed or made to keep their heads down so that they did not interfere. This is where the 'dipping wheel' came into effect.

All depended on the steadiness and courage of the leader and on his fellows following the plan closely. Forming up over the target in a large circle, much as the Stukas did against warship targets in the Mediterranean, a continual 'carousel' of aircraft was kept in motion that gave the defending gunners too many targets on which to concentrate. At the given moment and height the leader would break out of the circle and begin his attack.

As Polbin led down in a 70-degree dive, he would be followed at a 500 m–600 m distance by his number two, and a similar distance would separate the third peshka, and so on. As Polbin pulled out of his dive and released his bombs the second and third dive-bombers would be on their way down and the fourth would be starting his attack. In this way a continuous stream of dive-bombers would be hosing down to split the defensive fire. On completion of the attack the aircraft would rejoin the wheel to keep the cycle going and, with luck, keep the enemy bemused and bewildered. A sustained attack could thus be mounted in a very restricted area with minimum losses. And so it proved. Polbin's plans were given detailed trial and combat testing during the year by Colonel A.G. Fedorov and came through it with good results.

When the fighting got under way again in the spring the initial offensive, launched by the Soviet forces under Timoshenko against Kharkov in May, foundered and turned into a massive defeat. The Germans then launched their main blow, 'Case Blue', designed to take them through the Ukraine and on to the oilfields of Baku on the Caspian Sea. Once more the tried-and-tested blitzkrieg was initially successful and a wholesale retreat was made by the Russians to prevent the massed encirclements of 1941 being repeated. Eventually however a stand was made by the Soviet 62 Army to hold the strategic bridges over the river Don at Kalach. The German 6 Army, under von Paulus, was advancing against this great bend of the river towards the distant Volga and Stalingrad. On 29 July 1942, the opening moves began in what was to be a bloody struggle. On 28 July the order had been given to the defenders, 'Not another step back'. Close support missions were again flown continuously.

Ivan's regiment was thrown in to help stem the onrush as the Panzers moved up and surrounded 62 Army in the Verkhne-Businovki pocket. In four days' non-stop missions Polbin's dive-bombers claimed the destruction of 40 tanks and 50 soft-skinned vehicles, but it was not enough. One notable attack by Polbin's squadron at this time was that made on the German fuel supply dump at Morozovsk farm. Because it was so vital to them, the Germans had made elaborate attempts at camouflage and in addition had surrounded it with large numbers of flak guns and with fighter aircraft on constant standby. Despite this 150 Bomber Regiment made a determined daylight dive-bombing assault and Polbin and one wingman broke through all the defences and made two deliberate attacks, scoring direct hits and igniting the whole stock. This one attack had grave repercussions on the German advance as their tanks were held up by lack of fuel.

The Germans made a skilful and opportune advance across the river Chir and pushed forward. On 8 August the German pinzers closed around the Soviet army, trapping nine divisions, nine motorised and armoured brigades, 1000 tanks and 750 guns. On 16 August the great bridge across the Don at Kalach was taken intact and the Germans poured across towards the Volga.

At once desperate attempts were made to destroy the crossings from the air. These massed air strikes bore a marked resemblance to the Maas bridge debacle of the 1940 period in France. Massed formations of SBs and similar level bombers flew in groups of 160 at a time into the German flak and fighters and were wiped out. In desperation Polbin's peshka units were called up to do what they could against the massed flak defences. Polbin's dive-bomber sorties were described as 'the most formidable' of the Soviet air attacks at this time, but they also failed to achieve their objectives and soon Stalingrad itself was invested.

Over what was termed the Don front, 8 Air Army, to which Polbin's new unit 301 Bomber Aviation Division was subordinated, flew some 4000 sorties between 27 September and 8 October. For the counter-offensive, which commenced on 19 November and led to the encirclement and ultimate destruction of the German 6 Army, about threequarters of the 8 Air Army's sorties were given to supporting the assault by the Soviet 50 Army.

For his outstanding work in both leadership in the field and advances behind the scenes, and his tireless search to better his performance, Polbin received the supreme accolade. On 23 November he was made 'Hero of the Soviet Union'. He already held two Orders of Lenin, two Orders of the Red Banner, and went on to win the Order of Bogdan Khmel 'nitskii and the Order of the Patriotic War, First Class, as well as numerous other medals. All of which left him apparently unaffected, for his fierce devotion to his work was legendary.

The Germans again managed to hold the rout and even re-took some of the territory lost in the spring, but they were severely shaken. For the summer of 1943 a fresh offensive was planned, but of a far more limited ambition than hitherto, merely the pinching out of a large bulge in the front, known as the Kursk salient. Operation ZITADELLE was to be their last fling. Forewarned the Soviet forces prepared not only to defend tenaciously but to deliver a devastating counter-stroke. Production of the Pe2 had continued at a good rate in 1942, but had been somewhat hampered by the need to provide large numbers of the much publicised Shturmoviks and the demand for the peshka's Klimov inline engines for fighter aircraft requirements. However in 1943 production soared once more and by June almost all the front-line units had re-equipped with it. Another factor in the correct use of the Pe2 was the new dominance of the Soviets in the air. Increased demands from all fronts in the west had reduced the Luftwaffe's presence to an all-time low in the east and, save for areas of local concentration as at Kursk, the Soviets enjoyed large quantitative superiority in all arms. With a reduced threat from the German fighters, more and more of the less skilled Pe2 pilots could now use their mounts in the correct manner as dive-bombers. No longer were they forced to fly at heights above fighter performance as level bombers. They could now exploit the dive-bomber's accuracy against targets like gun-emplacements, tank concentrations, and bridges.

In readiness for the coming offensive Colonel Polbin was placed in command of 1 Guards Bomber Air Corps which was sent to reinforce 2 Air Army, under General S.A. Krasovski, on the Voronezh front. The German attack pushed off on 5 July 1943, but soon became bogged down. By 12 July the Soviets were ready to launch their counter-punch. This was to take the form of an armoured thrust by 5 Guards Tank Army from Prokhorovka towards Yakovlevo. Approximately one hour before they jumped off from their start positions Ivan led in with preliminary attacks, I Bomber Corps hitting with great success both tank concentrations and artillery positions in the line of advance. At 08.30 some 1200 Soviet and German tanks started to slog it out, with the intervention of the tank-busting dive-bombers, Stukas and Pe2s, of both sides in the greatest tank battle in history. In this participation the Pe2s came of age, as one Soviet historian was to write: 'The tactics of ground attack aviation flying in large groups enjoyed further development. Bomber aviation accumulated a great deal of experience in dive-bombing and in making concentrated attacks on units of as high as division strength.'

The methods of attacking small mobile ground targets and guiding aircraft to enemy air and ground-based targets received further experience also. By the end of August fresh Soviet offensives were begun to liberate the Ukraine, and again Polbin's unit was well to the fore with the 2 Air Army during the attempts to prevent the Germans withdrawing across the Dnieper. On the Steppe front I Bomber Air Corps led by Polbin made two very determined dive-bomber strikes on German strong points holding their two defence lines and flew 150 sorties in breaking these open.

Further promotion followed, to Major-General of Aviation, and other awards. Perhaps the strangest of his career took place during this period, a unique aerial dive-bomber combat. While returning from a mission over the front line in October with a force of 17 Pe2s Polbin came upon a unit of 18 Ju 87D Stukas about to make their dives on Soviet troops below. His own unit had not been spotted by the enemy and, while Polbin's own fighter escort diverted the German fighter cover, he took his much faster dive-bombers in to the attack. Knowing they were out-classed for speed, the Stukas jettisoned their bombs and prepared to defend themselves as they made a run for base. Ivan's Pe2s pursued them, managing to shoot down several en route and, on arriving over the airfield of Berezovka, sighted several more Ju 87s taking off. Attacks were continued against both groups, causing two of the German aircraft to collide while taking avoiding action. Within a few minutes it was all over and the Russian pilots later claimed to have destroyed a total of 13 of the German dive-bombers for the loss of only one of their own. Polbin himself was credited with the destruction of two of the Stukas.

After the fall of Kiev on 6 November the Russian offensive ground remorselessly on towards the western Ukraine during the next month, the troops of 1 Ukrainian front again being supported by Krasovski's 2 Air Army as they penetrated toward Zhitomir, Vinnitsa and Rovno. The growing supply of first-class aircraft reaching front-line units was increasing to a flood. In 1943 there were 35,000 machines and consequently units could be organised up to their old established levels. Air Divisions now expanded to three- and four-regiment compositions, with each regiment having an establishment of 40 or even 80 aircraft.

Production of the Pe2 was to total 11,427 by the end of the war, by far the largest of the aircraft type produced, and proof of its value. Despite this, in Britain at this period high-ranking RAF officials in Whitehall were still reiterating the idea that the dive-bomber was finished and that although 'it is understood that the Russians possess dive-bombers' that 'we have no information that they have proved as useful to the Russians as to the Germans'. At the time that this was being said around Whitehall, in March 1943 not only were the peshka regiments expanding faster than ever before but experience from the front was being worked on to give even greater efficiency to their application. The first Pe2 fitted with the new 1210 hp,

VK105RF engine, which boosted maximum speed to 361 mph, and a more streamlined cockpit, featuring a dorsal gun turret and other improvements, joined units that same month. With growing numbers came greater confidence in their correct usage. The idea of massed attacks to swamp ground defences was now practical and was put into effect. When flying in the small groups of one or two Zven'ya the dive-bombers were hard to defend and were often picked off by the marauding German fighters. Larger formations made the job of the protecting fighters easier in this respect. In the air, as on the ground, the Soviet Union's vast numerical manpower superiority, the long-vaunted 'steamroller', was able at last to be put to good use. Despite this overall policy there still remained plenty of scope for individual skill to be applied in certain circumstances, as Polbin continually showed. It was he who was the first to practise and perfect the 'sniper' tactic, the very epitome of individuality in the midst of mass. It was Polbin who taught this method to the regiments and divisions under his command. Narrow, precise objects, such as bridges or rail links, which had to be hit directly with a fine precision in order to be cut effectively, had long been prime Ju 87 targets when the Germans were on the offensive. Polbin and certain other selected Pe2 pilots were now able to repay the enemy in the same coin and thus seal the fate of thousands of enemy troops attempting to escape. Such targets were dive-bombed with exactness and some pilots, particularly Polbin himself, were credited with the ability to plant a bomb 'down a factory chimney'. In the great encircling operation of the Korsun-Schevchenkovskiy pocket the surrounded German forces were subjected to non-stop aerial assault and annihilated. This brought about the liberation of the whole of the Ukraine and Soviet Forces had advanced to the edge of Romania itself by early in February 1944.

On 5 February I Bomber Air Corps was re-designated as II Guards Bomber Aviation Corps. The special élite 'shock' units, like Polbin's, were re-numbered when awarded the coveted 'Guards' status. Equipped with the latest aircraft and manned by select aircrew, only four Pe2 units were so honoured. On 20 October Polbin was promoted from Colonel to Major-General of Aviation. He had long since passed the 100 combat-mission total, but he remained as keen and determined as ever. Whereas most of the Corps commanders assigned to tactical command had liaison jobs back on the ground at headquarters, where they utilised the growing radio communications net to control their forces, Polbin continued to fly with his regiment in mission after mission. By the end of 1944 he had clocked up 150 dive-bomber combat sorties.

In the spring of 1944 the Soviets had halted their great offensives and went over to the defensive in expectation of German counter-attacks. They also wished to prepare themselves for a whole new series of their own attacks which were aimed at clearing the remaining areas of the Soviet Union and Poland of the enemy and timed to coincide with the Allied break-out from Normandy which would tie down valuable German forces. In the summer the Russians struck. The Belorussian offensive was launched at the end of June 1944. It was aimed at Minsk with the task of wiping out the German Army Group Centre on the way. From Lake Nesherdo to Verba on a front 1000 km long were concentrated four Air Armies with some 6000 aircraft, 200 of them ground-attack machines, and including Polbin's Pe2s. The results of the application of such devastating air power was overwhelming and the Germans were crushed and forced to fall back with heavy losses of mechanised forces. Pe2s cut the Beresina bridge, trapping vast forces in the Bobruisk 'cauldron', the Eastern front's equivalent of the Falaise Pocket in France at the same time, but on a far grander scale. The end-result was the same however; wholesale massacre of German armour from the air.

As the front crumbled, the Germans hastily switched reinforcements from other fronts, again offering perfect targets to Polbin's dive-bombers. For example, on 14 July the German 8 Division was surprised on the main road to Brodny. Major-General von Mellenthin described the result: '8 Panzer was caught on the move by Russian aircraft and suffered devastating losses. Long columns of tanks and lorries went up in flames, and all hope of counter-attack disappeared.'

On the morning of 15 July the German counter-attack was pulverised before it could start by a mass dive-bombing attack which proved devastating. This began at 04.00, the leading groups crossing over the village of Zalozhtse at just under 5000 ft led by 4 Bomber Air Corps. Each group passed the control point at intervals of one to two minutes, each group passed by at precisely eight-minute intervals. The cumulative effect was overwhelming.

135 Pe2s of 4 Bomber Air Corps hit the Germans in sequence and were immediately followed by three groups of five dive-bombers. The first group was led by 2 Guards Bomber Air Corps commander Ivan Polbin himself; the second group of five by Colonel N.D. Gulayev of 8 Guards Bomber Air Corps and the third by Lieutenant-Colonel A.A. Novikov of 162 Guards Bomber Regiment. On a signal from the commander the Pe2s formed a circle over the German armour concentration near Plugow. The strong fighter escort split in two, patrolling at 4920 ft and 2300 ft respectively, the altitudes at which the dive-bombing commenced and finished. Then Polbin led the whole force into the assault.

Each Pe2 group made four dive-bombing passes each and when they had finished they were followed up by relays of ground-strafing aircraft and level bombers. The attack lasted for four continuous hours with more units feeding into the cauldron after that. In all some 3288 sorties were mounted on 15 July against the German tank formations and 102 tons of bombs per square kilometre were laid down. In the subsequent battle for Lvov, Polbin's 2 Guards Bomber Air Corps was assigned the right wing of the front and on 16 July they struck hard at troop concentrations in Sasov, Koltow and Bely Kamen. Sorties continued to be mounted until 22 July when the Germans in the 'Koltow Corridor' surrendered.

By the end of July the Soviet armies were over the Vistula and by mid-August into Estonia, Latvia and Lithuania as well as across the rivers Bug and San, at the gates of East Prussia itself. In the centre of each advance as usual flew Polbin, leading the way forward with his pinpoint missions. On 20 August it was announced on Moscow Radio that he had been awarded the Order of Bogdan Khmelnitsky, First Class, in recognition of his continuing services in the vanguard of the attacks.

The massive assaults of the 1 Belorussian and 1 Ukrainian fronts to clear Poland began on 12 January 1945. 3 Guards Army slammed its way westward through Wielun to Steinau by

6 February while, further south, 4 Guards Tank Army punched through Pinczow. 4 Panzer Army was smashed and the Russians fully established in Germany proper. They straddled the river Oder with bridgeheads at Brieg and Steinau. Between these two pinzers lay the city of Breslau (now part of Poland and known as Wroclaw), capital of the industrial area of Silesia. On 14 January Polbin celebrated his fortieth birthday but had no intention of being 'grounded' by age or instructions from on high. He was still leading his dive-bombers from the front when II Guards Aviation Corps was yet again thrown in as aerial spearhead when this exciting phase of the assault had first started.

On 17 January the troops of 1 Ukrainian Front developed their offensive and captured the towns of Przedborz and Radomsko which were described as important communications centres and defence strongholds, and, after forcing the River Warta, swiftly struck on to take the town of Czestochowa on that river. Polbin flew in combat action during this day's fighting and distinguished himself yet again. Two days later, with the same zest, he was again in the thick of it as Marshal Konev's troops took by assault and skilful outflanking movements the ancient Polish city of Cracow whose defences covered the vital Dabrowa coal region. Germany itself was entered on 21 January when the Soviet forces, advancing to the west of Czestochowa, broke through a strongly fortified defence system at her south-eastern frontier and, with Polbin's peshkas blasting the way ahead of them, invaded German Silesia along a 90-km front to a depth of 30 km, capturing in the process the towns of Kreuzburg, Rosenberg, Pitschen, Landsberg and Guttentag.

The pace was now breathtaking. On 25 January Polbin was again mentioned as performing notably during the advances which, the day before, penetrated even deeper into Silesia and resulted in the fall of Gleiwitz. On 26 January Polbin flew missions in support of the attack which took the town of Hindenburg, while next day Polbin was again commended for his courage in the assaults which led to the capture of the Dabrowa towns of Sosnowiec, Bedzin, Dabrowa, Gorna, Czeladz and Myslowice. The most important of the cities in this region was Beuthen, which was clearly doomed. On 28

January Polbin flew Pe2 missions in support of the final attacks on German defences around that town whose fall marked the expulsion of the enemy from the southern part of Upper Silesia. After a brief pause Marshal Konev's troops moved forward from Brieg on 4 February, advancing along the left bank of the Oder for 13 miles. A second prong began its assault, moving out at great speed from Steinau across the Silesian plain. On 11 February Polbin was recorded as playing a major part in the precision air attacks which accompanied the forcing of the river Oder to the north-west of Breslau reaching the fortress town of Gloghau on 13 February. Breslau was now surrounded but the Germans were now fighting on their own home soil and the reduction of the garrison at Gloghau was not easily overcome. Likewise the defenders of Breslau itself, under the command of Lieutenant-General Niefhoff, proved most stubborn opponents. In support of attacks against strong-points around the city the Pe2s were sent in to make precise strikes on 14 February 1945.

It was Polbin's 157th combat-mission. As usual his peshka led in a steep 70-degree dive against the well-dug-in Germans heavy gun positions holding up the advance. The German flak gunners were experienced and steady, tracking his spiralling aircraft carefully and opening up a furious barrage. Caught in a hail of exploding shells Polbin's Pe2 was badly hit and crashed in flames on the target, killing all the crew instantly.

Thus passed Ivan Semyonovich Polbin, dying at the peak of his prowess and with the ultimate fulfilment of his wishes so very close to completion. It was a sad blow to the dive-bomber arm he had done so much to build up and cherish. Their final victory flight over Berlin a few weeks later can be seen as both tribute and memorial to his work and dedication. He was honoured by the award of 'Hero of the Soviet Union' a second time, posthumously, on 6 April 1945. His name still lives on at his old pilots' school at Orenburg, which is to this day called the Polbin School.

An equally moving tribute was provided by the Soviet historian A.N. Kozhevnikov, who described Major-General Polbin as 'a talented leader, innovator and fearless pilot'. It is a fitting epitaph for the boy from the Mongolian foothills who died a hero in every sense of the word.

Epilogue

The examination of aspects of war can show people at their best, for under duress the better qualities as well as the baser qualities are highlighted and the plethora of superficial mannerisms, with which we cloak ourselves through our brief lives, are stripped away to reveal the true person below.

Modern aerial warfare has left little scope for individual heroism or skill, but, in the butchery of the Second World War, with its mass and indiscriminate area bombing and other horrors, some pilots could still achieve legendary status, particularly fighter pilots. For bomber pilots this was harder to achieve but in two cases was still possible: torpedo-bombing and, in particular, dive-bombing. It was mainly within these limited parameters that skill and precision, coupled with dedication, could still achieve results far out of proportion to numbers involved.

The much-derided dive-bomber led the German armies to quick, easy and cheap (in terms of lives lost on both sides) victories and the influence of the Stuka pilots was immense on the course of the vital land battles themselves.

Despite the enormous human and material cost involved the thousands of heavy bomber raids on Nazi Germany by the Allies between 1941 and 1944, strategic bombing, was a costly failure. German production of war materials actually increased enormously and Allied armies still had to fight every inch of the way from Normandy and Stalingrad to Berlin before the European war was ended. In those years the Allies had overwhelming superiority in the air, on sea and on land yet it took them three long years to reverse the gains the Stuka-led Panzers had made in a few weeks.

At sea also the pin-point elimination of important targets could influence whole campaigns in a way continual mass altitude bombing never did. Thus the British destruction of Dresden did not bring forward the end of the war by a single second, despite the carnage inflicted. But the attack by Major Enneccerus on *Illustrious* effectively closed the central Mediterranean to the big ships of the Royal Navy for two years enabling the Axis to send Rommel into Africa and keep him there and almost led to the capture of the Nile Basin.

Egusa led his dive-bombers against American, Dutch and British battle-fleets and eliminated them. As a result within six months inferior Japanese land forces were able to occupy the whole of South-East Asia and Allied air and land forces were powerless to prevent them doing so. Once the ships were sunk the oceans became Japanese and all else was inevitable.

Twenty years of boasting by the likes of Lord Trenchard and Billy Mitchell's followers about how they would eliminate warships with bombers led to nothing when put to the test in 1939, but with one deft and daring assault the much-derided Skua showed how such results could be achieved in fact rather than theory by using dive-bombing. Unfortunately the only ones who took any notice of the lesson Major Partridge and his compatriots thus imparted were the Germans and Japanese.

Even on the bitter Eastern Front, where a war of attrition with armies of millions locked in a mortal clash of ideology took place, dive-bombing could have enormous influence over the masses on the ground. The destruction of a strategic bridge could leave 100,000 soldiers trapped without hope of salvation. Dive-bomber pilots such as Hans-Ulrich Rudel on the German side could knock out 500 tanks, while men such as Polbin on the Soviet side absorbed the lessons and threw them back at the Germans with devastating effect during the final three years of the war.

Even in units of countries with slender resources, like France and Italy, dive-bombing maximised the best use of those resources ensuring that the majority of bombs dropped hit what they were aimed at. Thus blows struck by such pilots as Mesny and Cenni might not be able to reverse the inevitable but were more significant in stemming the tide than most other aerial intervention.

Since the Second World War the developments of the weapons of mass-destruction and the missiles to deliver them hold the entire world to ransom while the politicians of East and West continue their facile posturing regardless. Localised conflicts in Indo-China, Korea and Vietnam saw some limited use of dive-bombing, mainly by the highly skilled naval pilots of France, Britain and the United States but these were the final opportunities for such skills to be utilised. Electronic guidance and 'smart' bombs have taken over the eye sighting and bravery of the diving pilot. No doubt new skills will replace the old but it is doubtful whether ever again one pilot can have so much influence on a battle as any of the dive-bomber men described in this book. Each wrote his own unique page in the history of air warfare.

Bibliography

BOOKS

Alexander, J.P., *Russian Aircraft since 1940*, London, 1977

Bekker, C., *The Luftwaffe War Diaries*, London, 1967

Borgiotti, A., & Gori, Cesare, *Gli Stuka della Regia Aeronautica, 1940–45*, Modena, 1976

Brutting, Georg, *Das waren die deutschen Stuka-Asse, 1939–45*, Munich, 1976

Boyd, Alexander, *The Soviet Air Force since 1918*, London, 1975

Dickson, W.D., *The Battle of the Philippine Sea*, London, 1975

Dull, Paul S., *Battle History of the Imperial Japanese Navy 1941–45*, Annapolis, 1978

Francillon, R.J., *Japanese Aircraft of the Pacific War*, London, 1979

Jackson, R., *The Red Falcons: the Soviet Air Force in Action, 1919–69*, London, 1970

Kilbracken, Lord, *Bring Back My Stringbag*, London, 1979

Kozhevnikov, M.N., *Command and Staff of the Soviet Army Air Force in the Great Patriotic War, 1941–45*, Moscow, 1977

Lee, Asher, *The Soviet Air Force*, London, 1952

Mackenzie, Compton, *The Wind of Freedom*, London, 1943

Okumiya, M. & Horikoshi, J., *Zero: The Story of the Japanese Navy Air Force, 1937–45*, London, 1957

Obermaier, Ernst, *Die Ritterkreuz Träger der Luftwaffe, 1939–45, Vol. 2: Stuka und Schlachtflieger*, Mainz, 1976

Partridge, Major R.T., *Operation Skua*, Yeovilton, 1983

Poolman, Kenneth, *Illustrious*, London, 1955

Roskill, Stephen, *Naval Policy between the Wars, Vol. 2: 1930–39*, London, 1977

Salesse, Colonel, *L'Aviation d'Assaut Française*, Paris, 1968

Schliephake, Hanfried, *The Birth of the Luftwaffe*, Shepperton, 1971

Smith, Peter C., *Dive Bomber!*, Ashbourne, 1982

218 *Bibliography*

Smith, Peter C., *Battle of Midway*, London, 1976

Smith, Peter C., *Impact: the Dive-Bomber Pilots Speak*, London, 1981

Soviet Official Series, *Dvazdy Geroi Sovetskogo Soyuza (Twice Heroes of the Soviet Union)*, I S Polbin–Moscow, 1968

Soviet Official Series, *Krylatyye Syny Rodiny (Winged Sons of the Motherland)*, Moscow, 1975

Stafford, Commander E.P., *The Big 'E'*, New York, 1974

Taylor, Telford, *The Breaking Wave*, London, 1967

Thomas, David A., *Crete 1941: The Battle at Sea*, London, 1972

Tillman, Barrett, *Dauntless Dive Bomber of World War Two*, Annapolis, 1976

Tomlinson, Michael, *The Most Dangerous Moment*, London, 1976

ARTICLES, DOCUMENTS ETC

Abrail, Admiral, *Propositions de récompenses pour les Escadrilles AB1–AB2–AB4 de la Flotille du Bearn, Ordre No. 445 du 26 Mai 1940*, Amirauté Française 19 Juillet 1940

Air Ministry, *The Theory of Dive-Bombing*, London, 1938

Air Ministry, *Dive-Bombing: A Review of Policy*, 9 May 1940. AIR2/3176/S4583

Air Ministry, *Report of Air Attacks on HMS* Illustrious *on 10 January 1941, Operation MC4*, 26 January 1941. AIR23/5287

Commander Task Group 58.3, *Action Reports of Operations against Saipan, Tinian and Guam from units of Task Group Fifty-Eight point Three*, Office of Naval Records and Library 151927, Washington DC.

Flugsport, *Sturzflugbremsen*, Nr4/1941, Bd 33

Jozan (Capitaine de Corvette), *Comptes rendus des operations du 10 Mai au 26 Juin 1940, Amirauté Française*, 1944 (1 Sept 1940)

Larkin, Colonel A., *Preliminary Report of Marine Aircraft Group Twenty-Two of Battle of Midway*, US Marine Corps Archives, Washington DC

Leveille, Gaston (Capitaine de Frégate), *Le pont d'Origny*, 1972

Mesny, Admiral Gerald, *Le matériel n'a pas survivant*, 1970

Olszyk, Lieutenant Louis, *Iron Man of Dive Bombing*, Douglas Airview, 1944

Olszyk, Lieutenant Louis, ' "Iron Man" Glidden Sets Dive Bomb Record', *Chevrolet*, September 1944.

Ruhfus, Captain, *Uber den Einsatz des Kreuzers Königsberg bei der Beset-*

zung Bergens am 9 April und den Untergang des Schiffes am 10 April 1940 (307838/40).

Soviet Home Service, translated by BBC Radio Services: Transcripts of Broadcasts 1944–5

US Official, *Japanese Monographs: Outline of Armament and Preparation for War, Parts I, II & III*, 1922–41

US Official, *Japanese Monograph 166; China Incident – Naval Air Operations*, July–November 1937

US Printing Office, Washington DC, *Dictionary of American Fighting Ships*, pp. 327–8.

US Strategic Bombing Survey (Pacific), *Interrogation No USSBS 434-Shore-based Aircraft in the Marianas Campaign, Captain Akira Sasaki, IJN.*, 23 November 1945

US Strategic Bombing Survey (Pacific), *Interrogation No USSBS 448-Shore-based Aircraft in the Marianas. Captain Mitsuo Fuchida, IJN.*, 25 November 1945

Index